PRAISE FOR *BORDERLESS ECONOMICS*

"This is a thoughtful, entertaining and above all inspiring hymn of praise to the cultural, social and economic benefits of freer migration. Its conclusion should be noted by every politician running for office: immigration is an opportunity, not a threat."

—*Bill Emmott, author of* 20:21 Vision *and* Rivals

"For most, globalization has been about the movement of goods, services, technology and capital. As Robert Guest succinctly explains in this eminently readable book, globalization is actually about people—their migration, the networks they form and the ideas that they transmit through their mobility. In a world grappling with rising protectionist fever, this book is a warning that those nations who want to batten down the hatches and shut the free flow of people and ideas do so at their own risk."

—*Nandan Nilekani, chairman,*
Unique Identification Authority of India

BORDERLESS ECONOMICS

CHINESE SEA TURTLES, INDIAN FRIDGES AND THE NEW FRUITS OF GLOBAL CAPITALISM

ROBERT GUEST

BORDERLESS ECONOMICS
Copyright © Robert Guest, 2011
All rights reserved.

First published in 2011 by PALGRAVE MACMILLAN® in the United
States—a division of St. Martin's Press LLC, 175 Fifth Avenue, New York,
NY 10010.

Where this book is distributed in the United Kingdom, Europe, and the
rest of the world, this is by Palgrave Macmillan, a division of Macmillan
Publishers Limited, registered in England, company number 785998, of
Houndmills, Basingstoke, Hampshire RG21 6XS.

Palgrave Macmillan is the global academic imprint of the above companies
and has companies and representatives throughout the world.

Palgrave® and Macmillan® are registered trademarks in the United States,
the United Kingdom, Europe, and other countries.

ISBN: 978-0-230-11382-4

Library of Congress Cataloging-in-Publication Data

Guest, Robert.
    Borderless economics : Chinese sea turtles, Indian fridges and the new
fruits of global capitalism / Robert Guest.
      p.   cm.
    Includes index.
    ISBN 978-0-230-11382-4
    1. Diffusion of innovations.   2. Business networks.
3. Globalization—Economic aspects.   4. Immigrants—United
States.   I. Title.
HM846.G84   2011
303.48'209—dc23

                                                                2011022135

A catalogue record of the book is available from the British Library.

Design by Letra Libre

First edition: November 2011

10 9 8 7 6 5 4 3 2 1

Printed in the United States of America.

CONTENTS

INTRODUCTION

THE CURSE OF ISOLATION

I once attended a concert in North Korea. It was excruciating. The only songs that did not praise the Dear Leader, Kim Jong-Il, were those that glorified his late father, the Great Leader Kim Il-Sung. Some of the lyrics were a bit over the top. One song claimed that the Dear Leader could dispel raging storms with the sheer force of his personality. I had my doubts.

That the choir was mostly children made it worse. This was their education: the only worldview their totalitarian rulers allowed them to hear. As they sang a ditty called "We Must Always Be Prepared for the Sake of the Dear Leader," pictures flashed across a huge backdrop to reinforce the message.

There was a picture of the log cabin on Korea's sacred mountain, Mount Paekdu, where Kim Jong-Il was supposedly born. (Actually, he was born in the Soviet Union, where his dad served in Stalin's Red Army, but the official story sounds better.) There was a picture of the *kimjongilia*, a flower named after guess who? And finally, there was a painting of the junior god-king himself, mounted heroically on a rearing horse.

The painting looked familiar. Of course, I thought: it's that famous one of Napoleon crossing the Alps, by the nineteenth-century

French painter Jacques-Louis David. I looked it up afterward. The North Korean propaganda people had airbrushed Napoleon out of the portrait and replaced him with the equally short and pudgy Kim Jong-Il.

The crowd loved it—or, at least, they burst into wild applause. My guide, a party functionary whose job was to follow me around all day, woke up and clapped too. Then there was a power cut.

The tinny electronic music stopped. Darkness engulfed the audience. The choir stopped singing, and a thousand communists sat in mortified silence.

I felt a surge of sympathy. The party line is that North Korea's ruler is perfect—he even scored five holes-in-one on his first day playing golf, according to official sources.[1] Thanks to his wise leadership, the land he rules is a paradise, where contented farmers reap a bumper harvest every year. The penalty for suggesting otherwise is grim. North Koreans suspected of disloyalty can be sent to freezing labor camps, along with their families.

So none of those frightened people in that dark, silent theater could admit that the show was rotten. Instead, they all fervently pretended that nothing was amiss. They did not want anyone to suspect that they knew what was staring them in the face: that their country is a basket case. It is miserable, brutal, poor and so backward that its propaganda czars can't even keep the lights on during a musical tribute to the Dear Leader.

After a few minutes, a backup generator kicked in. The lights came on again, the synthesizers resumed their whining and the choir began again from the start of the song that had been interrupted. No one said a word about the power cut, then or afterward.

This is a book about connections. It is about people who cross borders, the ideas they bring with them and the networks they create. My argument is that migration matters more than most people realize, and that on balance it is a colossal boon to mankind.

Migrants sometimes cause trouble, to be sure. They disrupt local cultures and create social tensions. They compete with natives for jobs. Occasionally they commit crimes or plot terrorist outrages. But at the same time, the free movement of people makes the world richer, accelerates technological progress and helps disseminate good ideas, from genomics to democracy.

Migration is not well understood, not least because we tend to think in national terms. People in rich countries worry that immigrants will "swamp" their shores. People in poor countries fret about the "brain drain"—the exodus of doctors and engineers who seek fatter wages in the West.

What few people notice is that migration is no longer a simple, one-off event. People do not merely leave one country and take up residence in another. Often they circulate. They are born in one country, study in another and then return home. Or they work abroad and use the savings and experience they gain there to start businesses back home. Or they divide their time between two or more countries.

Most importantly, they build networks. A transnational family may have brothers in Kolkata and cousins in Cleveland. A graduate of a top American university may have classmates in both Bangalore and the Bay Area. Typically they stay in touch, swap ideas and alert each other to business opportunities.

As of 2009, some 215 million people were living outside the country in which they were born.[2] That is 3 percent of the world's population—and not just any 3 percent. Migrants tend to be more driven and dynamic than the people they leave behind. It takes courage to face the unknown, and get-up-and-go to get up and go.

That is one reason why diasporas are so important. The 60 million Chinese living overseas are among the smartest and most ambitious people their motherland has bred. Ditto the 25 million nonresident Indians and the legions of expatriate Arabs, Africans and Europeans.[3]

Moreover, because diaspora members typically have feet in (at least) two places, they are ideally placed to serve as bridges between them. The overseas Chinese connect China to the world and the world to China. The Indian diaspora performs the same service for India, and so on. *Borderless Economics* is about the miracle of migration, the dynamism of diaspora networks and the ways they enrich all our lives.

It is based on my reporting from nearly 70 countries, mostly for *The Economist,* the British newsmagazine that pays my salary and covers my hotel bills. Most of the countries I've visited benefit visibly from migration and the networks it creates. In later chapters, I'll describe how Indians in India have joined forces with Indians in the United States to build the world's biggest biometric database and the world's most attractive destination for medical tourism. I'll describe how the Chinese diaspora turbocharges China's incredible economic growth, and how it also promises to turn the world's last great dictatorship into a democracy.

I began with an anecdote from a country that enjoys none of the advantages of migration because I think it puts the rest of the book into perspective. North Korea is the most isolated place on earth. Its government has tried to seal it off from the outside world, save for the occasional shipment of costly cognac for the Dear Leader or spare parts for his nuclear weapons program. Hardly anyone is allowed into North Korea—I had to pose as a tourist and pay a lot of money to get a visa. (The regime does not like journalists.) Hardly anyone is allowed out, either.

The North Korean government tries to exclude outsiders because they might bring with them subversive ideas, such as capitalism, democracy and jokes about Kim Jong-Il's bouffant hairdo and platform boots. By closing its borders, however, North Korea also keeps out millions of ideas that might make its people less miserable, such as how to grow enough food for its 24 million people.

North Korea's extreme isolation is not the sole cause of its poverty, but it is an important one. A comparison with the more open, capitalist South Korea is revealing. The two nations share 5,000 years of history and culture, and were only separated in 1945. When Korea was split into communist and capitalist halves following the Allies' victory in World War II, the North was actually richer than the South, since it was where the Japanese colonists had built most of their factories.

Yet today South Koreans are 17 times richer than their northern cousins.[4] In the South, blue-collar workers have broadband Internet access in their homes; in the North they are banned from owning radios that can receive anything except the turgid official channel. Southern mothers fret that their children might not make it into the right university; northerners worry that their children might not make it to the age of five. Perhaps a million North Koreans starved to death during the 1990s. Today, North Koreans are six inches shorter than their southern cousins.[5]

South Korean cities by night are a carnival of merriment, with pulsating nightclubs, wide-screen cinemas, raucous drinking dens and restaurants serving every creature you can think of, smothered in chilli and garlic.* North Korea by night, seen in a satellite photo, looks completely dark, as if no one lived there. One night when I was eating dinner in the pitch black in a North Korean hotel, the waiter brought in a candle and tried to persuade me that the absence of electric light was deliberate, so that I could enjoy the romantic atmosphere of a candlelit meal.

The staggering difference between the two countries is due entirely to politics. The South allows free enterprise; the North does not. The South is open to foreign ideas; the North seeks ruthlessly to suppress them. When I lived in South Korea in the early 1990s, people constantly asked me how Westerners ran companies, held elections or raised their children. In North Korea, they did not ask questions at all. Instead, they subjected me to interminable lectures about the superiority of the *juche* idea (Kim Jong-Il's philosophy of national self-reliance).

Because I was single when I lived in South Korea, local friends assumed that I was looking for a wife and regularly tried to introduce me to eligible Korean women. In the North, marriage with an outsider is utterly taboo. The regime waxes hysterical about maintaining the nation's "purity" from foreign contamination.[6] It is like the Ku Klux Klan with nukes.

Some North Korean officials go so far as to insist that all good ideas emanate not only from North Korea but from the Kim family itself. Libraries there stock hundreds of volumes purportedly written by the Dear and Great Leaders, offering guidance on everything from politics to engineering. I visited a library in Pyongyang, the capital, with a friend. We asked the librarian if any of his customers ever read any books by authors other than the Kims. He could not name a single example.

---

* Including sea cucumbers, which look and taste like foot-long aquatic slugs.

WHY NETWORKS MATTER

People are smart. But alone, not even the most brilliant human could make a toaster. Not from step one. Not if he had to make the tools to mine the iron ore or drill the oil and refine it to make plastic. In 2009, a London-based artist named Thomas Thwaites tried to make a toaster on his own. Inevitably, he failed. Even when he cheated—for example, by using a microwave oven to melt metal—it took him months, cost a lot of money and yielded a fifth-rate product. Mr. Thwaites concluded that a modern consumer is helpless because he cannot be self-sufficient.[7]

A more rational reaction would be to rejoice that we do not have to be self-sufficient. Thanks to trade, the skills and labor of thousands of specialists—steelworkers, oil drillers, electrical engineers and so on—can be combined into a single, reliable product that costs $15 at Walmart. By working for two hours at the minimum wage, an American can afford something that he could not make for himself given a lifetime.

Actually, it is even better than that: when he buys a toaster, he is buying something that no human being alive knows how to make from scratch. Even the most gifted engineer at a toaster factory has no idea how to make the robots he uses on the production line or the computer he uses for his spreadsheets.

Or even the pencil he uses to doodle during meetings. As an economist called Leonard Read pointed out in 1958, making something as simple as a pencil requires the labor and expertise of millions of people: not only the loggers and graphite miners who provide the wood and the lead, but also the people who make the parts that go into the loggers' chainsaws or pour the concrete for the dam that supplies the pencil factory's electricity. "I am seemingly so simple," wrote Mr. Read, pretending to be a talking pencil. "Yet not a single person on the face of this earth knows how to make me."[8]

Technology advances because humans cooperate. To understand how this works, consider a prehistoric counterexample. Some 30,000 years ago, rising seas turned Tasmania, formerly attached to Australia, into an island. A few thousand inhabitants were cut off from all contact with the mainland. Their technology regressed. They forgot how to make bone tools, catch fish and sew skins into clothes.

It was not that the islanders grew less intelligent. Their problem was that they no longer had many people to trade with. It took a lot of effort, in those days, to learn how to carve needles out of bone. So long as there were plenty of people with whom to swap needles for food, it made sense for specialists to acquire such skills. But in a tiny, isolated society, there may have been room only for one or two needle makers. If they both fell off cliffs, the technology died with them. When the first Europeans reached Tasmania, they found natives whose only shields against the winter chill were seal fat smeared on their skin and wallaby pelts over their shoulders.[9]

Communities that turn inward tend to stagnate. History is crowded with examples: pre-Reformation Spain was a "center of learning and intellectual inquiry," writes David Landes, an economic historian, not least because it was "on the frontier of Christian and Islamic civilization and had the benefit of Jewish intermediaries."[10] But in January 1492 the Spanish monarchs Ferdinand and Isabella decided that Jews were a threat to the Catholic faith, and gave every Jew in the country four months to convert or leave, on pain of death. Then they offered the same deal to the Moors (North African Muslims who had recently ruled part of southern Spain).

Having expelled hundreds of thousands of heretics, Spain tried to prevent heretical ideas from entering the country as well. In 1558, importing foreign books without permission was made punishable by death. So was printing without a license. In 1559 the government drew up a list of banned books. Many were included for trifling reasons, such as having a Protestant author. Spaniards were barred from studying at foreign universities (apart from a few reassuringly Catholic ones in Italy). "[T]he diffusion of new ideas to society at large slowed to a trickle," laments Mr. Landes.[11] British historian Hugh Trevor-Roper argued that the Catholic backlash against Protestantism retarded southern Europe for 300 years.[12]

A globalized world is in many ways the opposite of ancient Tasmania, Spain under the Inquisition or modern North Korea: goods and ideas flow fairly freely from one place to another. "The success of human beings depends crucially, but precariously, on numbers and connections," argues Matt Ridley, a polymath and the author of *The Rational Optimist*.[13] Trade allows specialization. In narrower and narrower fields, people acquire deeper and deeper skills. Through trade, they share them. The fewer barriers there are to the free movement of goods and people, the more opportunities there are for ideas to meet and "have sex," as Mr. Ridley puts it.[14]

A network is more powerful than the sum of its parts. We see this in computing: a laptop without an Internet connection is just a calculator that won't fit in your pocket. We see it in biology, too: a single brain cell is useless, but 100 billion of them yoked together make a brain. And we see it in the world we live in: connect six or seven billion brains to one another and you have modern civilization.

This book is about the way those brains are linked. Because, of course, they are not all directly linked. Just as a brain cell has only a few thousand synapses, so the average person has only a few hundred acquaintances. An individual can know only a tiny fraction of what mankind knows collectively. So we all need a starting point, a place to plug into the global network.

For many people, that starting point is their tribe or ethnic group. People talk to people they know and with whom their share a common language. To make connections across borders—often the most fruitful kind—they tend to link up with their national diaspora.

This book is divided into eight chapters, followed by a conclusion. Chapter 1, **"Migrationomics: How Moving Makes Us Richer,"** explains how migration enriches mankind. Chapter 2, **"Bridges to China: Tales from the World's Greatest Diaspora,"** tells four very different stories about Chinese migrants. We meet Mei Xu, a woman whose business links Maryland with mainland China; James Riady, the scion of an old Chinese trading family in Southeast Asia; William So, a Chinese executive who lives in the West but is skeptical of it; and the staff at Alibaba, an Internet firm that helps Chinese people become gloriously rich without relying on the government. The aim of this chapter is to give a sense of the extraordinary variety of migrants' experiences, and the power of the networks they create.

Chapter 3, **"Diaspora Politics: How the Sea Turtles Will Turn China Democratic,"** argues that the overseas Chinese will undermine the Communist Party and eventually liberate their homeland. Chapter 4, **"Networks of Innovation: How Migrants Can Cut Your Medical Bills,"** looks at how diaspora networks such as India's are boosting innovation and bringing the world $69 refrigerators and $300 houses. Chapter 5, **"Networks of Trust: How the Brain Drain Reduces Global Poverty,"** argues that the outflow of educated people from poor countries actually makes those countries better off.

Chapter 6, **"Networks of Hate: Genocide, Terrorism and Crime,"** examines the dark side of tribal networks. It explains why the Tutsis refer to themselves as the Jews of central Africa, and how the Rwandan genocide of 1994 sparked the twenty-first century's worst war in neighboring Congo. It looks at how the virus of terrorism infects the *ummah* (the global community of Muslims), and what Muslims can do about it. And it describes how ethnic bonds make Nigerian criminals harder to catch.

The remaining chapters are about the United States. Chapter 7, **"'A Ponzi Scheme That Works': Why Migrants Choose America,"** argues that the United States' greatest strength is that people want to live there. Despite the recent recession, America still offers an unbeatable material standard of living for upwardly mobile migrants. It also offers a wider variety of niches than any other country. A migrant who likes quiet suburbs, Korean newspapers and conservative Christian churches where the sermons are in his native tongue can find precisely that combination in northern Virginia. A migrant who prefers a more urban, secular Korean lifestyle can find it in Boston or San Francisco. Gay or straight, Kenyan or Vietnamese, Catholic or Hindu, rural or metropolitan, there is a niche for just about anyone in America.

Chapter 8, **"The Hub of the World: Why America Will Remain Number One,"** argues that the nation's unique ability to attract and absorb migrants will allow it to remain the dominant power far longer than most people expect. Immigration not only provides the country with youthful energy and ideas. It also allows it to tap into every one of the world's diaspora networks. It gives the nation legions of unofficial ambassadors, deal brokers, recruiters and boosters. It dramatically increases innovation, dynamism and soft power. It makes America the hub of a connected planet.

The book concludes with a plea for freer movement. Migration is by far the most powerful weapon in the struggle against global poverty. More open borders are also in the interest of rich countries. Immigration is the only plausible corrective to the graying of rich societies. It is also the best hope for a more tolerant world. When rich countries allow migrants from poor countries to live and work within their borders, those migrants experience firsthand how a rich country works. When they taste the fruits of tolerance, pluralism and the rule of law, they often find them delicious. And sometimes they carry the seeds back home.

1

MIGRATIONOMICS

HOW MOVING MAKES US RICHER

When Cheung Yan moved to America from China in 1990, she noticed two things. First, that Americans threw away mountains of waste paper: heaps of junk mail, stacks of unread instruction manuals for barbecue sets and mountains of the Sunday edition of the *New York Times*.

Second, she noticed that fleets of container ships sail from China to America stuffed to the brim but go back half empty. The things China makes take up space: toys, televisions, steel girders and so forth. The things America exports to China, however, are often weightless: movies, patents, IOUs from the government.

Cheung Yan turned these two observations into a multibillion-dollar business. With her husband and brother, she set up a firm in Los Angeles to gather up American waste paper and ship it to China for recycling, where it could be done more cheaply than in America. Later, she set up her own factories in China to do the recycling.

She now turns American newspapers into cardboard boxes. These are then packed with Chinese electronic goods and shipped to America. When her firm, Nine Dragons Paper, went public in Hong Kong in 2006, she became rich. In 2011 her net worth was estimated at $1.6 billion, making her one of the wealthiest self-made women in the world.[1] Her business is part American, part Chinese: in other words, part of what financial historian Niall Ferguson calls "Chimerica." She came to the United States with an outsider's eye, and both countries benefited from what she saw.

The American dream has changed. The traditional immigrant success story went something like this. A plucky citizen of some foreign hellhole—Cuba, say, or Britain—decided to head for America. He braved stormy waters in a leaky boat to get there. He studied hard, worked hard, saved hard and ended up rich. His children went to Stanford or Cornell. By the third generation, his family was so thoroughly assimilated that his grandchildren had only the vaguest notion of what life was like back in the old country.

For most of American history, this stereotype was not far from the truth. Today it is in desperate need of an update. Immigrants still flee foreign hellholes, and they still flock to rich countries. They typically still find a good life once they arrive, and their children still thrive: think of Sergey Brin, the son of a Russian immigrant, who cofounded Google and is now worth $20 billion.[2] Or of Barack Obama, the son of a Kenyan goatherd, who has also done quite well in his chosen profession.

But for many migrants, moving from one country to another is no longer a simple, one-off event. Millions of people like Cheung Yan keep a foot in more than one place. Thanks to the Internet and cheap phone calls, it is much easier for a migrant to stay in touch with friends and relatives back home than it was a generation ago. Thanks to lower airfares, it is much easier to visit them.

It is also much easier to communicate with business partners back in the old country, which means it is easier to set up ocean-straddling businesses. The days when you had to be big to run a multinational enterprise are gone. These days, a "micro-multinational" might consist of one man in Virginia, his cousin in Hong Kong and a sheaf of contracts to supply American shops with fireworks made in mainland China.

Two big changes have made migration less likely to be one-off and one-way. One is the drastic drop in the cost of staying in touch. When AT&T's first transatlantic phone service opened in 1927, only one person could use it at a time, and it cost $75 for a three-minute call.[3] That was about a month's wages for a typical worker at the time. Today, anyone can call anywhere via the Internet-based chat service Skype for free. If the connection is good enough, you can even see your loved ones on the screen as you talk to them. The cost of air travel has not fallen quite as dramatically, but it has fallen. In the 1950s flying was a luxury reserved for the superrich. In 2009 scheduled airlines sold 1.6 billion tickets.[4]

The other big change is the spectacular rise of emerging economies such as India, China and Brazil. Some of the poverty-stricken hellholes whose brightest citizens used to flee in large numbers are no longer hellholes. They still have lots of poor people, but they are getting richer at an astounding pace. And that creates opportunities for their citizens, especially the brainy ones, which did not exist a generation ago.

China's economy has been growing at or near double digits for three decades. India's growth rate is only slightly slower. When an economy grows at 10 percent a year, it doubles in size roughly every seven years. Many of its businesses grow even faster—a well-run firm in China or India can easily grow by 20 to 30 percent a year. Such growth rates are incredibly hard to sustain in a mature economy. Small wonder so many smart young Chinese figure they can get rich quicker at home than in America.

Consider the story of Robin Li. Born in 1968 in Shanxi, China, the son of two factory workers, he spent the first 31 years of his life following the traditional path of an upwardly mobile migrant. He did splendidly at school and won a place at the State University of New York at Buffalo to study computer science.

After completing his master of science degree, he started work as a software engineer. He was good at it. By the late 1990s, he was a staff engineer at Infoseek, an American search-engine firm that was hot at the time. He was not rich, but he was well paid. By any reasonable standard, he had achieved the American dream.

But he was not satisfied with being what journalists Brad Stone and Bruce Einhorn call "a Silicon Valley cubicle jockey."[5] He met another ambitious young Chinese man, Eric Xu, a sales rep for a biotech firm. Mr. Xu decided to make a documentary about American innovation, and invited Mr. Li along to one of the interviews. The subject was Jerry Yang, the Taiwanese cofounder of Yahoo. Both men were impressed. "I got inspired," Mr. Xu later told *Bloomberg BusinessWeek*. "I'm sure

Robin got inspired, too, seeing an ethnic Chinese who created such a powerful company."[6]

Li and Xu went back to China. In January 2000, with backing from American venture capitalists, they founded Baidu, a firm that aimed to do for China what Google had done for the rest of the world. They succeeded. A decade later, Baidu was China's most popular search engine and Mr. Li was the richest man on the mainland, with a net worth estimated at $9.4 billion. Not bad for a former cubicle jockey.[7]

Thanks to his years living and working in America, Mr. Li is effortlessly cosmopolitan. His English is flawless, he shuttles to Internet conferences around the world, his American investors love him and he is on first-name terms with Mark Zuckerberg, the founder of Facebook.

Yet Mr. Li has accommodated himself wholly to the Chinese way of doing things. This is not just a matter of switching back to his old name, Li Yanhong. He takes the ruthlessly pragmatic view that the Communist Party calls the shots in China and that his firm must cooperate with its edicts, no matter how odious. If China's rulers want a search term blocked, Baidu blocks it. People in China who use Baidu to search for forbidden terms such as "democracy" or "free Tibet" find an error message on their screen. Mr. Li justifies such collaboration with censors by protesting that if Baidu did not obey Chinese law, it would be shut down.[8] Unfortunately, he is right.

Cheung Yan and Robin Li are prominent examples of an increasingly common phenomenon. Many migrants commute, literally or virtually, between two or more countries, taking advantage of what each has to offer. All this to-ing, fro-ing and circulating helps them create networks of contacts. And these networks are the central nervous system of the global economy.

Communication within diaspora networks is not new. Mayer Rothschild, the eighteenth-century founder of the Rothschild banking dynasty, sent each of his five sons to a different European financial center: Frankfurt, Vienna, London, Naples and Paris. This spread the family's risks—useful in an age of anti-Jewish pogroms—and gave it eyes and ears across the continent. The Rothschilds built a network of agents and couriers to keep themselves ahead of the news. When the

Duke of Wellington defeated Napoleon at the Battle of Waterloo in 1815, the head of the London arm of the Rothschild family heard of the British victory a whole day before the British government did, and made a fortune buying up British government bonds.[9]

Information remains as valuable today as it was 200 years ago. What has changed is that you no longer need an army of private couriers to deliver it. Today, a Pakistani immigrant in London can chat with his brother in Lahore every day, if he has time. He can stay in touch with the culture he left behind, by watching Urdu soaps on his laptop or reading blogs from Islamabad. He can sign an online petition complaining about the Pakistani government, or about some purely local issue, such as the noise pollution outside his mother's house. He can wire money to a business partner in Karachi or to his favorite mosque. He can fly home in a few hours, perhaps to meet a wife his family has chosen for him.

Via Facebook and other social-networking websites, he can keep up with old friends and new friends alike. Many people assume that the borderless Internet breaks down barriers of race and ethnicity. Sometimes it does, but mostly it serves to strengthen traditional bonds. A study by Ethan Zuckerman, a blogger and activist, of the top 50 online news sites in 30 countries found that most people get 95 percent or more of their news from domestic sources.[10] On Twitter, the ten most popular groups are joined almost exclusively by whites or exclusively by blacks, according to a study by Martin Wattenberg and Fernanda Viegas.[11] On Facebook, according to Mr. Zuckerman, only 1 percent of Israeli friendships are with Palestinians; for Greeks and Turks the figure is less than one-tenth of a percent.

John Kelly, who makes a living analyzing electronic social networks for Morningside Analytics, told *The Economist* that even when the Internet links people who live in different countries, the links are usually between people who share ancient cultural ties—that is, ethnic Greeks in Greece use it to communicate with ethnic Greeks in other countries.[12]

Techno-utopians will find this disappointing. Surely modern mankind has moved beyond primitive tribal loyalties? Dream on. Tribes still matter immensely. It is natural for people to feel more comfortable with others who share the same culture. It is easier for people to forge friendships with those whose values are similar and who speak the same language. That is why tribal networks remain so important—they are the principal framework within which people communicate and work together. What's new is that, thanks to mass migration, most tribal networks are now global.

THE MIRACLE OF MIGRATION

People are more mobile than ever before. There are some 215 million first-generation migrants, an increase of about 50 percent since 1990.[13] If first-generation migrants were a nation, they would be the world's fifth largest. Add in the descendants of recent migrants, and the number is even bigger. Yet even this figure would understate the importance of migration.

It takes energy and courage to leave the place where you grew up, where everything is familiar and grandma is always there to hold the baby when you are sick. So migrants tend to be strivers, doers and risk-takers. Everywhere they go, they are disproportionately likely to start businesses or make new discoveries.

For the migrants themselves, the benefits of migration are obvious. The gap between wages in rich and poor countries is much wider now than it was during earlier eras of mass migration. During the 1870s, when crossing the Atlantic was a ten-day ordeal, a mere twofold disparity in wages between Ireland and the United States was enough to propel a wave of Irish emigration. Today, wages in America are often ten times higher than those in the countries that send migrants to its shores. "While an American construction laborer works less than four minutes to earn enough to buy a kilogram of flour, it takes a Mexican worker more than one hour and an Indian construction worker just under two hours," observes Lant Pritchett, a Harvard economist.[14]

Which is why, according to a 2009 Gallup poll, 700 million people—16 percent of the world's adult population—would move permanently to a different country if they could.[15] Global inequality creates colossal pressure for people to move. And when they do move, global inequality falls (although the arrival of poor immigrants in a rich country will cause inequality to rise, at least temporarily, within that country).

When workers cross borders, their prospects are transformed. In the popular imagination, migrants from poor countries are horribly exploited when they arrive in rich countries. In reality, this is seldom the case. According to Mr. Pritchett, their wages become "almost identical to those of workers in the country they move *to* and almost nothing like those in the country they move *from*."[16] For example, a Salvadoran man with a high-school education would make on average $2,700 a year back home in El Salvador. If he moves to the United States, he would make more than eight times that: $22,611, according to the US Census Bureau. That is indistinguishable from the average earnings for an American man with the same level of education—$22,087.[17]

When rich countries open their borders even a little, they do far more good for the world's poor than they ever do by giving aid. A 2005 World Bank study estimated that if rich countries allowed just a 3 percent rise in their labor forces through easier immigration, it would deliver *$300 billion* in benefits to the world's have-nots. The cost to the host-country taxpayers would be zero—migrants who work pay more in taxes than they receive in government benefits. They also perform useful tasks. The same study found that the current residents of rich countries would benefit, to the tune of $51 billion a year, from an influx of newcomers willing to mow lawns cheaply or cap teeth skillfully.[18]

Contrast this with the cost-effectiveness of foreign aid. Some economists argue that foreign aid is mostly wasted or even harmful, since so much of it is stolen or used to prop up odious despots. I wouldn't go that far. Nor would Mr. Pritchett. But even if you assume that $70 billion of aid delivers $70 billion of benefits to the poor—an optimistic assumption—opening the borders a bit is still *infinitely* more cost-effective.[19]

Not everyone agrees that immigrants benefit the people who live in the countries where they make their new homes. Some natives find newcomers culturally threatening. Others believe that an influx of foreigners from poor countries depresses wages for the native born. Economists are divided as to whether this is really true. There are surely some people whose wages fall because of competition for jobs from migrants, but most studies have found this effect to be small or nonexistent. This is a subject we'll revisit at greater length in Chapter 7.

Against the possible losses for a relatively small number of citizens of rich countries, we must weigh the overall gains to rich countries and the staggering benefits to the migrants themselves. If people could move completely freely around the world (which is unlikely anytime soon), the total gains, by one estimate, would be around $40 trillion—40 times the potential gain from removing all remaining barriers to the global trade in goods.[20] As a tool for spreading the wealth, open borders make foreign aid look like a child's lemonade stand.

This chapter is about how migration makes the world a better place. But my aim is not merely to list the material benefits and costs. I also want to look at the way migration changes people; how it affects the way they think. Migrants usually have no choice but to become familiar with at least two cultures. So they see opportunities that are invisible to their monocultural neighbors, as Cheung Yan did, and they generate new ideas.

Immigrants are only an eighth of the population of the United States, but a quarter of the engineering and technology firms established in America between 1995 and 2005 had at least one immigrant founder, according to Vivek Wadhwa, of Duke University. And a quarter of international patent applications filed from America were filed by foreign nationals.[21]

The exceptional creativity of immigrants must be partly a selection effect—it is much easier to obtain a visa to work in a rich country if you have an advanced degree in bioinformatics than if you are a bricklayer. But there is also evidence that exile itself makes people more creative. William Maddux, of INSEAD (a French business school), and Adam Galinsky, of Northwestern University, conducted an experiment with MBA students, some of whom had lived abroad and some of whom had not, but who were otherwise similar.

The students were provided with a brainteaser. Each student was given a candle, a box of matches and a box of tacks and told to attach the candle to a wall so that it burned properly and did not drip wax on the table or the floor. The correct solution was to empty the tacks out of their box, pin the box to the wall and then put the candle inside it. The Duncker candle problem, as it is known, is considered a good test of creativity because it requires you to imagine something (the tack box) being used for a purpose other than its usual one.

The results were intriguing. Students who had lived abroad found the problem significantly easier than those who had not. Some 60 percent of the migrants solved it correctly, against 42 percent of those who had lived all their lives in one country. Angela Leung, of Singapore Management University, and Chi-yue Chiu, of the University of Illinois at Urbana-Champaign, found similar results in an experiment in which subjects were asked to find creative uses for plastic garbage bags.[22]

Migrants have to learn new languages and adapt to new environments and ways of thinking. This is exhausting, but mentally stimulating. A person who is constantly required to make sense of new situations should logically become more adept at doing so.

My own subjective impression, having spent most of my working life outside the country where I grew up (Britain), is that culture shock makes you think. I don't pretend that my life has been as challenging as that of a Cuban raft-rider or a Somali refugee. Far from it. But still, as a hard-up student in crazy-costly Tokyo in the early 1990s, I had to find ways to make ends meet in a strange city. I discovered, among other things, that because Japanese people do not like breadcrusts, Japanese bakers throw them away. So if you walk into a bakery and ask for a bag of *pan no mimi,* the man behind the counter will let you have it for nothing. That, I found, can stave off hunger till the next English-teaching job comes along.

As a young reporter in Africa in the late 1990s and early 2000s, I had to cope with roadblocks and rebels. I found it helped to stay calm and carry a conspicuous packet of cigarettes in my shirt pocket, to offer to any policeman or soldier who might otherwise demand a bribe to let me pass. And when I was detained by drunken, shirtless and gun-waving rebels during the Ivory Coast's civil war, I guessed that the wisest course would be to smile, chat politely and drink the fiery palm spirit they offered me, but not too much of it. And to wait for them to let me go, which they eventually did.[23]

Living in America (which I did between 2005 and 2010) was easier, since the cultural gulf was narrower. The main challenge was writing about American politics in a way that made sense both to students in Seattle and to bankers in Singapore—*The Economist*'s readers are roughly half American and half non-American. Dealing with the Internal Revenue Service required mental agility, too. They insisted for some time that I had no children, and therefore couldn't claim deductions for them. I was pretty sure I had three, since they were quite noisy.

Everywhere I travel, I see migrants adapting cleverly to unfamiliar environments. I've met Congolese refugees in Tanzania who created a trading system based on the bland rations doled out by the United Nations. I've met Koreans in Japan who, when locked out of white-collar jobs by bigoted locals, have made a fortune from operating noisy pinball arcades. In Brazil, I found that the proof is almost literally in the pudding: the national dish, *feijoada,* is said to have been invented by African slaves, whose owners gave them only black beans and the parts of pigs that no one else wanted to eat. With a few African spices and a dash of ingenuity, they created a culinary masterpiece.*

A WORLD WIDE WEB OF PEOPLE

Another big difference between migrants and less mobile folk is that migrants are more likely to form cross border networks. These networks serve two critical functions.

First, they speed the flow of information. A Venezuelan in Miami who hears that a local building site needs extra hands will swiftly alert his cousin in Caracas. A Chinese trader in South Africa who realizes that visiting soccer fans are desperate to buy deafening plastic *vuvuzela* horns will immediately tell a factory in Zhejiang to start cranking them out.

Second, diaspora networks foster a high level of trust. This matters: when you do business, you need to be able to trust the person you are doing business with. When you hire people, you need to know that they are neither lazy nor dishonest. Tribal networks make this easier. A good word from someone you know is worth a thousand résumés.

---

* Actually, the evidence for this story is inconclusive—it is hard to disentangle the Portuguese, African and native influences from many Brazilian dishes. But Brazilians assure me that it is true, and I like to think they are right. See http://www .virgiliogomes.com/chronicles/348-brazilian-feijoada-bean-stew.

Of course, trust can be misplaced or abused. Bernard Madoff, a fraudster, was able to inflate the world's largest-ever Ponzi scheme in part because he was so respected within elite Jewish circles. Several Jewish charities, from Yeshiva University to movie mogul Steven Spielberg's Wunderkinder Foundation, lost huge sums because they trusted Madoff.[24] They were shocked to have been robbed by "one of their own." But such cases are shocking precisely because they are rare.

The world's most flexible and resilient trading networks—the Chinese in Southeast Asia, the Indians in East Africa and the Lebanese in Latin America—are based on diasporas. A Lebanese diamond dealer in West Africa can send a bag of gems to a Lebanese trader in Europe without fear of being cheated, because he knows that if the other trader cheats him, he will be forever excluded from the network. That keeps everyone honest, and makes trading almost frictionless.

Diaspora trading networks have been powerful for generations, yet they have become even more so in the past three decades. As tariff barriers have fallen, global trade has exploded (albeit with a dip during the recent recession). Traders whose global networks were already in place were in a perfect position to profit from this boom. The economic opening of China and India (since 1979 and 1991, respectively) has given those countries' diasporas two massive new markets back home. Africa, too, is far more open to trade than it was in the 1980s, and this creates lucrative opportunities for Africans with connections in Europe, America and Asia.

In 2010 I asked Vish Mishra, an Indian American venture capitalist who invests in both India and America, how he found good firms to back and good people to manage them. He replied that personal introductions were absolutely crucial. "If you cold-call, you start from nowhere," he said. "It's laborious and tedious. If you know someone, you can move faster." He added, "The advantage of any network is you get to see things you might not otherwise see." Of course, you still have to make a decision, he noted, but networks "make the process far more efficient."[25]

Diasporas also accelerate the spread of big ideas. In Silicon Valley, more than half of Chinese and Indian scientists and engineers report sharing tips about technology or business opportunities with people in their home countries.[26] For those who study or work in America and then return home, the volume of information sharing may be even larger. A study by the Kauffman Foundation, a think tank in Missouri, found that 84 percent of returning Indian entrepreneurs maintain at least monthly contact with family and friends in America, and 66 percent are in contact at least that often with former colleagues. For entrepreneurs who return to China, the figures are 81 percent and 55 percent respectively. In addition, 45 percent of Chinese and 37 percent of Indian returnees make monthly or more frequent contact with professional associations in America, and 34 percent of Chinese and 17 percent of Indians are in touch at least that often with their American universities.

The subjects they talk about the most are customers (61 percent of Indians and 74 percent of Chinese mention this), markets (62 percent of Indians, 71 percent of Chinese), technical information (58 percent of Indians, 68 percent of Chinese) and business funding (31 percent of Indians, 54 percent of Chinese).[27] The tips about business and technology that migrants share with their overseas contacts are usually timely, relevant and believed, which makes them hugely valuable. Reading about last year's cool idea is of little use; hearing about next year's could make you rich.

Start-up firms in Silicon Valley, Bangalore and other technology hubs "are often global businesses from their first day of operations," observes University of California, Berkeley, professor AnnaLee Saxenian in *The New Argonauts: Regional Advantage in a Global Economy*, a brilliant study of ethnic networks in the technology industry. She continues,

> In this environment, the scarce competitive resource is the ability to locate foreign partners quickly and to manage complex business relationships and teamwork across cultural and linguistic barriers. This is particularly challenging in high-tech industries in which products, markets and technologies are continually redefined—and where product cycles are often nine months or less. First-generation immigrants like the Chinese and Indian engineers in Silicon Valley who have the necessary language, cultural and technical skills to function well in the United States as well as in their home markets have a commanding professional advantage.[28]

Ethnic networks boost business within countries, too. An Indian executive in Silicon Valley told Saxenian:

> I can approach literally any big company, or any company in the Bay Area, and find two or three contacts. . . . [A]ny software company must have at least two or three Indian or Chinese employees . . . and because they are there, it is very easy for me . . . to create that bond, to pick up the phone and say: "Swaminathan, can you help me, can you tell me what's going on?" . . . [H]e'll say: "Don't quote me but the decision is because of this, this and this." Based on this you can reformulate your strategy. . . . Such contacts are critical for start-ups.[29]

Diasporas today are imbued with "a new type of hyperconnectivity," reckons Carlo Dade, of the Canadian Foundation for the Americas, a think tank. He explains: "Migrants are now connected instantaneously, continuously, dynamically and intimately to their communities of origin. . . . This is a fundamental and profound break from the past eras of migration."[30]

By staying in touch with the countries they came from, migrants keep open the option of moving back. This is called "circular migration." It is extremely common. Exactly how common is hard to say, however, since most rich countries keep precise records of those who arrive but lousy records of those who return home. The best data about circular migration come from Australia, which tracks migration in both directions.

Graeme Hugo, of the University of Adelaide, crunched the numbers and showed that immigrants circulate in a huge variety of ways. Some go to Australia and stay permanently. Some go, stay a while, don't like it much and return home. Some go, stay long enough to pick up valuable skills and then return home to better jobs. Some stay for a while and then move back to look after their elderly parents. Some stay long enough to earn Australian citizenship and then move to a third country, such as the United States.[31]

The number of Chinese and Indian people living in Australia has shot up in recent years. And although Australia takes in many more settlers from Asia than it loses, there is a sizable reverse flow. For every three people who move permanently from China to Australia, one moves permanently in the other direction.[32]

The Chinese in Australia circulate furiously. They are the largest users of short-stay business visas. They make short trips home frequently. And many ethnic Chinese and Indians leave Australia for a third country, such as the United States, the United Kingdom or Canada. Scholars call this "escalator migration." Often, the immigrant really wanted to go to America all along, but could not get a visa. So he opts for a country that is easier to enter, such as Australia. Once he obtains an Australian passport, he applies to enter America as an Australian citizen, which is easier than trying to get in on a Chinese passport. Of course, he may then find that America is not everything he hoped it would be, and return to Australia.

All this barely begins to describe the different paths that migrants take.

They circulate like the blood in a human body, spreading money and ideas like food and oxygen. "I've stopped talking about migration," says Kathleen Newland of the Migration Policy Institute, a think tank in Washington, DC. "I've started talking about mobility instead. People move, but they don't have to choose between countries. They can keep a foot in two or more."[33]

A NEW WAY OF LOOKING AT THE WORLD

The lines on a map are clear. At each border, one country ends and another begins. But the real world is not so simple. Nation-states matter, to be sure. But it is often more accurate to think of the world as a complex and overlapping web of tribal networks based on ethnic and religious affiliations.

There are huge networks, such as those of the Chinese, the Indians, the Europeans and the Muslims. There are smaller but widely dispersed networks, such as those of the Jews, the Lebanese and the Mormons. The world looks different when you look at people rather than countries.

Consider the difference between China—that is, the People's Republic—and the Chinese people. The former is a state that occupies 3.7 million square miles. The latter is a tribe that stretches around the globe. Most of its members live in the People's Republic, but at least 60 million do not. Many hold foreign passports. Chinese people study physics in the United States, trade stocks in London, build oil pipelines in Africa and act as a conduit for trade and investment between China and every other nation. Lynn Pan, the foremost historian of the Chinese diaspora, writes of a "Greater China," which is "less a geographical region than a web of interconnections, one which radiates, like the circles of a pebble dropped in a pool, from coast to coast until it reaches the uttermost corners of the globe."[34]

What the Chinese do affects everyone else. American mortgages are subsidized by their savings. The price of grain has soared since they started eating more meat from grain-fed livestock. Africans have started to complain that they are the new imperialists.[35] Russians fear that they will overrun the vast empty spaces of Russia's Far East.

At the same time, however, the Chinese do not wholly control China itself. Nearly a third of China's landmass is home to people who are not Han Chinese (the majority ethnic group in China). The Tibetans belong to a tribal network that stretches many miles west, into India. Most yearn for autonomy. The Muslim Uighurs in the western region of Xinjiang, meanwhile, feel more loyalty to their ethnic group or to the global *ummah* (community of Muslims) than they do to Beijing.[36]

Protests against central control in these areas are common and sometimes violent. China's government is terrified of losing huge swaths of its territory. A free Tibet might fall into the sphere of influence of China's hated rival, India. An independent Xinjiang would take with it much of China's oil, natural gas, copper and iron ore. Beijing will do anything to prevent this, but repression only strengthens tribal solidarity.

The Han Chinese who live outside mainland China are largely (but not entirely) outside Beijing's control. There are 10 million ethnic Chinese in Indonesia, 7 million in Thailand, 6 million in Malaysia and nearly 4 million in the United States.[37] The number in Africa has more than doubled in two decades, from 99,000 in 1990 to an estimated 238,000 in 2009, and some say that figure is far too low. The number of Chinese in the Americas has nearly tripled over the same period, from 2.6 million to 7.3 million. According to the Taiwanese government, there were a total of 39 million Chinese living overseas in December 2009.[38]

That figure—39 million—is often quoted, but misleading. It does not include the 23 million Chinese people in Taiwan itself, for political reasons. Both the Chinese and Taiwanese governments consider Taiwan to be part of China. Beijing insists that Taiwan is a renegade province that must soon be reunited with the mainland. The Taiwanese government, for its part, claims to be the rightful ruler of all China, though it makes no serious effort to pursue this claim. I don't want to get mired in this argument. I'm going to include the Chinese in Taiwan in my discussion of the diaspora because they look and act like members of the diaspora. They live outside the Chinese mainland and are not subject to its rules. Like the Chinese in the United States or Australia, they are much richer than the mainland Chinese, and they can vote. So for the purposes of my argument, there are at least 60 million people in the Chinese diaspora.*

I need to talk about Hong Kong, too. A former British colony, Hong Kong has been part of the People's Republic of China since 1997, and no one disputes China's sovereignty over it. Yet Hong Kong's people have much in common with the diaspora. Under the "one country, two systems" formula agreed between London and Beijing, which is supposed to last until 2047, Hong Kong residents enjoy freedom of speech, association and assembly. They can even vote to elect members of a legislature, though Beijing has done its best to dilute Hong Kong's democracy.

Hong Kong is the commercial gateway to China, partly because of its superb natural harbor, but mostly because it is an island of transparent laws, first-world banks and enforceable contracts. Taiwan's links with the mainland are also vibrant. Some 800,000 Taiwanese citizens live on the mainland, and Taiwanese firms have invested at least $90 billion there. Trade across the Taiwan Strait

---

* Perhaps Taiwan will be reunited with the rest of China someday: nationalism is a sticky glue. But reunification will not happen peacefully until the rest of China is democratic. The Taiwanese are no more likely to give up the vote voluntarily than anyone else would be. The opinion polls are hardly ambiguous about this. Asked whether they wish to be reunited with the rest of China "as soon as possible," only 1 percent of Taiwanese people said yes.

is booming. Until 2008 there were no direct flights between Taiwan and the mainland, yet in 2010 some 1.6 million mainlanders came to look around, meet relatives, talk business and see the sights.[39]

Most of the foreign direct investment that flows into China is handled by the Chinese diaspora, loosely defined. In 2009 China received $90 billion of foreign direct investment (excluding investments in banks and other financial firms). Of this, $61.6 billion (68 percent of the total) came from places where the population was more or less entirely ethnic Chinese (principally Hong Kong and Taiwan). A further $3.9 billion came from Singapore, where the majority population is Chinese.[40]

These data may be misleading. Some of this foreign investment is not foreign at all. (Mainland Chinese businesses sometimes launder money through Hong Kong and invest it back into China. The aim is to make the money appear foreign in order to exploit Chinese government incentives for foreign investment.) Nevertheless, it is clear that ethnic Chinese are far more confident about investing in China than anyone else, and that non-Chinese who wish to invest there nearly always seek the assistance of a Chinese partner or intermediary.

The overseas Chinese serve as a bridge for foreigners who wish to do business in China. They understand the local business culture. They know whom to trust. In a country where the rule of law is, to put it mildly, uncertain, that knowledge can be the difference between success and failure. Studies show that American firms that employ lots of Chinese Americans find it much easier to set up operations in China without the crutch of a joint venture with a local firm.[41]

This fits with what we know about trade patterns between countries. The stronger the cultural ties between two nations, the more they trade with each other. Pankaj Ghemawat, of IESE Business School in Spain, calculates that two otherwise identical countries will trade with each other 42 percent more if they share a common language and 188 percent more if they have a common colonial past.[42]

The Chinese diaspora is the richest recruiting ground for the talent that China needs if it is to sustain its pell-mell growth. Between 2003 and 2011, more than 325,000 Chinese people returned to China after studying abroad—more than three times as many as returned in the whole of the previous three decades, estimates David

Zweig, of Hong Kong University of Science and Technology.[43] Still, at least two-thirds of the students who have left China since 1978 have stayed away.[44]

Foreign-educated returnees—known as *haigui,* or "sea turtles," because of a pun that doesn't work in English—are hugely influential in the most dynamic sectors of China's economy, such as technology, banking and anything that requires contact with the outside world. The Chinese government is of two minds about the sea turtles: It fears them, since they might bring subversive ideas back from their travels. But it also recognizes that China needs their skills.

The Chinese government's National Talent Plan, which it published in 2010, talks of an urgent need to attract back more overseas talent. The country is now too rich to keep growing at double-digit rates simply by shifting more people from rice paddies to factories, notes Henry Wang, an adviser to the Chinese leadership. The job of making cheap clothes, toys and electronics is moving to even cheaper countries, such as Vietnam. If China is to climb the technology ladder, it needs to pay more attention to talent, he argues.[45] And that means wooing the diaspora.

ELEPHANTS ABROAD

The Chinese diaspora is not the only one that crisscrosses the globe and links an emerging giant to everyone else. The Indian diaspora is smaller than China's but still huge, with at least 25 million members scattered across nearly every country.[46] Nonresident Indians, as they are called, are every bit as dynamic as the overseas Chinese. And their modern history shows some striking parallels.

Like the overseas Chinese, Indian emigrants have found commercial success in many countries, and sometimes suffered persecution because of it. Also like the Chinese, they have benefited immensely from the opening up of their ancestral homeland's economy since 1991.

Indians emigrated in large numbers during the nineteenth century. During the colonial period, the British encouraged (and sometimes forced) them to move to other parts of the empire. They laid railways in Africa, worked as clerks in East Asia and toiled in the plantations of Trinidad, Fiji and Suriname. Despite this arduous start, many Indians eventually prospered, finding niches as traders, bankers and tailors from South Africa to Singapore.[47]

Some of modern India's biggest firms were founded by members of the diaspora. Dhirubai Ambani, an industrialist, got his start in the port city of Aden (now part of Yemen), where he worked as a clerk for the British. He noticed that the face value of the local *rial* coins was less than the value of their silver content. So he put out word in the souks that he would buy every coin he could get. He gathered the coins, melted them down and sold the silver bullion. His operation was shut down after three months—the authorities were annoyed to see that all the coins were disappearing from circulation. But he made a mint, so to speak. "I don't believe in not taking opportunities," he once said.[48]

Mr. Ambani later took his opportunity-spotting skills back to India and built one of the country's largest conglomerates, the Reliance group. He died in 2002, but his empire continues to grow, despite a simmering feud between his sons, Mukesh, the elder, and Anil. Mukesh Ambani, who was born in Aden, was the ninth-richest man in the world in 2011.[49]

After independence in 1947, India's leaders turned their backs on the diaspora. Or, more precisely, they tried to shut India off from commercial contact with the world. They associated capitalism with colonial oppression: not surprisingly, since the initial British conquest of India had been carried out by a private enterprise, the British East India Company, which ruled much of India from 1757 to 1858. As Nandan Nilekani, an Indian software tycoon, later put it: "India's most significant experience with entrepreneurship was as a country captured by a business."[50] Mahatma Gandhi, the hero of the Indian independence movement, thought India should be a nation of self-sufficient villagers with spinning wheels. Indira Gandhi (no relation), India's prime minister from 1966 to 1977 and 1980 to 1984, described capitalism as one of the "dark and evil forces" undermining democracy.[51]

For most of the period after independence, the Indian government pursued the idea of *swadeshi* (self-reliance). It shut out foreign trade and erected a tangle of controls to curb domestic capitalists. This "license Raj," Nilekani explains, was enforced by bureaucrats who specialized in "the slow transfer of paper from desk to desk."[52] The difficulty of obtaining a license to do anything prevented new firms from challenging incumbents. This created "lazy monopolies, which held Indian consumers captive to products of terrible quality—yellow paper, refrigerators that didn't cool and cars that backfired on their way off the assembly line."[53]

The license Raj kept India poor and drove many of its most enterprising citizens to emigrate. Oddly, democracy itself gave members of India's upper castes another reason to leave. Universal suffrage quickly transferred power from the elite to the masses, since lower-caste Indians tended to vote for lower-caste politicians, who made sure that large quotas of civil-service jobs were reserved for members of their own castes. Upper-caste Indians were suddenly marginalized politically. Many of them took their skills and emigrated, or quit working for the government and found a niche in private business instead.

Devesh Kapur, a professor at the University of Pennsylvania, makes the intriguing argument that India's fragile democracy has survived largely because upper-caste Indians left the country. To explain: at independence, Indian democracy seemed unlikely to last. The country was mostly rural and illiterate, with only a tiny middle class. It suffered from multiple cleavages of caste and tribe, and had gone from colonial subjugation to one man, one vote at the stroke of a pen. In other countries where the elite's privileges were threatened like this, they fought back, using their wealth to subvert democracy or even back coups. In India, they emigrated instead.[54]

Mr. Kapur thinks this was because in India, the elites' status depended largely on their skills, which made it easier for them to move. (A pernicious tradition, persisting well into the 1970s, held that education was something for the upper castes alone. In West Bengal at that time, four-fifths of the children enrolled in schools were from the upper castes, as were 98 percent of those attending secondary schools.)[55]

Compare the Indian situation with neighboring Pakistan, where the upper classes derive their power from vast landholdings. They are rooted to the spot; they cannot walk away from their estates. Pakistani elites have more tools to subvert democracy—peasants vote the way the landlord tells them to, or they wake up homeless. Wealthy landowners dominate the army and the main political parties. They ensure that—amazingly—agricultural income is not taxed in Pakistan. In short, the elites have the motive and the means to block change.

All this helps to explain why democracy struggles to take root in Pakistan. Mr. Kapur notes that in the parts of India where vast feudal landholdings remained largely intact, such as in the state of Bihar, there has been far more political violence than in places where the elites were more mobile.[56] In the rest of the country, however, emigration provided an escape valve for elites who might otherwise have undermined the new democracy.

For a long time, India's government wanted nothing to do with the diaspora. The first prime minister after independence, Jawaharlal Nehru, was once a migrant himself, having been educated at Harrow School and Cambridge University in England. But he insisted that Indians who took foreign nationality should divorce India and bind themselves instead to their new homes.[57]

Even when Indians abroad suffered persecution, the government turned a blind eye. In 1972 Idi Amin, a murderous East African despot, suddenly expelled all the Indians from Uganda, where they were a commercially successful minority. He wanted to steal their banks and shops and give them to natives. Perhaps 70,000 Ugandan Indians were forced to flee. Amin's soldiers robbed and beat them as they left. India severed diplomatic ties with Uganda, but otherwise did nothing.[58]

Only gradually did India's government realize what a huge mistake it was to ignore the diaspora. By 1987, when a coup in the Pacific nation of Fiji drove ethnic Indians out of government and prompted crowds of them to flee, the Indian response was firmer. Rajiv Gandhi (Indira's son), the Indian prime minister, successfully pushed for Fiji's international isolation.[59]

One reason why India started to pay attention to nonresident Indians was that they were so conspicuously successful. In the early 1970s, an Indian lawmaker cheekily asked Indira Gandhi: "Can the prime minister explain why Indians seem to thrive economically under every government in the world except hers?" She had no good answer.[60]

Ethnic Indians in the United States are not merely richer than the average Indian; they are richer than the average American. At the time of this writing, the bosses of Citigroup, Mastercard and PepsiCo were all of Indian origin, as were the governors of Louisiana and South Carolina and the dean of Harvard Business School. Nearly 70 percent of the foreign-born Indians in America have college degrees, and 38 percent have advanced degrees.[61] The stereotype of the cerebral Indian has passed into popular culture. In Scott Adams's *Dilbert* cartoons, Asok the Indian intern has a brain so powerful that he can heat a cup of tea by holding it to his forehead and imagining fire.[62]

Because nonresident Indians are so widely dispersed, there is no single authoritative source of data on them. But Mr. Kapur has organized a number of useful measures, details of which are in his excellent book *Diaspora, Development and Democracy*. These include a huge, randomized "Survey of Emigration from India," in which 210,000 Indian households were asked questions about any friends and relatives they had living abroad. Mr. Kapur also built a database of 410,000 Indian households in the United States, put more detailed questions to 2,200 Indian American households and arranged for a study of the foreign links of India's elite.

He found that nonresident Indians come from the more prosperous, well-educated strata of Indian society. Mr. Kapur also found that the higher a family's social status, the larger its global network. Nearly a third of urban professional families in India know someone who lives abroad. About 10 percent say they have an immediate family member (such as a brother or a daughter) abroad. Another 16 percent say that a member of their extended family (such as a cousin) lives overseas.

By contrast, virtually no rural laborers have relatives abroad. (For them, striking out into the unknown means migrating to a city in India.) Some of the urban poor do move abroad. Several million live in the Middle East, sweating on construction sites and doing other jobs that Gulf Arabs would rather not do themselves. Their remittances keep the south Indian state of Kerala afloat. (I'll talk more about the power of remittances in Chapter 5.)

Indian migration has accelerated in recent years. There were about 450,000 Indian-born residents in America in 1990. That figure had quadrupled by 2009, to nearly 2 million.[63] Because so many Indian Americans are recent migrants, their links with India are still fresh, and therefore useful. Indian American venture capitalists back Indian-Indian software firms. Scientists and engineers in both countries collaborate furiously. Indian tycoons who might once have made their children learn the business by working in the family factory in India are now more likely to send them abroad to learn global standards.

For example, Rishad Premji, the likely heir to his father Azim Premji's Wipro software empire, spent time at Harvard Business School, the American consultancy Bain & Company and General Electric before joining the family firm. Siddartha Mallya, the son of Vijay Mallya, a flamboyant Indian drinks baron, cut his teeth at Diageo (the makers of Guinness stout) and Whyte and Mackay (a Scotch distiller) before returning to India.[64]

India's most innovative firms are now run by a class of brainy globe-trotters who are just as comfortable in Manhattan or Mayfair as they are in Mumbai. Ratan Tata, perhaps India's most admired industrialist, studied architecture and structural engineering at Cornell and then business at Harvard. Lakshmi Mittal, a steel magnate who is the richest Indian in the world, began his career in Indonesia and now lives in London.[65]

Many elite Indians are more at ease with traditional English customs than English people are. Pass through an Indian airport and there are stacks of novels by Charles Dickens and P. G. Wodehouse in the bookshop. The headquarters of Tata Ltd. in London, just opposite the Queen's gardens, are a throwback to a bygone age, with high ceilings, antique chairs and fussy tea sets. They also serve a type of English biscuit (cookie) that was popular in colonial days.

Global Indians schmooze easily at the talking-shops where the latest ideas in business, technology and finance are debated, from the TED conference in California to the World Economic Forum in Davos, Switzerland. They speak better English than the European delegates, and much better English than the Chinese ones. (Come to think of it, they speak better English than some of the English and American corporate bosses, too.)

Nonresident Indians bring ideas and investment back home, as I'll discuss in Chapter 4. But arguably the biggest favor the diaspora has done for India was to persuade it to open up to the world in the first place. They were not the only force—four decades of stagnation alerted India's leaders to the possibility that something was wrong with their economic model. But the diaspora was highly influential.

Palaniappan Chidambaram was a committed socialist until he went to Harvard Business School, but when confronted with America's widespread prosperity, he started to have doubts. Two-car garages and second helpings of dessert no longer seem remarkable to Americans, but to an Indian visitor, American abundance was simply astounding. During two tours as finance minister back home, from 1996 to 1997 and 2004 to 2008, he helped to push through free-market reforms. He argues that his fellow global Indians helped to open India up, in two ways:

> First, the phenomenal success achieved by Indians abroad by practic-
> ing free enterprise meant that if Indians were allowed to function in an
> open market, they could replicate some of that success here [in India].
> Secondly, by 1991 sons and daughters of political leaders and senior
> civil servants were all going abroad and studying abroad and living and
> working abroad. I think they played a great part in influencing the think-
> ing of their parents. I know a number of civil servants who were shut-
> tling between one ideology at home and one ideology at the workplace.
> They had been challenged by their children. What are you talking about
> when we are doing the exact opposite thing?[66]

The prime mover behind India's economic reforms was Manmohan Singh, who was finance minister from 1991 to 1996. Singh was (and is) a thoroughly global Indian. He was educated at both Cambridge and Oxford, worked for the UN and ran a think tank in Geneva before entering politics. As finance minister, he solicited the views of overseas Indians wherever he traveled. Indian businesspeople in Bangkok told him how easy it was to set up a business in Thailand, unlike in India. Indians in Singapore complained of the long delays they experienced when trying to obtain permission to invest in India. Mr. Singh promptly streamlined the rules.[67]

Mr. Singh and his fellow reformers reconnected India to the rest of the world. They tore down barriers to foreign trade. They chopped through the tangle of regulations that throttled private business. The economic growth they unleashed lifted hundreds of millions out of poverty and put India back on track to be a superpower. Mr. Singh was elevated to the job of prime minister of India in 2004. As I write, the Indian economy is charging ahead like a herd of (somewhat ill-disciplined) elephants. India's growth rate, once the laughingstock of the developing world, will probably outpace China's before long.[68]

2

BRIDGES TO CHINA

TALES FROM THE WORLD'S GREATEST DIASPORA

Every migrant's story is different. Most are worth hearing.

Take Thio Thiaw Siat, a Hakka* from Guangdong province in China, who moved to what is now Indonesia in 1858. It was a journey of 2,000 miles and he was only 17. That tells you something about him already. After he arrived, he made a huge fortune from trading tobacco, opium and booze, and from growing rubber, tea and coconut palms.

One day he wanted to sail from Singapore to China with three employees, including his German doctor. He sent a flunky to buy four first-class tickets on a German steamship. He was told that no Chinese were allowed in the first-class cabins—only his European doctor could travel in comfort.

Thio was furious. He placed an advertisement in European papers announcing that he was starting a shipping line of his own. It would carry only Chinese passengers, he promised, and would charge only

---

* The Hakkas are a subgroup of the Han Chinese, mostly hailing from Guangdong, Fujian or Jiangxi.

half the fare of the German lines. When the German company realized that he was serious, they apologized and invited him to travel first class. That was not good enough for Thio. He held his ground until the German merchant fleet allowed all Chinese travelers to buy whatever tickets they could afford.[1]

Chinese people have been leaving China for centuries. The first famous Chinese explorer was Zheng He, a fifteenth-century admiral serving the Ming dynasty. He sailed with a huge fleet as far as India, Arabia and East Africa, returning with camels, ostriches and ivory. But China's age of discovery did not last long. Later emperors decided that the wider world was not worth knowing about. Fearful that Chinese expatriates might trade, grow rich and plot against their rulers, the Manchu emperors ordered that anyone who left and came back should be beheaded.[2] A formal ban on emigration remained in place until 1893.

Despite the ban, legions of Chinese people emigrated in the nineteenth century. Life in China was harsh. The country was brutally hierarchical, prone to famine and ravaged by the Taiping rebellion, in which a man claiming to be Jesus's younger brother raised a vast army and laid waste to 17 provinces. Some 20 million people died during the Taiping revolt. Unsurprisingly, it prompted a wave of emigration.[3]

The twentieth century also gave Chinese people ample reason to pack their bags. The Japanese occupied Manchuria in 1931 and much of the rest of China from 1937 to 1945, fighting a devastating war against the Nationalists and the Communists. When the Japanese left, the Nationalists and the Communists fought each other.

After the Communists triumphed, Chairman Mao Zedong subjected his compatriots to social experiment after brutal social experiment. During the Great Leap Forward of 1958–61, he forced peasants into collective farms, causing mass starvation. During the Cultural Revolution (1966–76), he murdered people suspected of bourgeois sympathies and forced engineers and college professors to work as peasants in the fields or laborers in factories. Between 40 million and 70 million people died from his excesses.[4] Only through draconian restrictions on people's movements did Mao avert a mass exodus.

Today nearly every Chinese emigrant over the age of 30 has a chilling tale to tell. Li Ka-shing, a property developer whom *Forbes* ranks as the richest Chinese man in the world, fled to Hong Kong from the war-scorched Chinese mainland in 1940, when he was 12.[5] Jung Chang, a Chinese writer who now lives in Britain, saw her parents publicly humiliated during the Cultural Revolution, forced to kneel for hours in the rain with placards round their necks. *Wild Swans,* her account of her family's troubles, has sold millions of copies.[6] Younger emigrants recall the Tiananmen Square massacre of 1989, when tanks in Beijing crushed the bodies of protesters and the hopes of Chinese citizens who wanted the right to choose their rulers.

Small wonder so many Chinese people have sought their fortunes elsewhere. Some went involuntarily: nineteenth-century labor brokers in Hong Kong and Macau sent steamerloads of indentured "coolies" to toil in the docks of Singapore or the plantations of Cuba. Many had been "shanghai-ed": kidnapped and bundled onto ships against their will.

Yet others went voluntarily, to avoid starving at home or because they saw better opportunities abroad. They settled in Southeast Asia as traders. They rushed to California and Australia to pan for gold. They went wherever there was a living to be made: to Africa, to South America and eventually more or less everywhere.[7]

Wherever they went, they acquired a reputation for shrewdness and hard work. In the late nineteenth century Rudyard Kipling, a British poet, traveled through Singapore, Hong Kong and what is now Malaysia, and reported that he never saw a Chinese person asleep during daylight hours.[8] Rama VI, the king of Siam (now Thailand), referred to them as the "Jews of the East"—and he did not mean it as a compliment.

Like the Jews, the Chinese were often persecuted. In the United States, natives who feared that low-paid laborers were pushing them out of jobs sometimes lynched them. By one count, there were 55 anti-Chinese riots in the western United States in the late nineteenth century.[9] And in 1882, Congress passed the Chinese Exclusion Act, blocking further Chinese immigration until it was repealed in 1943.

In some parts of the world, persecution persists. I saw a flash of it in 1998, while covering a coup attempt in Lesotho, a tiny African nation known for its scenic hills and blanket-wearing cowherds. The capital, Maseru, was in chaos when I arrived. The army from neighboring South

Africa had come to restore order, but had failed miserably. Mobs of looters were ransacking shops and setting buildings on fire. The biggest local factories were owned by Chinese immigrants, who employed locals to make textiles for export. Many locals felt they paid excessively low wages. They were an easy target. I watched as rioters burned their factories and looted nearby shops. The Chinese factory owners fled. The police were too scared to intervene. So was I.

In Malaysia, resentment at the prosperity of the Chinese minority sparked an orgy of shop burning by native Malays in 1969, in which perhaps 200 people died. The government responded by passing a series of discriminatory laws designed to make the *bumiputras* (literally "sons of the soil," i.e., native Malays) as rich as the Chinese. Malays were given priority in university admissions and civil-service jobs, and private companies owned by non-Malays were obliged to transfer some of their shares to Malays. The architect of Malaysia's affirmative action policies later admitted that they prompted native Malays to treat university places as a right, and therefore to neglect their studies.[10] But the policies persist today, albeit in modified form.

In Indonesia, home to the largest Chinese minority in the world, discrimination was for a long time both blatant and intense. The Indonesian army believed that Red China was behind, or had at least inspired, an attempted communist coup in 1965. It snuffed out the alleged coup with white-hot savagery. In all, some 500,000 people were killed in the "Year of Living Dangerously," as Christopher Koch, a novelist, called it.

After the bloodletting, an officer called Suharto seized power and held it until 1998. He tried to force Chinese Indonesians to sever their ties with China. He banned Chinese-language newspapers, since his goons, unable to read Chinese, could not tell whether they were being used to transmit subversive messages from Beijing. The only exception was a dreary paper that was written first in *Bahasa Indonesia,* the local language, then censored and translated into Mandarin.

Suharto banned the teaching of Chinese in schools. He banned Chinese books, forcing Chinese Indonesians to smuggle volumes through customs in the folds of their clothes. If caught, they could usually bribe the customs official to look the other way, but the rules left them in no doubt that they were second-class citizens.

The Indonesian president even banned public displays of Chinese culture, such as signs in Chinese or celebrations of the Chinese New Year. That was wretched, recalls Aimee Dawis, the author of *The Chinese of Indonesia*.[11] It was only when she went to school in Singapore, she told me, that she realized that the New Year celebration could involve joyful dragon dances in the streets.

Suharto may have oppressed Chinese Indonesians, but he also liked doing business with them. Precisely because they were members of a tiny and unpopular minority, they posed no political threat to him. A native Indonesian billionaire might have parlayed his money into political power, but there was no danger of an ethnic Chinese billionaire doing so.

The cozy ties between the Suharto regime and certain Chinese tycoons made Chinese Indonesians in general less popular. And the army played a fiendish double game, sometimes deliberately provoking anti-Chinese riots so that it could crush them and then tell everyone what a good thing it was that Indonesia had a firm leader to keep order.

Since democracy came to Indonesia in 1998, however, relations between Chinese Indonesians and the *pribumi* have been smoother. The pogroms have stopped. Daily interactions are less acid. Ms. Dawis remembers enduring catcalls as she walked in the streets of Jakarta in the 1990s. Laborers would call her *amoy* (a word for a Chinese woman that carries lewd overtones).[12] John Riady, a young Chinese Indonesian businessman, recalls how, as a child playing soccer against native Indonesians, they would taunt him by suggesting that he go back to China and sell electronics.[13] In recent years, however, neither Mr. Riady nor Ms. Dawis can recall receiving any racist taunts at all.

Four themes crop up time and again in my conversations with members of the Chinese diaspora. First, they are delighted that China has sloughed off Maoism and started to grow richer. Second, they notice that people take them more seriously since China has become a serious power. Third, they want to help their motherland. Finally, they assume that the rewards for doing so will be more than just a warm glow of patriotic satisfaction.

There are nearly as many ways for migrants to engage with their homelands as there are migrants, and the information revolution has made all of them easier. To give a taste of this infinite variety, here are some of their stories.

FROM BEIJING TO BETHESDA: MEI XU
AND HER MINI-MULTINATIONAL

When Mei Xu was born, her prospects looked wretched. It was 1967, the height of the Cultural Revolution. Mao's Red Guards were leading witch hunts against anyone suspected of disloyalty to the Communist Party, and Mei's family had been prominent capitalists.

Her father's family had owned sugar plantations; her mother's family, textile factories. They lost everything after the Communists seized power in 1949: their homes, their businesses, their personal belongings and "most importantly, a normal life," sighs Ms. Xu. All four of her grandparents died young. She never met any of them.[14]

Mei's mother was a school principal. Her father was a professor turned engineer. Because they were well educated, they were denounced as enemies of the people. Almost every night, they were summoned to undergo public chastisement. In front of jeering crowds, they were forced to renounce their bourgeois heritage and vow to start a new life as communists. "My childhood was about being locked in a small room at home while my parents went to be 'reeducated,'" remembers Mei.

Her parents never complained. Mei thinks this was either because they had been brainwashed—her mother spent part of her youth in a labor camp—or because they were terrified of saying the wrong things. To survive, the family kept a low profile. Mei recalls her mother teaching her communist ideas about equality. But she also found time to teach her to appreciate art and beauty.

After Mao died in 1976 and China began to open up, Mei's life took a turn for the better. The government suddenly realized, after decades of gazing inward, that not nearly enough Chinese people spoke foreign languages. So it invited foreigners to come and teach at special foreign-language schools. The aim was to train a new cadre of diplomats and trade officials. Such schools were hard to get into, but Mei was studious and a quick learner. She passed a battery of tests and won admission to a foreign-language boarding school in Hangzhou, near Shanghai. Her parents wept for joy.

She entered the school at the age of 12 and immersed herself in the English language and Western culture. She discovered the art of the Renaissance. She found she loved the Dutch Old Masters, and preferred their realism to the abstraction of so much Chinese painting.

She attended university in Beijing. While there, she worked part time for the World Bank and for the UN. She enjoyed this tremendously. It allowed her to make use of her language skills and travel all over China. She made friends from all around the world, since the bank was brimming with German consultants and Danish engineers. She helped arrange funding for schemes to install water pumps in villages, and learned a lot about getting things done.

Then, in 1989, "a big thing happened in Beijing," as she describes it. The People's Liberation Army slaughtered the people in Tiananmen Square. Because the protesters were largely students, the government became suspicious of students in general. Many were sent to the countryside to be reeducated.

Mei was ordered to spend a year working in a mineral warehouse in Dalian. The highlight of her day was to sign a piece of paper on a clipboard to confirm that a truck had picked up its appointed load. There was no intellectual stimulation, and no opportunity for Mei to use her language skills. So she applied to go to university in the United States.

She was accepted by the University of Maryland, where she studied journalism, graduating in 1992. She had intended to go back to the World Bank, but the bank was short of cash that year because of the first Gulf War. (The elder President George Bush was spending so much money on expelling Iraq from Kuwait that he skimped on some of his other obligations, such as funding the World Bank.) Mei instead found a job in New York at a firm that exported high-tech medical equipment, such as ultrasound machines, to China. But she was uninspired.

The company put her up in a hotel near Bloomingdale's, an upmarket department store. "That was very dangerous," she laughs. Mei has a taste for pretty things. But she noticed that the household goods at Bloomingdale's were much less exciting than the clothes. Clothes shoppers were spoilt with choice, with a vast selection of designs by the world's most creative fashion gurus. But if you wanted to put something chic on your table or in your living room, the store did not have much to offer. Mei saw a gap. She decided to fill it.

She and her husband, David Wang, decided to set up their own business. They had no children, no mortgage and no responsibilities, so they felt able to take a risk. They began by contacting friends back in China and asking them to send over samples of Chinese-made goods that might sell well in America. They took a selection to a trade show in North Carolina in 1994. Of all their wares, Chinese-made candles sold the best. So they started experimenting in their basement, melting wax in old Campbell's Soup cans. Instead of using solid colors and plain scents, such as lavender or vanilla, they whipped up striking mottled designs and subtle botanical fragrances.

At first, they had their candles made in Chinese factories belonging to other people, but after a while, their business was large enough to need a factory of its own. Mei proposed that her sister, a computer scientist in Hangzhou, open a factory there. Mei's sister jumped at the chance and quickly hired a team of candle experts.

Their first big break was persuading Target, an American chain store, to stock their products. Their candles were so popular that Target bumped up its order from $2 million worth to more than $8 million. Their factory could not cope. They had to find extra capacity, and fast—they had only two months to meet the Christmas rush. To make matters worse, the whole country was taking time off to celebrate the Chinese New Year. Mei called all her friends and searched frantically for a factory that could help her fulfill Target's order. She succeeded, with no time to spare. "Someone who does not know China could not have done that," she points out. Her firm, Pacific Trade International, now generates about $100 million in annual sales.

Even a relatively low-tech business such as candle making evolves rapidly. Mei no longer manufactures in China; she has moved basic processes to Vietnam. Her firm is truly multinational. The most imaginative parts of the design process are performed by highly paid Americans in Rockville, Maryland. More routine design work, such as drawing sample patterns in various colors to show customers, is done by designers in China. In 2010 she opened a factory in Maryland to meet urgent orders from customers who cannot wait.

China is no longer just a source of cheap labor, says Mei. It is increasingly a place from which good ideas flow. And it is potentially a huge market. For now, her sales in China are modest. Many Asians see candles as a fire hazard. So Mei hopes to figure out other ways to fill Chinese homes with delightful fragrances. And perhaps she can tempt them with other small luxuries: she also owns a firm called Blissliving Home that sells brightly colored furniture, wall hangings and duvet covers, among other things.

Mei lives in Bethesda, Maryland, outside Washington, DC.* She travels often between the United States, China and Europe. She worries sometimes about the rise of nationalism in China, which she detests. There is no need to divide the world into opposing camps, she reckons; everyone can benefit through peaceful exchange.

You don't have to love fancy candles—personally I couldn't care less about them—to draw lessons from this story. Migration creates opportunities. Mei used her knowledge of China and America, and her connections in both countries, to build a multinational business from scratch. As it expands, she creates jobs on both sides of the Pacific. In a small way, she binds China and America together. And most of what she does would have been impossible a generation ago.

When China was closed to the outside world, the overseas Chinese had no hub; their trading networks mostly linked Chinese exiles in one foreign port with Chinese exiles in another foreign port. They still do that, but they also penetrate deep into the Middle Kingdom. And they not only trade but also invest billions in brick-and-mortar businesses. Consider how the Riadys, a wealthy Chinese Indonesian family, have changed with the times.

---

* It's a lovely place, checkered with well-tended lawns, crowned with azaleas and populated by agreeable suburbanites. But the welcome sign that describes Bethesda as "A World of Excitement" is exaggerating somewhat. I lived there for five years, during which time the only drama on our street involved rumors of a rabid raccoon.

FROM JAKARTA TO FUJIAN,
VIA ARKANSAS: THE RIADYS

When John Riady was 13, his parents woke him up in the middle of the night. He was whisked to the airport, where he boarded a flight for Hong Kong. The year was 1998. Thanks to a debt crisis, Southeast Asia's economies were in freefall. Indonesia's president of 31 years, Suharto, was about to be toppled. Mobs of native Indonesians were attacking shops and businesses owned by ethnic Chinese. John Riady's family is ethnic Chinese, and one of Indonesia's wealthiest. They survived the riots, but they were shaken.

Mr. Riady's parents and grandparents stayed behind in Jakarta to look after the family business. It was a frightening time. Rioters burned down one of their malls in Jakarta, killing 86 people.[15]

I met Mr. Riady in 2011 at his office in Jakarta, a city of tedious traffic jams and exquisite skewered beef in peanut sauce. Democracy has brought peace to Indonesia. Corruption is still a huge problem, but native Indonesians no longer feel that their views count for nothing. Because life is improving, fewer *pribumi* feel the urge to find scapegoats. Race relations are smoother, as are relations between the Muslim majority and non-Muslim minorities. (The Riadys, for example, are Christians.)

Despite the progress of the past decade, few Chinese Indonesians take peace for granted. Mr. Riady talks of the constant need to nurture democracy and to promote religious tolerance. Though only in his mid-twenties, he runs a daily newspaper, the *Jakarta Globe,* which supports pluralistic ideas. He studied law at Columbia University in America, so he has given some thought to such issues as civil rights and free speech. The family money, of course, buys a useful megaphone.

The Riadys have been in Indonesia for nearly a century. John's great-grandparents ran a batik shop. His grandfather, Mochtar Riady, built the family fortune after World War II. He started out among the bicycle traders of Jakarta, many of whom had roots in the same Chinese province, Fujian. A relative helped him get started, and soon he was thriving. In 1960, he went into banking. He later admitted that at the time, he "couldn't tell the left from the right of a balance sheet."[16] Yet he raised the cash to buy an ailing bank—some

$200,000—by tapping the network of Chinese lenders he had met while selling bicycles.

He then built a business by tending to a neglected niche market: the Chinese Indonesian firms that dominated bicycle making in a country whose roads were dominated by bicycles. He quickly learned how to read accounts, but always insisted that the essence of banking was something else. "To me, banking isn't a business of buying and selling money," he said. "It buys and sells trust."[17]

In the 1960s and early '70s, Mochtar bought and turned around three banks, each time using his contacts to find a sector that was starved of credit, and then supplying it. After bicycle makers, he financed textile firms, farm businesses and importers. In 1975 he forged an alliance with another Chinese Indonesian tycoon, Liem Sioe Liong, buying a stake in the bank at the center of Liem's sprawling business empire and helping to manage it better. In 1976 Mochtar started calling his empire the Lippo Group, from the Chinese words *li* (energy) and *pao* (treasure).

Rosabeth Moss Kanter, a professor at Harvard Business School who has produced a study on the Riady family, argues that for the Lippo Group, "networking is not just supportive of the business strategy; networking is the business strategy." Ethnic ties, she writes, "can serve as an entrepreneurial springboard while more universal business alliances are formed."[18] Mochtar Riady would likely agree. "Without a network, we can do nothing," he once said. The Riadys nurtured their *guanxi* (connections) carefully, sometimes buying stakes in firms owned by their business partners to demonstrate that they wanted the relationship to endure.

Since the Chinese diaspora is widely dispersed, the Riadys found it easier than they might otherwise have done to enter markets far from home. They spread from Indonesia into Hong Kong and Singapore. In the 1980s, they moved into the United States, hooking up with Chinese American firms engaged in transpacific trade.

Where possible, they forged ties with non-Chinese movers and shakers, such as Bill Clinton, whom James Riady (John's father) got to know as governor of Arkansas. This link later caused the Riadys serious embarrassment. James Riady was fined $8.6 million in 2001 for steering donations from foreigners to American political campaigns, which is illegal in the United States.[19] James said afterward that he had learned his lesson: "Business and politics do not mix."[20] American newspapers still describe him as disgraced, though his offense would barely raise an eyebrow in Indonesia.[21]

When China opened up, the Riadys came knocking. Until 1990, they could not easily do business with their ancestral homeland because the Indonesian government frowned on it. But in 1990 Jakarta restored normal diplomatic ties with Beijing. Mochtar Riady promptly spent eight months touring China by car, taking stock of the country's progress, sniffing out opportunities and, of course, forging new friendships.

The Riady empire was badly battered during the Asian financial crisis of 1997–98. Panicked investors pulled their money out of nearly every Southeast Asian country, and Indonesia suffered more than most. The Lippo Group tottered on the brink of bankruptcy. Only by painful and aggressive restructuring did it avoid collapse.

But since then, the Riadys have found new opportunities in the homeland their family left nearly a century ago. John Riady told me that the first time he visited mainland China, in 1998, he was repelled by the squalor and the dysfunctional plumbing. Within five years, however, the infrastructure had improved so much that "it was like night and day." Roads, buildings, you name it—it was all better, he told me.[22]

Modern China understands the value of tapping into its diaspora network. The government has set up an entire ministry to deal with the overseas Chinese. Mr. Riady never ceases to be impressed by the hospitality he is shown whenever he visits China, which is at least twice a year. "They really make us feel at home," he says. The family is building a variety of businesses, from supermarkets to restaurants, in second-tier Chinese cities. The scale is super-sized, says Mr. Riady. Even a relatively unknown Chinese city may have several million inhabitants, all rapidly acquiring a taste for the nice things money can buy.

It is fashionable to deride both family firms and conglomerates. In the West, the conventional wisdom is that firms should be focused and professional—that is, they should concentrate on one or two things they do exceptionally well, and stay out of other businesses. And they should be managed by professionals, rather than the founder's children or grandchildren.

The Lippo Group runs afoul of both these rules. It is big (with 35,000 employees) and sprawling (it has interests in banking, insurance, property, retail, health care and media). Yet that may not be a bad thing. In developing countries, where political instability is common and the rule of law is unreliable, specialization is much riskier than it is in the West. If you put all your eggs in one business, you may wake up one day to find that the president's cronies have taken over that sector, and you are left with nothing.

Western firms put their trust in the law. Emerging Asian firms do not have that luxury. Instead they put their trust in their relatives or friends, and they spread their risks both geographically and across industries. James Riady is based in Indonesia; his younger brother, Stephen, is based in Hong Kong. Besides Indonesia, Hong Kong and mainland China, the Lippo Group operates in Singapore, Macau, the Philippines and South Korea.[23]

The Riadys used to build up companies and hang onto them. Now they build them up and sell them. That keeps the empire liquid, and therefore more secure. A shopping mall can be torched. A mine can be nationalized. Cash, by contrast, is easy to park in safe places and can be moved quickly when the need arises. Having lived through the mass killings of 1965, the financial meltdown and riots of 1997–98 and the ups and downs of the Suharto dictatorship, Chinese Indonesian families such as the Riadys have learned caution.

A family conglomerate like the Lippo Group is unlikely to generate any technological breakthroughs. It is not that sort of business. But it does help to spread capital, contacts and the basics of modern management to areas where most Western firms fear to tread, from the islands of Indonesia to the midsize cities of the Middle Kingdom. And despite all the controversies that surround the Riadys, that is no small service.

BROKE AMONG THE BARBARIANS: THE HARD LIFE OF A CHINESE EXPATRIATE

Chinese firms are increasingly global. They scramble for oil and copper in Africa. They scout for investment opportunities in the United

States and Europe. They are starting to set up offices throughout the world. Naturally, they are sending out Chinese executives to run them.

Expatriate Chinese executives are a relatively new phenomenon. Their situation is in many ways like that of a Western expatriate, but there are glaring differences. Western expats in China have typically moved from a liberal democracy with a sluggish economy to an authoritarian state with a fast-growing one. Chinese expats in the West have done the opposite. Each journey presents its own challenges.

Expats are different from other migrants. They arrive on foreign shores with the security of a job and a salary. Their assignments are temporary: they expect to return after a few years. They are less entrepreneurial than other migrants: more cogs in a corporate machine than fortune-seeking adventurers. Nonetheless, they are an important and growing part of the networks that link China and other emerging markets to the rest of the world.

Life for a Chinese expat is less peachy than you might imagine. Consider the food, for a start. English meat pies, says William So, groping for a tactful way to phrase this, "are dry and have no flavor." British nosh is no longer as awful as it was 30 years ago, he concedes. But prices in London are exorbitant, and Chinese executives posted abroad do not enjoy the same lavish pay and perks as Western expatriates in China, especially if they work for state-owned firms. Back home, Chinese managers have housemaids. "They are not used to cooking for themselves," says Mr. So, a telecommunications executive. When sent to work in rich countries, "they even have to clean their own toilets," he chuckles.[24]

Mr. So probably finds life in London easier than many other Chinese expatriates do. His English is excellent, not least because he was educated at a British boarding school. ("It was like a prison," he says: surrounded by cow-filled fields and a 45-minute walk from the nearest town.) He also studied computer science at Imperial College, London, which he enjoyed rather more.

When I spoke with Mr. So, he had just stepped down as the chief executive of the European subsidiary of China Unicom, a huge telecoms firm owned by the Chinese government. Freed from the corporate hierarchy, he could speak more frankly than most Chinese executives. He had been in charge of China Unicom's operations not only in Europe but also in Africa, a continent now packed with home-sick Chinese who want to call home. Much of his job involved working with European companies, some of which use China Unicom's infrastructure to connect calls between Europe and China.

Executives at Chinese firms who are posted to the West often come without their families, he explains: "They don't have the kind of expat package that pays for the kids' education and the wife's shopping." This makes for a lonely, gloomy time, unless the expat in question is young, single, fluent in English and gregarious.

In China a senior executive at a state-owned firm is a big fish. Waiters and receptionists grovel before him. The police treat him with deference. In the West he is just another middle-aged man in a suit.

Even as China Unicom's head man in Europe, Mr. So was paid a paltry Chinese salary plus a small cost-of-living allowance. His allowance was only 30 percent more than that of the most junior employee, he says. He managed to live reasonably well in London only because he had some investments, having founded and sold a small Internet company called Beijing Online before the dot-com bubble burst in 2000. He also owned some property. Without those cushions, his time in Britain would have been less comfortable.

Western expatriates in China are typically there because they want to be. Some find the culture fascinating. Most expect to make good money and burnish their résumés. A stint in China helps a Western executive rise to the top.[25] Yet the converse is not true. Chinese executives, especially at state-owned firms, win promotion by cultivating the right people, and those people live in China. Even a few years away from your connections can mean they go cold, quashing your chance of promotion. If you are a senior Chinese manager and you get posted abroad, it may mean you are not doing very well at home, says Mr. So—and if you work for a state-owned firm, you cannot refuse to go.

Young Chinese white-collar workers may enjoy the adventure of a foreign posting. Some want to learn about other cultures, improve their English, go clubbing and generally have fun. Mr. So suspects that women tend to have a better time than men. (Perhaps they find the culture less sexist. Perhaps they are luckier in love.) Men who have left their families behind, by contrast, can't wait for their tour of duty to end.

Many struggle with the language. Mr. So says that some of his expat colleagues spoke hardly any English, which is obviously a handicap. The Beijing subway has plenty of signs in English, but good luck finding any in Chinese on the London Underground. In theory, a Chinese firm in the West could hire locals who speak Chinese to help out. But in practice, such people could earn far more working for a Western firm in China, so they are hard to recruit.

Still, it's not all hardship. The one thing about the West that every Chinese expatriate appreciates is the air. "It's much cleaner," says Mr. So. "Everyone comments on this." British people are quite pleasant, too. They are very polite, he continues. When you go into a shop, you do not get the feeling that anyone is hostile. "But if you go into a pub and try to debate Chinese politics, it would be very hard," he says.

Another plus about working in the West is that the rules governing business are relatively straightforward. "Everything is transparent," says Mr. So. If you want to obtain a license to do something, you don't need to spend money bribing an official or hiring a go-between; "you just download the form from the Internet and apply."

Relationships between companies are simpler, too. In China, Mr. So explains, companies assume that customers will do business only with someone they like. They spend vast amounts of time wining and dining clients in private booths in swish restaurants. Western firms do this too, but not nearly as much.

Differences in corporate etiquette are a minefield. If a Chinese vendor gives a presentation and the customer asks a lot of questions he can't answer or raises potential problems, the vendor will be distraught, says Mr. So. He will assume that the customer does not like him. But if the customer is Western, it probably just means that he wants more information. "People [in the West] look at the facts, not the person," he says.

Another problem for Chinese expatriates is that "views of Chinese companies outside China are quite negative," Mr. So notes. "Most Chinese blame the media," he adds. Chinese brands lack cachet outside the domestic market. At home everyone recognizes names such as China Unicom, Lenovo or Bank of China, but most Europeans or Americans would struggle to name a single Chinese brand.

Westerners tend to assume that Western firms are superior, complains Mr. So. They think a big Western bank will be sounder than Bank of China, even though the Western bank has been in financial trouble. This attitude makes it hard to sell directly to Western consumers. (Of course, such stereotypes tend to change when the underlying facts change. As Chinese products improve, Western consumers will eventually notice—just ask the Japanese or the South Koreans.)

A final headache for Chinese expats is that when you move to an oppressive Western capitalist society, you encounter a working class that can throw its weight around. Europe's toiling masses sometimes go on strike, leaving streets unswept and commuters stranded. Chinese expats find this shocking. Though there are stoppages in some factories in China, no one strikes in public services there. "If they did, there would be trouble," says Mr. So.

Having quit his job, Mr. So decided to strike out on his own. He plans to use his contacts, technical expertise and language skills to help Chinese businesses in Africa connect with Europe and China, he told me. And he plans to stay in London, at least for a while, despite the food.

TECHNO-TURTLES: THE RETURNEES WHO POWER THE CHINESE INTERNET BOOM

One of the difficult things about living in China is that no one knows what is really going on. The government is opaque. Basic statistics that would be freely available in other countries are treated as state secrets. The private media are ruthlessly censored. The state-owned media produce two types of news: expurgated reports for public consumption and more-accurate ones destined only for the eyes of senior officials.

The Internet is challenging this dreary status quo. The Chinese government censors the web, of course, but it has still dramatically increased the access that ordinary Chinese people have to information. Outsiders seldom appreciate just how much difference that can make to life in a dictatorship. Nor do many people realize how much the expansion of Internet use in China has depended on the efforts of foreign-educated and -trained Chinese entrepreneurs and engineers.

Consider Alibaba, China's most popular e-commerce firm, which is run by an Americaphile and packed with returnees.

The first thing you notice about Jack Ma, the boss of Alibaba, is his size. He is so short and thin that his unofficial biographers wonder whether he was malnourished as a child. (He was born in 1964, as the aftereffects of the Great Leap Forward famine lingered.[26]) Yet he is charming and thoughtful, and because half a billion people use his various online services, the room goes quiet when he speaks.

In a country where tycoons are often the children of politicians, Mr. Ma stands out. He grew up an outcast, since his grandfather had supported the Nationalists against the Communists during China's civil war. He learned English from the radio and by striking up conversations with foreign tourists strolling by the scenic lake in his hometown of Hangzhou. (The lake is still considered a tourist attraction, but when I visited in 2010, it was invisible beneath the smog.) As a teenager, he made extra cash by pedaling tourists around in a pedicab, pointing out the sights and practicing his language skills on them.[27]

He twice failed to get into university, but eventually won a place to study foreign languages at an obscure school in his hometown. After graduating, he found a job teaching English at a technical college. After five years, he struck out on his own, setting up a translation agency in Hangzhou. At this point, he had never been abroad, but he had earned a reputation, as Shiying Liu and Martha Avery write, as "marginally more familiar with things foreign than others in Hangzhou."[28] So when the local government needed someone to go to America to kick-start stalled negotiations with a potential American investor, they sent Mr. Ma.

That mission was a flop. But while he was in America, Mr. Ma stumbled on the Internet. It was in 1995, when the technology was still fresh. Sitting for the first time in front of a computer linked to the web, he typed the phrase "Chinese beer" into a search engine. No results appeared. He tried again with other Chinese products. Still nothing. He saw an opportunity.

There was no Internet in China at the time, so Mr. Ma's first web pages—advertising his translation service—were hosted in the United States. His crude website—little more than a name and an email address—went live at 9:30 one morning. By the evening, he had received five inquiries: three from the United States and two from Japan.[29] He was hooked.

In 1999 Mr. Ma founded Alibaba, a firm whose aim was to help small vendors find customers and suppliers online. It grew like a bamboo forest. By early 2011 Alibaba.com claimed 57 million users, including some from nearly every country in the world. Another Alibaba Group website, Taobao.com, founded in 2003, sells to consumers. It is like a scrappy cross between Amazon and eBay: it operates an online mall where vetted sellers can hawk their wares, and a site where anyone with a Chinese identity number can sell anything legal to anyone. It generates money through advertising. It claimed a staggering 370 million customers in 2011—more than the entire US population. Business is "pretty good," Mr. Ma concedes with a smile.[30]

Alibaba's staff boast of the businesses they have nurtured, both big and small. One Chinese village had a stack of rabbit meat, having skinned the creatures for fur. The chief asked for suggestions, and the winning one was to sell the lot on Alibaba.com. More commonly, clients are small firms that want to link cheaply to the global market. Manufacturers in Turkey or Britain use Alibaba to find cheap suppliers in China without having to go there. Buyers can read reviews that others have written about each seller, which fosters trust, though it is far from foolproof.

I visited the Alibaba campus in Hangzhou. It looks much like the offices of a zippy firm in Silicon Valley. The architecture is airy and *feng shui*–compliant. Employees enjoy ping-pong and free massages. Gray hairs are as rare as neckties. A huge statue of a tubby, naked man dominates the courtyard. Apparently it represents the company's values, but no one I met could explain how.

At the heart of the operation is a "live data monitoring room," where a dozen huge screens and flashing maps show just how many people are buying and selling on Alibaba websites, and where. There are Chinese firms trading with foreign ones, Chinese individuals buying clothes from one another and, no doubt, Chinese exporters disguising goods as gifts to avoid customs duties. (This is not Alibaba's fault. Tax-dodging is a national sport in China.)

To get all this off the ground, Mr. Ma needed *haigui*, sea turtles. He is no technology expert, and he began his business in a country

where web experts were thin on the ground. So he hired disproportionate numbers of ethnic Chinese who had lived, worked or studied
abroad to senior posts in his new company. They brought essential
skills and contacts. Some understood the Internet. Some understood
the Western buyers that Mr. Ma hoped to connect with Chinese sellers.
Others knew the Western investors whose capital Alibaba would need
to expand. (Alibaba Group attracted big investments from America's
Yahoo and Japan's Softbank.)

Joe Tsai, Alibaba Group's chief financial officer and a founding
member of the firm, brought Wall Street savvy. He had been a vice
president of Rosecliff, a New York management buyout firm, and
had worked for an investment firm belonging to Sweden's Wallenburg
banking family. He recruited Brian Wong, a bright young Chinese
American who is Alibaba.com's head of global sales.

"I wanted to help China," says Mr. Wong. He had considered
becoming a doctor or joining a UN development agency. But then he
realized that he could make more of a difference by helping to bring
e-commerce to his ancestral homeland. Just as McDonald's raised
standards in China in simple ways, such as by having clean restaurants, so Mr. Wong feels that he can help raise the quality of life in
China by introducing Chinese businesses to e-commerce.

He explained this to me over sumptuous slices of fatty pork—our
dining companion called it "bacon on crack"—at an agreeable Can-
tonese restaurant in Hangzhou in late 2010. Mr. Wong says that working for Alibaba is not exactly a hardship. "It's like doing Peace Corps
work, only with stock options."[31]

China has millions of small entrepreneurs but a primitive financial system. To boost traffic through his websites, Jack Ma set up an
online-payment portal, Alipay, in 2004. It grew fast. (It did not hurt
that PayPal, an American rival, had immense difficulty obtaining a
license to operate in China.) By 2011 Alipay claimed that 550 million
people were using its payment system worldwide and that more than
500,000 Chinese merchants accepted it. In some Chinese cities people
use it to pay their utility bills.[32]

Next came Ali-loan. It does not lend money directly, but works
with banks, which typically have no idea if a small borrower is creditworthy. Mr. Ma, by contrast, has a trove of data from his own sites

revealing whether small firms pay their bills on time. He can also bundle together firms that know each other, so that a seller can help guarantee a bank loan to a regular customer. The proportion of loans recommended by Ali-loan that went bad was a trifling 0.35 percent in 2010—in other words, this service could be massively expanded.

Mr. Ma's greatest challenge with the Alibaba Group is to build trust. Business in China is rife with fraud, and the legal system is little help. Persuading customers that it is safe to buy goods from Chinese vendors they have never met is not easy. Richard Wang, a former Shell executive from Texas who was running Taobao's international business unit when I spoke to him in November 2010, says the firm strains every muscle to kick peddlers of shoddy or counterfeit goods out of its network.[33]

It sometimes fails. In February 2011 Alibaba revealed that an internal audit had uncovered serious wrongdoing by some of its own staff. About 100 sales staff and a few of their managers had either negligently or deliberately allowed some 2,236 sellers to dodge safeguards meant to protect buyers, the firm admitted. David Wei, the London-educated boss of Alibaba's business-to-business e-commerce website, resigned for failing to prevent the breach, although he was not personally implicated.[34]

Critics say the scandal will irreparably tarnish the Alibaba brand. More sympathetic observers retort that the firm came clean and sacked the miscreants. Plenty of other Chinese firms have hushed up scandals rather than resolve them. Given the Wild West mentality that prevails in China and the pace of Alibaba's growth—from zero employees to 22,000 in little more than a decade—it is perhaps surprising that the firm has not stumbled more often.[35]

At any rate, the scandal appears not to have dimmed Mr. Ma's ambitions. Alibaba has a huge and barely exploited asset: the incomparable data it has gathered about the spending habits of China's emerging middle class. At the time of writing, the firm was cagey about what, exactly, it planned to do with this information. It was also at pains to insist that it would not violate anyone's privacy.

Still, it seems unlikely Alibaba will just sit on this goldmine. It could use customer data to identify trends and help companies anticipate what consumers want. Given the paucity of accurate data in

China, this would be extremely valuable. Or it could try to kick-start consumer credit in China. At the time of writing, Ali-loan did not charge for its credit-scoring service for business borrowers, and a company spokesman told me the firm had no plans to do so. But such a venture would make sense: a small commission on each loan would be almost pure profit. And there is no practical reason why the group should limit itself to helping businesses borrow money. Another glittering prize would be to help Chinese consumers to obtain credit, too. Very few can do so at the moment. Many would surely like to.

This is a politically sensitive area, however. The government largely controls the allocation of credit in China. Through state-controlled banks, it funnels the nation's savings to large, politically favored firms. An expansion of credit to the little people might be seen as a threat to this cozy arrangement. Also, the Communist Party is terrified of credit bubbles, which might spark unrest if they burst.

It is surely not Mr. Ma's intention to undermine the government. (It would be extremely dangerous for him even to entertain such an idea.) But as China's private sector grows ever larger, it will inevitably reduce the degree to which Chinese people depend on the state.

Already, China's private companies employ 92 percent of the country's non-agricultural workers, by one estimate. Big, well-connected firms may hog all the cheap credit, but small private firms are the engine of China's growth. The number of private companies registered in China grew by more than 30 percent a year between 2000 and 2009, according to China Macro Finance, a research outfit in New York. And their return on capital was 10 percentage points higher than the paltry 4 percent notched up by firms owned wholly or partly by the state, according to Qiao Liu and Alan Siu, of the University of Hong Kong.[36]

It is hard to look at a firm like Alibaba and not be excited. By creating a cheap trading platform for small businesses, Jack Ma is helping the Chinese middle class to grow. If he can democratize the allocation of credit, too, he will increase the power of Chinese individuals and reduce the relative importance of the state.

That said, all predictions about China must be taken with a dash of monosodium glutamate. Given the head-spinning pace of change there, Alibaba could be wiped out by a competitor or a scandal by the time you read this book. But the story so far illustrates how a business that is empowered by technology and hooked up to the best ideas the world has to offer can make a big difference to people's lives.

THE REVOLUTIONARY POWER OF MIGRATION

Though the tales in this chapter are quite different from each other, they all share a common theme: that migration empowers individuals and creates networks that are outside the control of the state. Mei Xu's candle company creates legions of jobs and connects Chinese designers to the outside world. The Riady family brings investment to the Chinese hinterland and forges links between previously isolated cities and Southeast Asia. Chinese expatriate executives such as William So learn firsthand about democratic politics and the rule of law, even if they don't like everything they experience in the West. And e-commerce firms such as Jack Ma's Alibaba and Taobao help millions of Chinese entrepreneurs prosper without state backing.

Add these strands together and multiply it by the number of Chinese who have lived, worked or studied overseas. The result is a clear and imminent threat to the dictatorship in Beijing—which is the subject of my next chapter.

3

DIASPORA POLITICS

HOW THE SEA TURTLES WILL
TURN CHINA DEMOCRATIC

Sarah Chang thinks the Communist Party is doomed. She keeps quiet about it, though. To agitate openly for democracy in China requires heroism, and heroes are rare in any society. Ms. Chang is not an activist, just a young office worker in Shanghai who knows unfairness when she sees it.

Sarah is clever and works hard. But because she is not a member of the Communist Party, many doors are closed to her and many privileges are out of reach. She watches with disgust as officials enrich themselves in illicit ways and abuse the people with impunity. And she is not alone.

It is hard to measure public opinion in China. Most Chinese people almost certainly appreciate how much better life has grown since Mao Zedong died. Polls often indicate that more than 80 percent are satisfied with the direction their country is going in.[1] Some experts even believe that ordinary Chinese are reasonably content with their government.[2]

But opinion polls are an unreliable guide in a country where the government's ears are everywhere and expressing the wrong view can cost you your job or even your liberty. What people tell their friends in private is often quite different from what they tell strangers who call them up and ask them sensitive questions.

If the nation's millions of blogs are anything to go by, many Chinese people are deeply disenchanted with their rulers. Sarah Chang (which is not her real name) is an avid reader of online political chatter. In October 2010 she heard a new catchphrase. "Everyone online was saying, 'My dad is Li Gang,'" she recalls. She had no idea what this meant, so she did a quick search. It turned out that the son of Li Gang, a senior police officer in the city of Baoding, was driving drunk and ran down two roller-skating students, killing one of them. When stopped and questioned, he had allegedly shouted: "Make a report if you dare; my dad is Li Gang!"

News of the incident went viral. There were poems and pop songs with the refrain "My dad is Li Gang!" Sarah remembers a silly joke that made the rounds, in which a primary-school child gets a bad grade and is ordered to go and see the principal. He refuses, saying: "My dad is Li Gang."

The scandal embarrassed the party. Li was forced to make a televised apology.[3] His son was arrested. Drunk drivers who cause fatal accidents are sometimes executed in China, but Li junior got away with a six-year jail sentence for "crimes causing traffic casualties." The Lis reportedly paid the family of the dead girl $70,000 not to press for stiffer charges.[4] How a modestly paid public servant got hold of such a large sum is anyone's guess.

Sarah thinks the rich and powerful in China are all like Li Gang's son. "They all take advantage of their power," she says. The only difference, she reckons, is that Li Gang's son was stupid enough to boast about his connections, rather than discreetly asking his father to quash the charges against him.

STRONG BUT BRITTLE

Dictatorships are brittle. Zine el Abidine Ben Ali ruled the North African nation of Tunisia for 23 brutal years. He looked secure right up until December 2010, when a young fruit-seller who had been robbed and insulted by the police set fire to himself and died. Simmering fury at the corrupt regime boiled over. Within a month, mass protests had forced President Ben Ali to flee to Saudi Arabia.

In Egypt, President Hosni Mubarak ruled for nearly 30 years and showed so few signs of retiring that Egyptians muttered grim jokes about him behind closed doors. In one, the angel of death comes to Mubarak and tells him that he must bid farewell to the Egyptian people. "Why?" asks Mubarak. "Where are they going?"[5] Yet when Egyptians saw how easily their cousins in Tunisia had thrown out their dictator, they rose up and threw out Mubarak. It took only 18 days.[6]

China is different from Egypt or Tunisia. It is not a crude dictatorship with an obvious villain at the helm. Its rulers use force when they deem it necessary, but most of the time they rely on high-tech surveillance to monitor dissidents and sophisticated censorship to restrain public debate. Also, unlike Egypt or Tunisia, the Chinese government has presided over an economic miracle since the late 1970s. Its growing urban middle class sees life improving every year. Political turmoil might imperil a generation of gains. Why would they risk it?

Many Chinese are understandably terrified of turmoil; they had enough of it under Mao, who tried to remake society from scratch. His utopian schemes killed tens of millions, impoverished the survivors and taught Chinese people to dread political upheaval.[7] But after the Great Helmsman's death in 1976, pragmatic leaders took over. Declaring that "to get rich is glorious," Deng Xiaoping allowed Chinese people a large measure of economic freedom. Peasants were allowed to keep the food they grew. Entrepreneurs were allowed to set up businesses. The pent-up dynamism of the world's most populous nation was unleashed. Hundreds of millions of Chinese people lifted themselves out of poverty. Chinese consumers threw away their dreary jumpsuits and donned designer threads.

Political repression eased, too. Under Mao, notes Perry Link, an American China specialist, you could be jailed for griping about your cat, since snitches were everywhere and the Chinese word for "cat" sounds a bit like the Great Helmsman's name.[8] Today, people are largely free to do what they like. They are free to travel abroad, if they can afford it. They are free to grumble in private. But they are not free to choose their rulers.

The ruling Communist Party brooks no opposition. The most important decisions are made in secret by the nine members of the Politburo Standing Committee, all aging men with jet black hair that appears to have been dyed. None has ever faced a real election.

To be fair, China does allow voting, but only at the most local level. Many villages choose their own chiefs. This is an important reform since Mao's day, and one that many people value. But the power of village chiefs is circumscribed: few would risk offending the party, and many are overshadowed by its local representative, who often calls the shots on all important matters.

The party is a huge and secretive organization. It has 78 million members—about 6 percent of the Chinese population.[9] Its cadres are sent to watch over banks, state-owned companies, local government and any other organization important enough to keep an eye on. In recent years it has pushed hard to set up cells within private companies to spy on them.

The party may not be democratic, but it is somewhat meritocratic. Would-be members must pass an exam to join, or prove their talents in some other way. The top leaders are all highly intelligent. But because the party wields unaccountable power, it attracts the sort of people who enjoy being powerful and unaccountable.

Many are staggeringly corrupt. Local party bosses prey on the people, especially in rural areas. They seize their land and sell it to their developer chums. They award contracts and permits to cronies. Sometimes they simply help themselves to other people's money—by one (rather speculative) estimate, 40 percent of taxes extracted from peasants have no basis in law and never reach public coffers.[10]

China's economic growth, however, has benefited multitudes. Between 1990 and 2010, the proportion of Chinese people living in absolute poverty (i.e., $1 a day) fell from 60 percent to 10 percent.[11] That is a staggering achievement. But the fruits have not been evenly spread. In 2010 China had 800,000 millionaires, but also 400 million people who lived on less than $2 a day.[12]

Wealth often depends on political ties, which makes China's inequality even more galling. In 2007, a blogger called Liu Yide (undoubtedly a pseudonym) leaked what he said were the findings of a secret report by the state-backed Chinese Academy of Social Sciences, which showed that 91 percent of the people in the People's Republic with personal fortunes of more than 100 million yuan ($13 million at the time) were close relatives of senior officials.[13] According to the *China Youth Daily,* a communist paper, China spends five times more on entertaining local government officials than it does on educating children up to the age of 16.[14]

Corruption is probably the number-one complaint against the party. By the government's own figures, the country sees 80,000 or 90,000 mass protests every year, many of them violent. The protesters' grievances typically concern predatory local officials, who may have stolen their land or allowed a well-connected factory to pollute it.[15] In addition, some 280,000 labor disputes were taken to civil court in 2008, as workers demanded a fairer share of the fruits of growth.[16]

The party blames corruption on corrupt individuals. From time to time it makes an example of the worst offenders by shooting them or giving them lethal injections. It also allows people to air grievances about graft, so long as they do not challenge the Communist Party's monopoly on power. But that monopoly is the root of the problem: it is precisely because officials are accountable to neither voters nor the law that they can get away with being so crooked.

Typically, their victims' only recourse is to trudge to a big city and petition a higher level of government. But local officials do not like tattletales, so they sometimes send thugs to kidnap and torture them in seclusion. The Chinese government denies the existence of "black jails," as they are known. But groups such as Human Rights Watch have gathered copious evidence that they are common.[17]

China's authoritarian state cannot last forever. The party no longer stands for a coherent ideology. No one even pretends anymore that it is building a communist paradise. It has tried, with some success, to portray itself as the champion of Chinese nationalism. But the party's popularity depends first and foremost on continued rapid growth, which will someday falter. It is relatively easy to grow fast when you are catching up with the rest of the world, importing its technology and cherry-picking its best ideas. It gets harder as you get richer and have to start innovating to keep growing.

Before long, China will hit roadblocks. Thanks to the one-child policy,* it will grow old before it grows rich, sapping its enterprises of energy. Its financial system is opaque and riddled with bad debts, since state-directed banks are forced to lend vast sums to incompetent state-owned firms.[18] China's banks could crash. So could its stock market or its overheated housing market. All societies face economic crises from time to time, but in democracies there is a safety valve—voters can toss out the politicians who let the crisis occur. China has no safety valve.

If a sudden shock causes China's living standards to fall sharply, can the single-party state survive? I suspect that it will not. This is a controversial view. The party has been in charge for so long that people take its dominance for granted. Past predictions of democracy coming to China have always proven wrong. But it would take extraordinary skill and devilish luck to keep more than a billion Chinese people down forever. I do not believe that the Communist Party is as skillful as its admirers insist. And I do not believe that its luck will last indefinitely.

In previous ages, tyrannical regimes lasted for centuries. But those were the days when the only alternative to an odious despot was a slightly less odious despot. Today, there is an obvious alternative to tyranny. And the more contact China has with the rest of the world, the more Chinese people will be exposed to that alternative.

This is why the Chinese diaspora will play such an important role in bringing democracy to China. Its members are the bridge between China and the free world, over which subversive ideas may pass.

The main impetus for democratic reform will come from within China. Such a great transformation must be home-cooked or it will be rejected. But the overseas Chinese will act as supporters and enablers of the coming democratization. They will accelerate its arrival, in five essential ways:

The power of example. To people who say that democracy is alien to Chinese culture, the pithiest retort is: what about Taiwan? The

---

* For decades the Chinese government has used coercive methods to prevent couples from having more than one child. The rules have relaxed somewhat, especially in rural areas, but China is still a nation of only children.

island's inhabitants are 98 percent Han Chinese,[19] yet Taiwan has been a thriving multiparty democracy since 1996. Indeed, the overseas Chinese can cast ballots in nearly all the countries where they settle, so long as they naturalize. The only major state that denies the vote to Chinese people is China. As contact with the diaspora increases, this anomaly will chafe.

The diaspora provides a safe haven for dissidents and a hub for democratic ideas. From the safety of San Francisco or Taipei, uncensored information and heretical ideas constantly seep back into China itself.

The number of mainland Chinese who study abroad has surged. For the Chinese elite, sending your children to an American college is the ultimate status symbol. Bright youngsters who study in the United States notice that democracy need not spell chaos. Since many of these students return to China and eventually attain positions of influence, this trend will make China more receptive to democratic reforms.

The diaspora helps make China more prosperous. This could strengthen the party, since it takes credit for everything that goes right. But history suggests that rising incomes lead to a more assertive middle class, which soon demands a say in how it is ruled.

Links with the diaspora help spread new communications technology around China. The country's tech industry is powered by entrepreneurs who have studied or worked abroad. They have helped to hook up hundreds of millions of Chinese people to the Internet in a startlingly short time. Despite censorship, the widespread availability of new communications tools makes it harder for the Chinese government to control the national conversation, and easier for dissidents to organize.

I will deal with these five points in turn.

THE POWER OF EXAMPLE

Most of the 60 million overseas Chinese live in free countries. Taiwan, the second-largest Chinese polity on earth, is a rambunctious democracy. Its people are richer than the mainland Chinese and live without fear of arbitrary arrest. Some 800,000 Taiwanese citizens live on the Chinese mainland, where they chat freely and often to mainlanders. And 1.6 million mainlanders visited Taiwan in 2010.[20]

Hong Kong, under the "one country, two systems" deal that preceded its handover from Britain, is subject to Beijing but retains many freedoms. The Hong Kong Chinese can say, write and publish what they like. They do not live in fear of being robbed by corrupt policemen or tax officials. Their laws protect both their bodies and their property. They can vote for a legislature, although Beijing has done its best to keep that legislature toothless.

Lynn Pan, a historian, describes Hong Kong as "a refuge for heterodoxy and political subversion" and a "prime nursery" for expatriate democratic protest.[21] Shortly before the 1997 handover, she observed that seven out of ten Hong Kong Chinese either had fled from Communist China or had at least one parent who had done so. Half a million of them took to the streets to show solidarity with the pro-democracy protesters in Tiananmen Square in 1989.[22]

Partly as a result of their freedoms, Hong Kongers are seven times richer than mainland Chinese and live nearly a decade longer. Mainlanders made more than 10 million trips to Hong Kong in the first six months of 2010, a number that had risen by 27 percent in a year.[23] If nothing else, Hong Kong is a showcase for the rule of law, and it is a showcase that an increasing number of mainlanders can gawk at.

A Chinese person can win full political rights in the United States simply by being born there. Though a tiny minority, Chinese Americans participate wholeheartedly in public life. Elaine Chao was labor secretary under George W. Bush. At the time of writing, Steven Chu was Barack Obama's energy secretary. Gary Locke, whose family originally came from Guangdong, did not speak English until he was five but was still elected governor of Washington State. Barack Obama later appointed him commerce secretary, and then ambassador to China. When Locke addresses Chinese audiences, he stands as a living reminder that not every ethnic Chinese politician is afraid of the ballot box.

Chinese Thais can also vote in their adopted country, as can Chinese Australians and Chinese Brazilians. Even the 10 million Chinese in Indonesia, who until recently were subject to discriminatory laws and attacks by racist mobs, now have more political rights than the Chinese in China. Any mainlander who travels or has friends in the diaspora must swiftly become aware of such blatant disparities.

A HUB FOR UNCENSORED INFORMATION

In the winter of 2010, I had a long chat with Sarah Chang. It was around the time that Liu Xiaobo, a Chinese dissident, was supposed to receive the Nobel Peace Prize. Liu could not make it to Oslo for the ceremony, however, because he was in jail. An empty chair on the podium symbolized his absence.

I spoke to Sarah over the Internet. We had each downloaded a program that let us talk without fear of the party listening in; I won't say what it's called. When the party hears of a hole in the Great Fire-wall of China (the popular name for the ring of censorship that the Chinese government has erected around the Chinese Internet), it immediately seeks to plug it. One human-rights campaigner warned me that if I were to reveal that I was using a particular program to talk about democracy with people in China, the government would assign 20,000 people to shut it down.[24]

Liu Xiaobo's writings are banned in China and news about him is censored. The official line is that he is a traitor. The sole shred of evidence for this is a joke he once made about how agreeable life was in Hong Kong under British rule.[25]

Sarah knows the official line is rubbish because she has read Liu's uncensored work. She downloads software that enables her to set up a virtual private network outside the Great Firewall. "You basically jump over the firewall," she told me. Then, by using Google's Chinese-language search engine, she can find material her government does not want her to read posted on servers in Hong Kong, Taiwan or the United States.

The software she uses was created by a Chinese American in California who makes it available for free online. By the time you read this book, the Chinese authorities will probably have found a way to block it. But Sarah will have found another way over the firewall. There are many similar programs out there. "There's a lot of demand for them," she says. "There are lots of people like me."

One of the forbidden tracts that Sarah has read is "Charter 08," a manifesto that Liu Xiaobo cowrote and published online in 2008. It has now been posted on countless websites around the world. It is powerful stuff, yet painfully reasonable.

One-party rule has led to "a long trail of human-rights disasters," it says. Today these include "endemic official corruption . . . growing inequality . . . pillage of the natural environment . . . [and] a sharpening animosity between officials and ordinary people.[26]

"Change is no longer optional," it goes on. To avoid "the possibility of a violent conflict of disastrous proportions," the government must consent to some radical reforms: freedom of speech, freedom of the press, freedom of association, freedom of movement, an independent judiciary, equality before the law and free elections.

Every important political post should be subject to "periodic competitive elections" based on the principle of one person, one vote. The scope of the government's power should be limited and defined by a written constitution. Power should further be "balanced among different branches of government," thus upholding "the traditional Chinese political ideal of 'fairness in all under heaven.'"[27]

Sarah read Charter 08 as soon as it was published. "I thought it was great," she says. "He's calling for something we don't have in China. And that's really brave."

Many observers argue that manifestos such as Charter 08 have a limited appeal. Ordinary Chinese people are too busy making money to have time for abstract ideas such as democracy, they say. Yet the ideas expressed in Charter 08 are vivid and simple to understand. The authors deftly summarize the ways in which abusive rulers make daily life worse.

For example, Liu Xiaobo and his fellow dissidents call for the abolition of the two-tier household registry system. This sounds dull, but is not. China has a system of residence permits, called *hukou,* which resembles the pass system in apartheid South Africa. People with a city *hukou* can live and work there freely. Those with a rural *hukou* can enter a city only as guest workers. Such internal migrants—and there are perhaps 200 million of them—do not have the same rights as city *hukou*-holders to social services such as schools and clinics. In effect, they are foreigners in their own country.

The government said it would liberalize the *hukou* system in 2005, but cities can still exclude anyone they like, and often do. Yukon Huang, a former head of the World Bank's office in China, estimated for me that real freedom of movement would prompt a quarter of a billion peasants to move to the cities.[28]

The *hukou* system has many supporters. Many city folk don't want peasants clogging their schools or erecting slums on their doorsteps. Nor do they want outsiders competing with them for jobs—or for women.

Guy Sorman, the author of a rather skeptical book about China called *The Empire of Lies,* describes a rule in Shanghai that allows a Shanghai man to obtain a *hukou* for his non-Shanghai wife only after 15 years of marriage—but makes no provision for a Shanghai woman to marry a man from elsewhere. Asked why not, the mayor's office told Sorman that it was unthinkable that a Shanghai woman would marry an outsider.[29]

The *hukou* system was designed to help control the people, but it is so flagrantly unjust that it stirs up anger against the party. Sarah Chang lives in Shanghai but comes originally from a less prosperous city, so she has no Shanghai *hukou,* and little prospect of ever receiving one. "It's not fair at all," she complains. "I pay as much tax as a local, but get no benefits: no [city] pension, no health benefits, nothing." If she were to have a child, she says with a sigh, "there's no way I could get him into a local school."

It is impossible to know whether most Chinese citizens would find democratic ideas persuasive. But you can tell how much the Chinese government fears them by the efforts they make to silence them. In the days before Liu Xiaobo's Nobel ceremony, prominent dissidents throughout China found that their mobile telephones and Internet connections stopped working. Many were arrested or invited for a "chat" with national security officers.[30] In the days after the Jasmine Revolution in Tunisia in 2011, when online messages circulated calling for similar street protests in China, the party flooded the proposed rallying points with police, arrested anyone who showed up and even blocked Internet searches for a traditional song about jasmine flowers.[31]

Dissidents often find ways around these curbs, however. When the censors blocked online messages that mentioned Liu Xiaobo, his admirers circulated pictures of an empty chair instead. The phrase "empty chair" was swiftly banned, too. So they circulated comments in praise of other people with the family name Liu, which is too common to ban. Or they deliberately misspelled his name to fool the firewall, just as online hucksters offer you "Xtra str0ng V1agra" to get past your spam filter.

A newspaper in Guangzhou published on its front page what appeared to be a dull story about preparations for a sporting event. Savvy readers noticed, however, that it included a picture of three empty chairs, along with five cranes, a bird whose name in Chinese ("he") sounds very similar both to "congratulations" and to the first character of the word for "peace."[32]

Information that the Chinese government wishes to suppress can always be published outside the Chinese mainland. This includes not only dissident tirades but also accurate accounts of modern Chinese history. For example, in 2008, Yang Jisheng published *Tombstone*, a history of the famine of 1958–61, when between 35 million and 40 million Chinese people starved to death after Mao Zedong forced them into collective farms. The party still shrouds this man-made catastrophe in euphemism, referring to it as the "difficult period lasting three years."

Yang spent nearly two decades secretly gathering material from official archives around China. As a journalist for Xinhua, Beijing's official news agency, he had plenty of excuses to be snooping in old files. The result was a meticulously researched and exhaustively footnoted account of one of the twentieth century's cruelest episodes, which laid the blame squarely at the ruling party's feet. Bookshops in Hong Kong sold stacks of copies.[33]

The Communist Party seeks to control Chinese history, and to whitewash its own bloody role in it. Books like *Tombstone* make that harder. More broadly, the existence of a Chinese-language free-speech zone outside China makes it harder for the party to control debate within China's borders. Granted, only a minority of Chinese people have the skills to leap over the Great Firewall or the means to go book shopping in Hong Kong. But it is no longer a tiny minority, and news spreads quickly.

A SAFE HAVEN FOR SUBVERSION

When I first spoke with Bob Fu, in December 2010, he was grappling with a cyberattack. Hackers were bombarding his website, a hub for underground Christians in China, with so many messages that it crashed. Fu was certain that the Chinese government was to blame, though he could not prove it. He was also sure that the hackers would return.

Mr. Fu works in Texas—in Midland, an oil town whose best-known daughter is Laura Bush. He runs an organization called the China Aid Association, which fights against the mistreatment of Christians in China. For example, when the Chinese authorities find an underground church and arrest its members, one of them may get word to one of Mr. Fu's mainland contacts. China Aid then springs into action.

Mr. Fu tries to get a lawyer to defend the detainees. He and his staff write up the facts and post them on their website, along with video footage of battered believers and interviews with the relatives of those who have disappeared. This information is then disseminated throughout China by any means possible: text messages, anonymous group emails and so forth.

Christianity is not illegal in China, but Christians may only belong to registered churches, and the government only allows churches that seem tame. The same rules apply to all religious organizations. They must register a place of worship and refrain from conducting religious services anywhere else, so the state can keep an eye on them. If the government disapproves of their leaders, they are banned. In effect, an atheist regime claims the right to veto any Chinese believer's choice of priest or congregation.

Mr. Fu fell foul of this rule. He was teaching English literature at a university for Communist Party members in Beijing and leading an illicit Bible-study group in his spare time. When the authorities found out, he was fired and jailed for two months, along with his wife, a fellow Christian. His interrogator told him that Western governments were using Christianity as a weapon to overthrow the Chinese state. Upon their release, Mr. Fu and his wife were placed under house arrest. She became pregnant, which was another black mark, because the couple did not have a permit to have a baby. A friend with connections warned the Fus that they were about to be arrested again, so they fled the country. They won asylum in America in 1997.

Why did Mr. Fu expose himself and his family to such danger? Why did he not just join one of the approved churches, or read his Bible quietly on his own? Because he takes his faith seriously. He is an evangelical Christian: he overflows with the urge to share his beliefs with others. He is outraged that the Chinese government does not permit this. "If you pass out a Christian pamphlet outside an official church building, that's illegal," he complains.

When Mr. Fu arrived in America, he was struck by the easy availability of information. He kept hearing about Christians in China being arrested. So he decided to publicize their plight.

In one case, the authorities in the city of Linfen, in Shanxi province, decided to shut down an unregistered church that was getting too popular. Early one Sunday morning in September 2009, 400 police officers, officials and hired ruffians burst into a half-built church and viciously beat the worshippers who were sleeping inside. Twenty people required treatment, but local hospitals were ordered not to give them blood. Seventeen buildings were ransacked. Bulldozers crushed the half-built church to rubble.

The next day, a crowd of 1,000 Christians assembled to pray in the rain on the site of their demolished church. That irked the authorities. Ten church members were charged with such offenses as "unlawfully occupying agricultural land" and "gathering to disturb the traffic order." After a trial that lasted only a few hours, five were given prison sentences of up to seven years. The other five were sentenced to two years of "reeducation through labor." All claim to have been beaten while in custody.[34]

A church member alerted China Aid with a text message. Mr. Fu helped to hire eight lawyers to fight the case. Although they lost, China Aid did succeed in collecting and publishing reams of documentation, including footage of the destruction and the injuries sustained by the worshippers. Since this is now safely posted on Internet servers in the United States, it cannot be suppressed. News of the persecution at Linfen spread fast along China's underground Christian grapevine.

When fighting a case, Mr. Fu's lawyers cite the Chinese constitution, which guarantees freedom of religion. If China's rulers felt bound by their own supreme law, they would have to allow the acts of worship for which Christians are charged. Mostly they do not. But occasionally China Aid's lawyers win a case.

On July 15, 2007, police in Jianshi county, in Hubei province, burst into a private home where a dozen Christians were praying. They dragged them away and charged several with "making use of an evil cult . . . to undermine the enforcement of State laws." Nine were sentenced to a year or more of "reeducation through labor"—in other words, prison camp.

China Aid hired a lawyer called Wu Chenglian to represent some of the accused. (Others refused representation, perhaps fearing that it would annoy the authorities even more.) Mr. Wu managed to get them off. In January 2008, the Hubei Provincial Reeducation Through Labor Administration Committee (the panel's bureaucratic title speaks volumes) decided that the sentences were unjustified, and four of the nine were released.[35]

It is impossible to say how much China Aid's work undermines the one-party state. Clearly, the actions of campaigners inside China are more important. Those on the ground have a more nuanced understanding of what is going on in the area where they work. But for any dissident group, having a hub outside the country is immensely valuable. It means that a record is kept of the government's abuses—a record that the government cannot erase. It means that this information is accessible to Chinese Christians, so that they know they are not alone.

The Chinese government fears groups it cannot control. The devout are especially suspect, since they are loyal to a higher power than the Communist Party. They are also more numerous than the Chinese government likes to admit. Beijing claims that there are 100 million religious believers in the country, but a survey in 2007, reported in the state media, found that there were 300 million—31 percent of Chinese adults.

About two-thirds of these were Buddhists, Taoists or followers of Chinese folk religions. Officially sanctioned Christian churches (Protestant and Catholic) claim about 20 million members, but underground Christian churches are much larger. Extrapolating from surveys, the

Washington, DC–based Pew Research Center estimated that there are between 50 million and 70 million closeted Christians in China. There are also about 50 million Muslims. And Falun Gong, a spiritual movement, claims 70 million followers—although this number cannot be verified since Falun Gong is persecuted more vigorously than any other faith and its members are nearly all hiding, abroad or in jail.[36]

Falun Gong stresses gentle exercise and high morals. Other countries deem it harmless, but the party is terrified of it because its adherents are so numerous and have shown themselves capable of organizing large protests quickly. How scared is the party of Falun Gong? I once asked the manager of a door-to-door sales firm in China what challenges he faced, and he sighed that it was hard to get permission for pep rallies for his sales staff, because the government suspected that members of Falun Gong might use them as a smoke screen for their own meetings.

Faith fills a void that communism cannot. And the faithful can be stubborn. Even when the regime's torturers apply electric shock batons to their genitals, says Mr. Fu, Christians often find the strength to endure. Some are so ready to be martyred that secular human-rights campaigners accuse them of recklessness, under their breath.

IN SILOS, BUT NOT SILENCED

Several dissident groups forced into the shadows in China operate openly abroad. For example, Falun Gong's founder, Li Hongzhi, lives in North America. His followers run websites in dozens of countries and several languages. They also run a multilingual newspaper (the *Epoch Times,* based in New York), a television channel (New Tang Dynasty Television) and a radio station that streams into China via the Internet. They lobby Western governments to lean on Beijing to stop persecuting their co-religionists. They file human-rights lawsuits in American courts against Chinese politicians. They encourage Chinese people to quit the party. They even engage in cyberwarfare. Falun Gong members include many Chinese American engineers who write censorship-dodging software and distribute it for free. And when the Chinese government hacks their websites, they hack back.[37]

Likewise, campaigners for a free Tibet work primarily out of India, where their "government in exile" is based, in Dharamsala. From this safe haven, the Dalai Lama broadcasts his message of nonviolence and autonomy. In March 2011 the Dalai Lama said he wanted to step down as the political leader of the Tibetan exiles, while remaining their spiritual leader. The next month Tibetan exiles elected a Harvard academic, Lobsang Sangay, as their new prime minister.[38] The Chinese government was outraged. The Beijing-appointed governor of Tibet howled that the Dalai Lama's succession should be decided the old fashioned way, by waiting for him to die and then finding his reincarnated spirit in a young boy. It may seem odd that a godless party should preach reincarnation, but then, small boys are easier to push around than elected adults.[39]

Both inside China and outside, dissidents tend to work in silos. Activists tend to focus on one area of injustice, rather than the whole system; they may privately support many different causes, but the groups keep their objectives narrow. To do otherwise would give the government yet another excuse to arrest their allies in China. This tendency to specialize prompts some to scoff that exiled Chinese dissidents are hopelessly divided. This misses the point. Granted, there have been personality clashes. But disparate movements can come together very quickly when the time is right, as the revolutions in Tunisia and Egypt in 2011 showed.

In the meantime, there are advantages to working in silos. If Chinese dissidents all united into a single group, the Chinese government would find it laughably easy to infiltrate. Instead, they form shape-shifting networks that the authorities find harder to track. They are cautious about their message, too, attacking the symptoms of one-party rule—corruption, torture, land grabs and so forth—rather than directly confronting the system itself.

Many dissidents, if asked, would deny that they seek to overthrow the party. Many prefer the safer reply: that they wish only to reform the way China is governed. Yet the drip-drip effect of their work highlights how unaccountable rulers misrule and encourages people to stand up to them. Gradually, this will foster a climate in China that says that autocracy is not inevitable, and that the alternative might be better.

A few dissidents are blunter about their ultimate goal. Mr. Fu, of China Aid, for example, demands freedom of religion, freedom of assembly, freedom of expression and a government that upholds the rule of law. Once China has those things, he told me, "Democracy will inevitably follow."

THE SEA TURTLES RETURN

There has been an explosion in the number of mainland Chinese who have studied in the West. For elite parents, nothing matches the cachet of sending their child to Harvard. For the brightest Chinese students, a scholarship to a foreign university is the gateway to a fabulous career.

Since Deng Xiaoping first decided, three decades ago, that China must learn from the West, more than 1.6 million Chinese have studied abroad for at least a year, with the largest share (37 percent) going to the United States. Many more have gone on shorter study trips. And the pace at which Chinese students leave for foreign shores is accelerating: according to China's education ministry, 130,000 Chinese citizens studied abroad each year between 2007 and 2009.

This number includes many who were sent abroad by the Chinese government itself. China's rulers are shrewd enough to understand that rich countries, for all their flaws, do many things better than China does. So they send an army of technocrats abroad each year to find out how Europe tackles pollution, how Singapore keeps civil servants honest, how America fosters entrepreneurship, and so on.

In all, more than 500,000 Chinese people have returned home from foreign countries, mostly in the past decade. "The current wave of returnees is undoubtedly the largest foreign-study movement in Chinese history," notes Cheng Li, a scholar at the Brookings Institution.[40]

Many of these "sea turtles" end up in positions of influence. Cheng Li calculated in 2010 that 21 percent of China's ministers and assistant ministers were foreign-educated. And the number of sea turtles on the Communist Party's Central Committee has been rising steadily, from 6 percent in 2002 to 10.5 percent in 2007. Cheng Li predicts that it will rise yet further, to 15 to 17 percent, when a younger generation of party leaders takes over in 2012.[41]

Several of the older generation of Chinese leaders studied abroad, too, but they tended to study in communist countries. Jiang Zemin, China's president from 1993 to 2003 (and, more importantly, Communist Party chief from 1989 to 2002), honed his engineering skills at the Stalin Automobile Works in Moscow. Li Peng, the prime minister who urged his colleagues to crush the students in Tiananmen Square, also studied engineering in Moscow.

The younger generation of sea turtles, by contrast, nearly all studied in advanced democracies such as the United States, Britain, Germany or Japan. (Somehow, they figured they wouldn't learn as much in North Korea or Cuba.)

Cheng Li's 2010 study of sea turtles found many in exalted posts. Li Yuanchao, who spent time at Harvard's Kennedy School of Government, is in charge of the Communist Party's Organization Department. This is one of the most important jobs in China. He is in charge of personnel within the party, deploying cadres from one job to another in the civil service, in state-owned firms and in local government. Cheng Li speculates that Li Yuanchao's time at Harvard must have affected him, since he launched a program to promote more sea turtles within the party. Another returnee, Wang Huning, who went to the University of California, Berkeley, was in charge of the Central Policy Research Center—the party's propaganda machine.

Returnees dominate China's financial leadership. Zhou Xiaochuan, the head of the central bank, attended Santa Clara University in California. Guo Shuqing, the chairman of China Construction Bank, studied at Oxford University. Liu He, an economic adviser to the party's leaders sometimes dubbed "China's Larry Summers," also went to Harvard.

Sea turtles dominate Chinese think tanks to a "truly remarkable" extent, notes Cheng Li. This matters. Mao Zedong ignored experts, but his successors pay them close heed. Hu Angang, a returnee from the United States who took charge of the Center for China Studies, is widely credited with persuading President Hu Jintao to take into account damage to the environment when measuring economic growth. At other think tanks, returnees are often "the face, brain and soul" of the organization, says Cheng Li. At the China Center for Economic Research at Beijing University, which regularly briefs decision makers in the government, all 24 faculty members studied abroad.

Sea turtles run China's best universities and laboratories, too. Wang Huiyao, the head of the Center for China and Globalization in Beijing, calculated in 2010 that 78 percent of Chinese university presidents were returnees, along with 81 percent of the Chinese Academy of Sciences, 54 percent of the Chinese Academy of Engineering and 72 percent of the directors in charge of key government research labs.[42]

Some scholars argue that the sea turtles' presence at the highest levels is not terribly important. Because the party encourages loyal overseas students to snitch on their classmates, those who plan to return to China steer clear of politics. They study hard to become better technocrats and return home uninfected with unsettling democratic ideas.

There is perhaps some truth to this line of thinking. Among sea turtles, the most outspoken political writers are often virulently anti-Western. The authors of such nationalist best-sellers as *China Is Unhappy* and *China Can Say No* were foreign-educated. Yan Xuetong, a prominent professor of international studies at Tsinghua University in Beijing, studied at ultraliberal Berkeley but came back arguing that democracy was not for China. Converting to a liberalized system, he told me, would slow China's economic growth. "You ask people, if the price of freedom of speech is to reduce your salary, do you still want it? I doubt even in the United States that people would say, yes, please reduce my salary."[43]

There is little evidence, however, that democracy does reduce salaries. Chinese students who spend time in advanced democracies surely notice that the people there earn far more than the average Chinese worker. They must also notice that the air is cleaner and the political systems more adept at resolving disputes peacefully.

But those who return harboring democratic sympathies have good reason to keep quiet about them. If you were planning to be China's Mikhail Gorbachev, you would hardly brag about it. The fact that the one-party state's fans are noisier than its foes does not mean they are more numerous.

A few influential sea turtles have spoken openly about the need for reform. Yu Keping, a former visiting professor at Duke University who later became an adviser to President Hu, wrote an essay entitled "Democracy Is a Good Thing." In it, he acknowledged the shortcomings of democracy: it "can make certain very simple matters become complicated"; it "often involves repeated negotiations . . . thereby decreasing administrative efficiency"; and it offers opportunities for "sweet-talking political fraudsters to mislead the people." Nevertheless, he wrote, "democracy is the best political system for humankind."[44]

Yu Keping's prescriptions are somewhat vague, leading skeptics to wonder whether he wishes to adopt the word *democracy* but use it to mean something quite different. Yet he has the basics right:

"[O]fficials must be elected by the citizens, and they must gain the endorsement and support of the majority of the people."[45]

For some time, there has been a debate within the Communist Party as to whether and how to allow more political opening. Occasionally, hints of it can be heard in public. Wen Jiabao, the premier, caused a stir in 2010 when he said that China's economic gains might be lost if the country does not reform politically. He backpedaled after the Arab revolutions of 2011 shook party leaders to the roots of their dyed-black hair. In public, he said that reform should be "gradual," "orderly" and "under the leadership of the party."[46] No one knows what he or his colleagues say in private.

The sea turtles bring two welcome qualities to China's political debate: they understand how free countries work, and they fear the party less than other Chinese do. They have skills and contacts, so they know they can always move abroad again. This makes them harder to push around.

For example, when Teng Biao, a foreign-educated human-rights lawyer, was arrested for visiting a colleague, he protested that the police had no right to detain him. When they dragged him to a cell and started to beat him, he coolly recited chapter and verse of the laws they were breaking. Even when they threatened to bury him in a hole, he refused to shut up.

Writing about his ordeal afterward, Teng asked: "If it had not been for my status as a teacher [at the China University of Politics and Law], a doctor with a degree from Peking University, a famous human-rights lawyer, a visiting scholar at Yale, could I still have shown as much courage? I very much doubt it."[47]

History provides many examples of returnees swaying politics. Vladimir Lenin plotted the Russian revolution while exiled in Munich, London and Geneva. Many of the leaders of South Africa's antiapartheid struggle agitated from safe havens in Britain or Zambia. One of them, Thabo Mbeki, later became president. Between the cold war years of 1958 and 1988, some 50,000 Soviet citizens visited America through cultural exchange programs. Nearly all were members of the cultural, scientific or intellectual elite. Upon returning, they brought with them ideas and attitudes that helped to pave the way for *glasnost*—and ultimately, the collapse of the Soviet Union.[48] Migrants are "agents of democratic diffusion," as Clarisa

Perez-Armendariz, of the University of Texas, who has written a study on the subject, puts it.[49]

PROSPERITY BREEDS DISSENT

As I discussed in earlier chapters, the overseas Chinese help China grow richer. And as any country grows richer, it is more likely to turn democratic.

If we look around the world, there is a strong correlation between income and democracy. All rich countries—bar a few oil sheikh-doms—are democracies.[50] Poor countries are disproportionately despotic. This does not prove that prosperity fosters democracy. It could be the other way around—that democracy fosters economic growth. Perhaps both propositions are true: freedom and prosperity feed each other. Or there could be another factor that promotes both democracy and prosperity.

In 2008 four economists at MIT, Harvard and Columbia University published a paper called "Income and Democracy" that purported to show that income has no effect on a nation's level of democracy. The correlation between the two disappears entirely, they insisted, when you take into account factors that might influence both. For example, they controlled for past savings rates (which should influence economic growth but have no effect on democratization) and for changes in the wealth of each country's major trading partners (ditto). Democracy probably arises in some places but not others, they concluded, because different nations make different political decisions at certain "critical junctures" in history.[51]

Yet when Erich Gundlach, of the Kiel Institute for the World Economy in Germany, and Martin Paldam, of the University of Aarhus in Denmark, conducted a similar study, they reached the opposite conclusion. They controlled for different variables, such as climate (farming is easier in temperate zones) and geography (coastal nations find it easier to trade). They claim to have proved that in the long run, income is by far the most important cause of democracy.[52] They concluded that foreign attempts to impose democracy by force were likely to fail, but that fast-growing countries were likely to evolve into democracies of their own accord. Others have found similar results.[53]

This debate may never be settled. Human societies are maddeningly complex. Even the most brilliant econometric model can capture only a fraction of what is really going on. But I find the idea that wealth fosters democracy compelling.

When people are struggling to feed themselves, they have no time to fret about political freedom. But as they grow richer, they tend to get uppity. They grow accustomed to having choices: which type of bread to buy, which brand of jeans to wear, which school to send their children to. In the marketplace, they discover that their opinions matter. If one mobile-phone company displeases them, they can switch to another. Why, they start to ask, can they not dump their government, too? China's economic reforms, wrote Sun Xiaoli, a professor at one of the government's top training schools, have introduced "the principle of competition," which is now "leaking into the political system."[54]

The Chinese Communist Party faces a dilemma. So long as most people are getting richer each year, it has a reasonable chance of staying in power. But as people grow richer, they also become more independent-minded. They start to form associations, from trade groups to tennis clubs to community organizations that grumble about traffic jams. And as Alexis de Tocqueville wrote in his great study of nineteenth-century America, this "multitude of particular little societies" is the foundation on which democracy can be erected.[55]

China's maturing economy will create fresh challenges for the ruling party. To keep getting richer, China must move from merely copying other people's ideas to generating more of its own. "[Y]ou cannot plagiarize your way to pre-eminence," as one writer put it.[56] To foster innovation, the Chinese government needs to encourage critical thinking, rather than mere rote learning, in schools. It needs to allow its people easier access to ideas and information. It needs to keep sending its brightest minds abroad to study, and it needs to make intellectual life in China exciting enough to entice them back.

Yet China's censorship casts a shadow even over disciplines that are not censored. Discussions about physics, for example, are free and open, but because other areas, such as politics, are stifled, it is hard to attract the world's best scientists to China. Rana Mitter, a professor of Chinese Politics at Oxford, argues that China's censorship will ultimately retard its innovation:

[S]cientists know that they do not operate in a vacuum. To work in an institution which is known for restricting freedom of academic expression will, ultimately, be problematic for a scholar's standing. Few scientists of repute, after all, would choose to work at a US college run by fundamentalists who deny evolution, however significant the funding they are offered.[57]

This is a delicate problem for China's rulers. On the one hand, they can't afford not to allow a freer flow of ideas; on the other, the free flow of ideas is deeply threatening to any dictatorship. They will try hard to cherry-pick the rest of the world's scientific and technical ideas from the political ones. But the two are hard to separate. Scientific inquiry and democratic debate involve similar habits of mind, in particular a willingness to question authority.

THE TUG-OF-WAR OF TECHNOLOGY

Facebook did not cause the Tunisian revolution of 2011, but it did allow angry Tunisians to see, in an instant, just how many other people shared their revulsion for the regime. Nor did Twitter topple the Egyptian dictator Hosni Mubarak, but it did help the protesters against his tyranny to organize.

As I mentioned in Chapters 1 and 2, the overseas Chinese play a crucial role in bringing new communications tools to China. Chinese Americans have funneled venture capital to Chinese IT firms, and foreign-trained engineers have helped China to leapfrog to the latest technology. In 2011 China had 400 million Internet users, 100 million bloggers and 850 million mobile-phone accounts.[58]

Modern communications tools empower individuals. When radio and television were the main channels of mass media, it was relatively easy for a despotic government to control the flow of information.* The first aim of any rebel army (after liberating the national brewery) was to capture the national broadcaster. No longer.

---

* Short-wave radio broadcasts by the British Broadcasting Corporation and Voice of America, it should be noted, helped to spread accurate news behind the Iron Curtain and into China during the Tiananmen protests.

Nowadays, mass communication is decentralized, which means that information is hard to control. Millions of people have smartphones. If the police start shooting protesters, they know that someone will film and broadcast it. So they will not be able to pretend that it never happened, or that they acted in self-defense.

Twitter, the leading American microblogging service, is banned in China, but there are local alternatives, such as QQ.com and Sina.com. Microblogs are hard to censor because they are instantaneous and broken into small chunks. An individual message may be impossible to understand unless you have also read the ones that came before it. This makes it hard for the regime's filters to spot a subversive message before it spreads.

In September 2010, for example, local officials in Jiangxi province ordered a family's home demolished, prompting three of its members to set themselves afire and jump off the roof. A local newspaper tried to report the story, but the censors quickly suppressed it. Two of the sisters set off for Beijing to complain to the central government. Local police tried to stop them, so they locked themselves in an airport bathroom and sent text messages to reporters begging for help.

One journalist began reporting the story live with a series of microblog posts. Others joined in. The story spread fast, and even when the government tried to delete all the messages, it found it could not, because so many had been forwarded to readers' friends, and their friends' friends. A photo of the two sisters' miserable faces was reposted on Sina.com nearly 3,000 times.[59]

Using such strategies, journalists and even ordinary people can broadcast from their homes, from coffee shops and from the street. Deng Fei, a mainland journalist who investigates corruption, microblogs to 2.45 million readers—more than the paid circulation of any American newspaper.

Communications technology can support tyranny as well as undermine it. Iran's government checks the Facebook pages of ethnic Iranians visiting Iran to see if they have dissident friends. During the cold war, the communist government of East Germany allowed its people to watch Western soap operas on television, and surveys found that those who did so were less angry about the regime than those who did not. Evgeny Morozov, a journalist based in Belarus, an oppressive former Soviet state, argues that the Internet "has provided so many cheap and easily available entertainment fixes to those living under authoritarianism that it has become considerably harder to get people to care about politics at all."[60]

Many strong-arm regimes use online methods to spread their own propaganda. In countries where everyone assumes that official newspapers are full of lies, this can be insidiously effective. Anonymous blog posts by government hirelings may be believed if the propaganda is subtle enough.

Morozov is right to be suspicious of the most breathless predictions about the democratizing power of technology. After all, many tyrants were toppled before Twitter existed. Political change will always depend more on human bravery than on bytes. But decentralized communication technologies still confer on individuals powers that were once reserved for governments. That must make a difference. As Ying Chan, of the China Media Project, a Hong Kong–based watchdog for journalistic freedom, observes: "We live in an era when we receive and dispatch news anytime and anywhere, a time when the human spirit and information flow like running water, gathering and dispersing with warp speed. How can bureaucrats suppress such forces of nature?"[61]

A BORDERLESS WORLD HAS STANDARDS

The more contact China has with the rest of the world, the more pressure it will feel to meet the minimum moral standards that the world expects of a civilized nation. People from different countries and cultures disagree about many things, but few would argue that a nation should be stuck with a government that its people never chose and do not want.

China is so powerful that other nations seldom voice their disapproval. But the country's leaders understand that the rest of the world considers them morally inferior—and they must know in their hearts that the rest of the world is right.

When Hu Jintao visited Japan in 2008, a young child asked him why he had wanted to be president. He replied that he had not wanted the top job. "It was the people in the whole country who voted me in," he said, adding that he could not let them down. His predecessor,

Jiang Zemin, made the same outrageous claim on an American television program in 2000, insisting that he "was elected, too."[62] Such hypocrisy is revealing. The most powerful men in China recognize that their authority cannot be justified without lying.*

It may be unfashionable in some circles to argue that morals matter in politics, but they do. A regime that ceases to believe in itself is weakened, sometimes fatally. The Soviet Union was not overthrown by force, but because hardly anyone wanted it to survive. Armed resistance barely scratched South Africa's white-supremacist government, but the regime collapsed when white South Africans tired of being global pariahs.

Chinese dissidents are not plotting a violent revolution. China has had those before, and they brought more misery than joy. Bruce Gilley, the author of *China's Democratic Future,* predicts that change will come peacefully and from within the Communist Party itself.

Mr. Gilley posits that discontent will grow until a crisis of some sort sparks massive street protests. The party will not order the army to shoot the protesters because its leaders will be divided—even more so than they were in 1989. Even the hawks within the party will not be confident that the army would once again obey an order to massacre civilians. In 1989, some 150 officers wrote an open letter stating their abhorrence of the impending carnage in Tiananmen Square. Since then, the People's Liberation Army has grown more professional, and more reluctant to involve itself in domestic politics.[63]

As the protests spread, some party leaders will calculate that they need to make concessions. The tipping point will come when enough senior party members start to believe that democratic change is inevitable. Once they believe this, it will be in their selfish interest to back it early, enhancing their chances in China's first free elections. Mr. Gilley, a former correspondent for the *Far Eastern Economic Review,* predicts that an alliance of liberals and pragmatists within the elite will eventually overcome conservative resistance.[64]

---

* Jiang could argue that he was telling the truth in the sense that he was elected by the National People's Congress, but that is not what any American viewer would understand by the term "elected" and he damn well knows it.

Gilley's is a plausible scenario. I make no guess as to how exactly democracy will come to China, only that it will happen, and sooner than many people expect. China cannot buck history forever. Nor can it link itself so intimately to the world's advanced democracies without catching the democratic bug.

One overseas Chinese businessman, who is well connected enough to be a friend of the family of Xi Jinping, the likely president of China in 2013, told me that the foreign-educated children of the elite may not want democracy tomorrow, but they think it is "inevitable" eventually. "I think they are planning for it," he says.

There is evidence that he is right. A survey of China's new rich by Bain & Company, a consultancy, found that 57 percent of those with assets worth more than $1.5 million have considered emigrating, and 10 percent have actually completed the paperwork for a country that lets you immigrate if you invest enough. The second most common reason given for wanting to leave (after "education") was "wealth safety."[65]

What does this mean? Many of these people no doubt acquired their stash in corrupt ways and fear being caught. Others know it's unwise to assume that the current political system will last forever. And if the Communist Party falls, its successor might investigate those who grew rich from their links to it. Small wonder the Chinese elite crave the security of a foreign passport.

Sarah Chang, the web-surfing office worker in Shanghai, admits that she has only a rough notion of what living in a democracy might be like. "If you've never had beef before," she muses, "how do you know what it tastes like?" But she is sure that she will find out. "Will change happen in my lifetime? Definitely."

Consider, for a moment, what that would mean. A billion Chinese would suddenly be free. No one knows what use they might make of that freedom. Doubtless they will elect bad governments as well as good ones. But the choice will finally be theirs. As Bao Tong, a former high-ranking communist, once put it, a democratic China "will fundamentally change the balance between good and evil in the world."[66]

4

NETWORKS OF INNOVATION

HOW MIGRANTS CAN CUT YOUR MEDICAL BILLS

Hundreds of millions of Indians cannot prove they exist. They have no birth certificate, no driver's license and no social security number. This makes their lives difficult in many ways.

For starters, they find it hard to obtain from their government the services it has promised them. Consider this shocking example. One of the Indian government's biggest welfare programs involves distributing cheap grain to the poor. In a country where half the children under five are chronically malnourished, this ought to be a lifeline.[1] But it is a frayed lifeline at best. As a senior Indian official explained to me one warm morning in New Delhi, two-thirds of the grain intended for the poor is stolen or adulterated. Yes: *two-thirds*.

It works like this. First, the government buys truckloads of grain. Then it sells it at a steep discount to a network of 500,000 public distribution stores around India. These distributors are supposed to sell a fixed ration of subsidized grain to every poor person in their area.

The system is laughably easy to scam, however. Having taken delivery of a truckload of cheap grain, a distributor often sells it to local shops at full price. This is illegal but immensely profitable, since the difference between the subsidized price and the market price is huge. Hungry peasants lose out. The distributor may turn them away empty-handed by pretending that the government grain never arrived. Or he may sell them rotten or adulterated grain mixed with cheaper, less nutritious materials, such as gravel.

The system is corrupt because there are no effective checks. If a middleman swears that he has delivered so many bags of rice to so many thousands of peasants, there is no easy way to tell if he is lying. To expose his corruption, you would have to track down the people he says he sold it to. They probably live miles away, along unpaved roads, in villages where no one has a formal address and scores of people share the same name. It is a nonstarter.

But suppose the merchant had to prove that each ration of grain had gone to a specific individual with a unique identity number backed up by biometric data? Then it would be much harder to cheat the system.

A biometric identity system could help address a lot of problems in India, from rampant voter fraud to the trouble poor people have obtaining credit. So Nandan Nilekani, an Indian software billionaire, volunteered to help the government build one.

The government thought this was a wonderful idea. But there was a snag. India has more than a billion citizens. The proposed biometric database would have to cover ten times more people than the largest one ever built (the database used by the US Bureau of Citizenship and Immigration Services to track people entering the United States). India is still a poor country, and its government has a long record of botching large infrastructure projects. Mr. Nilekani's dream seemed impossible.

So he turned to the Indian diaspora for help. He called up ethnic Indians who had done well in the information technology industry in America and offered them a chance to do something for their motherland.

They jumped at the opportunity. Before long, they were Skyping their friends and urging them to join in. Since every bright Indian in Silicon Valley knows other bright Indians in Silicon Valley, the news spread fast.

The project was enticing for three reasons: First, it presented a colossal technical challenge. Second, it offered an opportunity to improve the lives of millions of poor people. Third, it appealed to the migrants' patriotism.

By sending word out through the diaspora grapevine, Mr. Nilekani was able to pull together a team of ethnic Indian IT superstars on very short notice. One of them, Raj Mashruwala, had helped to set up the number-crunching system for the New York Stock Exchange. Another, Srikanth Nadhamuni, had helped to set up a multibillion-dollar health-IT firm in California. Others had worked for whizzy tech firms such as Google and Snapfish.

The team set up a whiteboard in a rented apartment in Bangalore, ordered a ton of junk food and started brainstorming. "It was like a start-up in a garage," bubbles Mr. Nadhamuni. "There were lots of people like me who had experience in getting things to market very quickly."

They formed a flat organization with no hierarchy and no fussing over job titles. Had it been a standard Indian government project, they might have wasted months trying to figure out who reported to whom and who would get the most lavish perks. But the Indians from California cared nothing for bureaucratic titles. Since most of them were already wealthy, they did not care about perks, either. And since they were used to Silicon Valley deadlines, they took it for granted that they would work punishing hours. The first brainstorming session lasted for 13 straight hours, Mr. Nadhamuni recalls. The program went from start-up to rollout in little more than a year.

I flew to India in January 2011 to watch people enroll in the new program. I met Mr. Nadhamuni in his office, a sparse and functional room in a block on the edge of sprawling Bangalore. The writing board on his wall was scrawled with figures and flowcharts. Outside his door was a warren of activity: engineers tweaking code, stress-testing the database, monitoring enrollments and assessing which bits of equipment were the least likely to break when dropped on a hard dirt floor. (It would all have to work in remote villages, so it would have to be tough.)

Mr. Nadhamuni is tall and affable, with simple habits and a ferociously logical mind. He is a strict vegetarian, which is the norm in southern India. He also finds it hard to cope with spicy food, which is not.

We talked about his background. Living abroad, which he had done for much of his adult life, made him see India differently, he said. Having seen how smoothly most things work in America, he found it hard to accept the potholes and hassles that bedevil Indian life. He recalled how, as a student at Louisiana State University, it took him only ten minutes to fill in an application for a social security number. Few things are that easy in India.

His assistant brought us two extra-sweet cappuccinos. Mr. Nadhamuni was reminded of an anecdote from his Silicon Valley days. He was working for Jim Clark, a serial entrepreneur who founded or cofounded three separate billion-dollar businesses: Silicon Graphics, Netscape (now part of AOL) and Healtheon (now called WebMD).

Mr. Clark was a tornado of a man, constantly charging around and shaking things up, but he also knew how to stroke the talent. His bright young employees complained that the coffee at Healtheon was foul. "We could work in a garage, but we couldn't work without good coffee," recalls Mr. Nadhamuni. "So one day [Jim Clark] drives in on a BMW motorcycle, into the building, booming. And we said, 'We need a coffee machine. And not just any coffee machine. We need a La Pavoni [an expensive Italian brand].' He said: 'OK, let's go get a La Pavoni.' And we went out and got a big machine."

The culture of Silicon Valley is about floating big ideas and then making them happen—fast. Healtheon started as a sketch so simple that Mr. Clark could draw it in a few seconds. It consisted of a diamond. At each corner was a single word. The words were: "doctors," "payers" (i.e., insurers), "providers" (e.g., hospitals) and "consumers" (i.e., patients).

Clark's pitch to investors was these four groups were hopeless at communicating with each other and wasted hundreds of billions of dollars each year on treatments that did not make anyone healthier. With better use of IT, he argued, the system could work more efficiently.

His presentation lasted only 20 minutes. Its climax was a four-word command. The American health-care market was worth $1.5 trillion a year at the time (this was in the mid-1990s). Healtheon would trim the fat and keep a chunk of the savings. "You do the math," said Mr. Clark. Investment bankers salivated.

Mr. Nadhamuni was among the small team of software maestros who brought the Healtheon vision to life. Mr. Clark "had a thing for Indians," according to his biographer, Michael Lewis. "As a concentrated group," Mr. Clark reckoned, they were "the most talented engineers in the Valley . . . *and they work their butts off.*" He affectionately called them "my Indian hordes."[2]

Healtheon did not resolve America's health-care problems (more on that later). But Mr. Clark and his team did create a business that survived the dot-com bust of 2001 and continues to prosper today. In June 2011, WebMD was worth $2.8 billion.[3]

Having earned a tidy sum, Mr. Nadhamuni left Silicon Valley in 2002 and went home to India. He wanted to help those less fortunate than himself, so he took an unpaid job running a new foundation, which he set up with Nandan Nilekani, to promote the use of the Internet to improve government services for the poor.

He discovered that the poor in India are extremely mobile. Unlike China, India has no laws that restrict the free movement of people from one place to another. Rural Indians often move to cities to find temporary work laying bricks or mopping floors. In all, India has at least 42 million internal migrants.[4] Yet a poor Indian's ration card works only in his home state. Without proof of identity, India's creaky welfare system cannot keep track of those who move. Vaccination programs are a nightmare, since their success depends on jabbing nearly everyone, which is hard to do when you don't know who has already been jabbed and who has not. With little idea of who the needy are or where to find them, rational budgeting is impossible. So when Mr. Nilekani asked if he would like to help set up a national identity system, Mr. Nadhamuni said, "Of course."

I drove out to the countryside with Mr. Nadhamuni to watch people being enrolled. Crowds of them sat in the shade, waiting in line outside town halls or one-room schools. Many were subsistence farmers, shorter and thinner than the fleshy urbanites who operated the iris scanners. Goats and chickens nibbled and pecked in the dust nearby.

Everyone filled in a form with his name and approximate date of birth. Those who could not read—which included plenty of the adults—had someone else do it for them. Everyone was friendly to the inquisitive foreigner—farmers were happy to show off the forms they had just filled in. Looking at their birthdates jolted me a bit. Everyone I had thought to be a decade older than me turned out to be a decade younger. Heavy toil under a hot sun ages a face pitilessly.

Having filled in the paperwork, each applicant placed his fingertips on a scanner. Some farmers had illegible fingerprints—years of hoeing and weeding had worn their ridges down. The scanner operators gave them a damp cloth to moisten their fingertips, which helps the ridges stand out.

Next, each applicant stared at another scanner, which captured his irises. Another camera then snapped a digital photograph of his face. These images were uploaded to a computer.

Within a few weeks, each applicant received a universal identity number (UID) tied to his unique biometric markers. The people I talked to seemed pleased. In a village called Belgumba, a shoe hawker named Muneer Ahmad said he expected to be able to use it "for all kinds of things," from obtaining a ration card to getting a loan to expand his modest business. "I can't pay the interest that loan sharks charge," he told me. "I'd get killed."

An office worker in the small town of Tumkur called K. J. Manjunathswamy rejoiced that wherever he traveled in India, a biometric identity number would prove who he was. It would help him enroll his children in schools and slice through the bureaucratic tangle at banks. Previously, opening an account had taken hours, sometimes days. "They'd ask for a million signatures," he frowned. "It's always: 'Get me this form. Get me that form.'" All that would soon become much easier, he predicted.

A reliable way of identifying people would also smooth financial transactions. Some 42 million poor households in India toil for a government program that guarantees them up to 100 days of work at the minimum wage each year. The money is welcome; the trek to the bank to collect it is not. Mr. Nadhamuni told me how Ram, a peasant in Madhya Pradesh, must walk four miles to the bus stop, travel nearly nine more, clinging to the roof of a bus, wait two hours at the bank and then do it all again in reverse. This trip swallows a fifth of his earnings. Every ticket costs precious rupees. And then there is the opportunity cost—the money he loses by missing a day's work.

The identity scheme could help Ram avoid this hassle. The plan is to supply scanners to village shops and link them to distant banks via mobile phones. Ram will be able to walk in, scan his fingers and authorize the bank to transfer his money to the shopkeeper's bank account. The shopkeeper will then advance Ram the money, minus a small fee.

Shopkeepers are excited. I spoke to B. C. Manjunath, who runs a tiny *kirana* store in Tumkur selling boiled sweets, soap and single eggs. He saw two ways to profit. As well as charging fees, he would benefit from customers with more cash in their pockets. At present he said he had little choice but to extend credit. Customers owed his family 20,000 rupees ($440), interest free—a crushing burden for such a small business.

Mr. Nadhamuni believes that his team of local and diaspora Indians has generated three innovations that others might want to copy.

The first is the way they use cloud computing. Cloud computing is the harnessing of huge amounts of computing power on machines that may be anywhere in the world ("in the cloud"). Private companies use the cloud all the time, renting capacity when they need it from such firms as Google or Amazon. The UID team wanted something cheaper and more secure. Many Indians worry that the scheme will allow an invasion of their privacy, and Mr. Nadhamuni is anxious to assuage their fears. His team hit on the idea of using vast numbers of secure government computers that otherwise sit idle at night. Millions of machines in dark, empty government offices now help him with his number-crunching.

Second—and unusually for a government program—the UID team has used completely open-source software and an open-standards platform. Open-source software means that the scheme will never be shackled to a particular software firm—a problem that afflicts many government projects around the world. Open-standards means that anyone can graft new applications onto their system. India's state governments could use it in schools, to help them monitor each student's progress. If a student migrates from one state to another, his school records could move with him—something that often does not happen today.

Businesses will be able to use it, too. Verifiable identities would make all kinds of insurance much cheaper. Auto insurers will be able to price risk more accurately when they have a reliable way of discovering, for example, that a man applying for insurance in Mumbai has previously been convicted of drunk driving in Delhi.

Microfinance should start to work better, too. In India the fashionable business of making small loans to the poor has run into huge problems because no one can keep track of how many loans an individual has taken out. UIDs should make it easier to tell whether a farmer asking for a loan already owes money to ten other microfinanciers. And if lenders can judge more accurately whether each borrower is creditworthy, it will make credit cheaper for everyone.

Even with strict controls for privacy, the UID program will help companies understand more about the population they serve. "It would be fantastic for just about any business," says Shivinder Singh, a hospital executive who appears later in this chapter. There is a caveat, of course: the system must work. The main challenge is ensuring that the data are accurate. If they are not, the identity numbers will be worthless. And that brings us to the team's third nifty innovation: the way they motivate the private contractors who do much of the work.

When an individual is enrolled, his biometric data must be compared with everyone else's to ensure that there is no duplication: i.e., that each Indian has one—and only one—identity. This is harder than it sounds. Sometimes the workers who show people how to place their fingers on the scanner accidentally scan their own fingerprints. It is essential that the UID scheme's central computers detect such mistakes and reject all duplicated applications for identity numbers. As enrollments hit a projected peak of about 1 million a day, the system will need to carry out a staggering 14 billion matches per second.

The UID team wanted to hand this task to private contractors. But since the task is unprecedented, no private firm could know how much work it might involve. So if the whole job were to be contracted out in one go, bidders would be reluctant to offer their best price, in case it turned out to be harder than they realized. And once they won the contract, they would have no incentive to do a better job than the contract specified.

So instead of awarding the contract in a conventional way, the UID team devised a dynamic model. There are three contractors (Accenture and L-1 Identity Solutions, of the United States, plus Morpho, of France). The firm that does the fastest, most accurate job gets 50 percent of the work; the others get 30 percent or 20 percent. This allocation is reassessed frequently, so if the second-best firm starts doing better, it picks up some work from the leading firm. In other words, each contractor is constantly competing against the other two. That keeps everyone sharp.

Word of this neat idea is already spreading. When Mr. Nadhamuni gives speeches abroad, officials from agencies that spend a lot on IT— such as the FBI—buttonhole him as he steps off the stage and demand to know how it is working.

The scale of the UID venture is mind-boggling. Mr. Nadhamuni's team was feeling quite pleased after logging the first 500,000 people— until they remembered that this represented less than one-half of 1 percent of India's population. An Australian at a project discussion joked that, once it was over, he could go home and register everyone in Australia over a long weekend.

As of June 2011, more than 9 million people had been enrolled in the UID program.[5] They'll have to pick up the pace to enroll 600 million people by the end of 2014. It could all end in failure—plenty of Indian government projects have. But this time the need is so palpable and the people in charge so rigorous that I am optimistic. When the world's largest democracy brings its offshore brains onshore, wonders ensue.

THE NATTERING NABOBS OF INNOVATION

In a comic strip my ten-year-old son Peter finds amusing, a schoolboy named Calvin builds an "atomic cerebral enhance-o-tron" to help him with his homework. Placing a kitchen colander hooked up to imaginary electrodes on his head makes his brain so large that he brags he can reduce all natural laws to "one simple, unifying equation." (Alas, he forgot to write it down.)[6] Diaspora networks are like Calvin's colander: a nation that has one is like a man with two brains.

Atal Bihari Vajpayee agrees. In a 2003 speech, the then–prime minister begged nonresident Indians to help their motherland. "We do not want your investments," he said. "We want your ideas. We do not want your riches; we want the richness of your experience."[7]

Recent emigrants from India are a clever bunch. Among Indian professional households with a relative abroad, a hefty 78 percent say that that relative has a postgraduate degree.[8] To get a job in Silicon Valley, an Indian has to pass through the narrowest of funnels. A typical first step is to win admittance to one of the Indian Institutes of Technology (IITs), a network of elite universities. You need to be a first-rate student just to take the entrance exam. And among these first-rate students, the competition is ferocious: only 1 in 60 wins a place. Indians joke that when a student enrolls at an IIT, his spirit ascends to America; after graduation, his body follows.[9]

"Anyone with the brains to get into the IITs *and* the gumption to get himself to the United States [must be] capable of all manner of miracles," writes Michael Lewis in *The New New Thing,* a book about Silicon Valley.[10] California's Indian engineers have "the lust for the kill" and are "ferociously, recklessly competitive," he observes. They are also enterprising. Vivek Wadhwa, of Duke University, and AnnaLee Saxenian, of the University of California, Berkeley, discovered that between 1995 and 2005 more than 15 percent of the startups in Silicon Valley had at least one Indian cofounder.[11]

Brainy Indians still emigrate in large numbers every year. But as India's economy has started to grow fast, many have turned around and headed home. The numbers are hard to verify. Indian emigrants who still have their old passports can waltz back into Delhi without attracting notice. But the movement is clearly big. The Indus Entrepreneurs, a club for overseas Indians, estimates that at least 60,000 Indian IT professionals have moved back.[12]

Some stay; some don't. Of the UID launch team, Mr. Mashruwala eventually returned to America, whereas Mr. Nadhamuni plans to stay in India permanently. He loves the rhythm of Indian life, the excitement of his job and the chance to raise his children near their grandparents.

But he has not wholly left America. He wants his children to go to university there. His sister still lives in Houston (his mother, who lives in Mysore, not far from Bangalore, teaches her Texan grand-children classical Indian singing via Skype). Among India's intellectual elite, ocean-spanning family setups like Mr. Nadhamuni's are now common.

When ethnic Indians in different countries talk to each other, ideas bounce across borders. That is important in itself: a huge part of progress consists of spreading good ideas to places where people have not yet heard them. But there is another benefit to the constant nattering that goes on within ethnic networks. As good ideas are passed around, they evolve. Insights are taken apart and recombined in millions of individual brains. Then they are fed back into the network. After a while, new ideas emerge.

It is hard to measure how knowledge moves through ethnic networks, but Harvard scholar William Kerr has done some brilliantly suggestive research. He looked at the names on US patent records. He guessed that an inventor called Wang was probably of Chinese origin, while someone called Martinez was probably Hispanic. He discovered that foreign researchers cite US-based researchers of their own ethnicity 30 to 50 percent more often than you would expect if ethnic ties made no difference.[13]

It is not just that Chinese scientists in Beijing read papers written by Chinese scientists in America. It is also that geeks like to gossip. In casual conversation, Chinese scientists in America will often alert their old classmates in Beijing to intriguing research being done at the lab across the road. And the information flows both ways.

A great virtue of science is that it is both universal and colorblind. The value of an experiment depends not on the ethnic background of the experimenter but on whether her results are replicable. But scientists themselves are social creatures bound together by ethnic, religious and school ties. They may email someone they don't know with a specific query, but for an idle chat, they will surely call someone they know. Likewise, if they stumble upon some data that a friend might find useful, they will probably forward it to him.

"Ideas do not move effortlessly across space," wrote Edward Glaeser, a Harvard economist.[14] He was talking about the benefits of cities, in which creative people can cluster and swap ideas in gyms and coffee shops. But his insight applies equally well to the human interactions that diaspora networks promote. You can learn a lot from a book about, say, architecture or chip design. But you will probably learn more by working with an architect or at a chip-making firm.

Personal connections matter even in the meritocratic world of science. With so much more information whizzing around the Internet than any individual can absorb, often the most useful thing is knowing people who can tell you which scientific paper to read, whom to hire for your project, or which venture capitalist might be interested in your idea. In short, technological progress depends more on personal ties than most people realize.

Companies that do business in India are acutely aware of the talent in the diaspora and are eager to harness it. I cornered a few Indian bosses at the 2011 World Economic Forum in Davos and asked them what proportion of their top people had worked or studied abroad. Natarajan Chandrasekaran, the chief executive of Tata Consulting Services, thought for a moment and replied: "All of them."[15] Others said much the same thing.

Once you start looking for examples of diaspora collaboration, they are everywhere. For example, Godrej & Boyce Manufacturing, a big family firm based in Mumbai, has developed a $69 refrigerator—the world's cheapest. This engineering miracle was conceived through a marriage of ideas generated by Indians in India and by Indians overseas.

Jamshyd Godrej, the company's chairman, lives in India, but has spent a fair bit of time overseas—he studied mechanical engineering at the Illinois Institute of Technology. Through a fellow alumnus, he met C. K. Prahalad, an Indian-born professor of management who spent time in both India and the United States, ending up at the University of Michigan. The late Professor Prahalad influenced Godrej profoundly. One of his insights was that there is money to be made from serving the poor, because there are so many of them. Prahalad called this "the fortune at the bottom of the pyramid" and wrote a much-cited book of that name.[16]

Godrej saw applications for his own line of work, which is making household appliances. Only 1 or 2 percent of rural Indian households own a fridge. A standard model costs $200 and guzzles power. Few peasants can afford such extravagance. So Godrej asked his best engineers to see if they could develop a frugal fridge. The team introduced an early version, based on thermoelectric cooling, in May 2009.

Around this time a trio of Indian American engineers dropped by. Uttam Ghoshal, Himanshu Pokharna and Ayan Guha were in India to visit relatives, but they had a good idea and they wanted to show it to someone who could put it into practice. They knew the Godrej name; as a student in Mumbai, Mr. Ghoshal walked past the Godrej factory every weekend.

Mr. Pokharna wheedled an introduction from a young member of the Godrej family, exploiting the fact that both had been at Wharton, the business school affiliated with the University of Pennsylvania. Eventually, the three engineers got an appointment to see a vice president, G. Sunderraman.

They showed him their idea for a superior cooling engine. It was based on technology used to cool laptop computers and servers. (Mr. Ghoshal used to be a master inventor at IBM.) They thought it might work in a standard fridge. They were told it would be perfect for the Chotu Kool (the name means "little cool"), a new fridge that Godrej was designing for the bottom of the pyramid.

So now, the Chotu Kool uses a light and compact cooling chip and a fan. Unlike conventional fridges, it can run on batteries, which is handy in villages where the power supply is fitful or non-existent.

The Chotu Kool is an example of frugal innovation, one of the most important trends to emerge from developing countries in the past decade. People in India and China are extremely price-sensitive, but they still want fridges and televisions and cars. To serve them, companies have to redesign products from scratch. They have to ask, what does this product need to do? In the case of fridges, Godrej noticed that Indian villagers go to the grocery store every day. So a fridge would not need to be big. The Chotu Kool is light and portable: it is only one-and-a-half feet tall and two feet wide. Godrej is now working with Ghoshal's firm in Texas, Sheetak Inc., to make the Chotu Kool more efficient in time for a mass-market rollout in late 2011.[17]

It's safe to say that this innovation wouldn't have originated in the United States. Americans like their fridges to be huge. (A nice chap I met at a National Rifle Association convention once explained to me that he needed to be able to fit a whole moose in his freezer, since he liked to eat what he killed.) But Americans might warm to the idea of a cool box for camping trips that keeps chilling for days.

Frugal technology can be applied to any area where people want to save money. For example, Tata Chemicals has codeveloped a water filter that harnesses rice husks (a common waste product) and nanotechnology to make Indian water safe to drink. This nifty little device saves lives—some 2 million Indians die each year from drinking dirty water—and it only costs about $20.

Another part of the Tata Group, Tata Steel, has built a prototype for a house that costs only $500 and can be bought in a shop.[18] Vijay Govindarajan, an Indian professor at Dartmouth College's Tuck School of Business, is trying to crowdsource an even cheaper one. In a blog post, he challenged inventors to design a durable home with water filters and solar panels that could be mass-produced for only $300 per unit. More than 900 inventors responded.[19]

Making simple products need not mean making primitive ones. Frugal inventors often leapfrog from an old technology to a barely known one, bypassing the intermediate stage. Some take advantage of the very latest techniques in miniaturization and advanced materials. Many make products that are better as well as cheaper.[20]

Not all frugal inventions will be hits. Tata Motors' much-hyped $2,000 car, the Nano, launched in 2009, has since run into roadblocks. As my colleague Adrian Wooldridge wryly reported, "Some [Nano] cars have suffered from what Ravi Kant, the vice chairman of Tata Motors, calls 'thermal incidents' and his customers call 'catching fire.'"[21] Yet someday, a Chinese or Indian firm will build a cheap car that people do want to buy. The profits would be immense—Asia's multitudes of commuters are sick of being knocked off their scooters.

Another area crying out for frugal innovation is health care. Poor countries struggle to supply basic medicine to their people. Rich countries are grappling with soaring medical bills as their populations age. New tools being developed in India and China could help address both problems. And much of this innovation is driven by the blending of diaspora know-how with local brainpower.

I visited the vast research campus that GE Healthcare's Indian arm runs in Bangalore.* It is an imposing place: a walled village of office blocks gleaming in the south Indian sun, crammed with laboratories and whirling with white coats.

The chief technology officer, Munesh Makhija, showed me around. He is a tall, high-browed man, born in India but educated in Indiana. After working for a telecoms firm in Chicago for a decade, he joined GE in Milwaukee in 2003. He asked to be sent to India, he said, because he wanted to watch a giant emerge, and because he wanted his children to reconnect with their grandparents.

Mr. Makhija showed me some of the gizmos developed by GE in India. Most were not merely 10 percent cheaper than the standard alternative but an order of magnitude cheaper—a handheld heart scanner, for example, cost $500 instead of $5,000.

The Mac-i ("i" is for India) is the smallest, simplest electrocardiography (ECG) machine I had ever seen. It has only three buttons, so you don't need much training to use it. It gives a printout that looks like a bus ticket, with heart readings and a simple analysis ranging from "Normal" to "See a doctor." A nurse—or even someone with no medical training at all—can look at it and get a pretty good idea whether or not you need to trudge to a city to find a hospital. As I mentioned earlier, for a poor Indian a trip into town can mean losing a whole day's wages, so this is precious information.

I held a Mac-i in my hand. It was impressively light: no heavier than a carton of orange juice, and less likely to burst if dropped. GE made it robust enough to cope with heat, humidity, dust, flies, rutted roads and being trampled by cows. Since a typical rural clinic in India gets only a few hours of electricity a day, the Mac-i can run on batteries. And the batteries can be recharged on one of the country's ubiquitous mobile phone–like chargers.

Most importantly, it costs only nine rupees (less than 20 cents) for an ECG test. At a clinic it would cost between 150 and 300 rupees; at

---

* GE Healthcare is a global company headquartered a stone's throw from my house in Buckinghamshire, England. It is an offshoot of GE (formerly General Electric), an American conglomerate that grew from a seed planted by Thomas Edison, the inventor of the lightbulb.

a fancy urban hospital it could set you back 1,000 rupees.[22] Granted, there you'd get an air-conditioned waiting room and a nice cup of tea thrown in. But for someone who makes a dollar a day, the Mac-i offers a more affordable way to avoid premature death. (Five million Indians a year die of heart problems.[23])

The next step, promised Mr. Makhija, will be to use mobile-phone technology, which is already widespread in India, to transmit readings from a portable ECG to a cardiologist hundreds of miles away.

At GE, I saw several other frugal machines, along with their pricier counterparts. There was a fancy digital X-ray machine, for example, that could move a patient around robotically and cost $1.5 million—and a basic version that cost *only one-hundredth as much,* and was simpler to use. On the downside, you have to move the patient around by hand; on the plus side, India is not short of hands.

One of the advantages of having lived in the United States, says Mr. Makhija, is that you can see what the future might look like and devise a plan for getting there faster. Looking at India, he says, "you start to see patterns that the US has already been through"—and can perhaps learn from American mistakes.

Working in India has tremendous advantages, too. Because India's problems are so huge, they force you to think creatively. Take telemedicine (supplying medical services from afar). "Elsewhere, you want it because it's often cheaper and more convenient," says Mr. Makhija. "Here, you need it because of the distance." India has only 6 doctors per 10,000 people, compared with America's 27, and hardly anyone in rural India owns a car, so getting to the hospital in a hurry is simply not an option.[24]

For their part, Western firms such as GE are often happy to send ethnic Indian staffers back to India, because they know that these employees are more likely to understand the local market and less likely to commit cultural blunders, like the one Ford once made with the electric windows in a car it was trying to sell there. (It installed them for the front seats but not the back ones. What Ford failed to realize was that anyone in India who can afford a Ford probably has a driver, so they were giving the better windows to the servant rather than his boss. That model did not sell well.)

PARVINDER SINGH'S PARSIMONIOUS SONS

To find out more about frugal medicine, in early 2011 I visited a hospital in Delhi owned by Fortis, a private company founded and run by global Indians. Brothers Malvinder and Shivinder Singh are the chairman and managing director, respectively. Both have MBAs from Duke University in North Carolina.

Neither was born hungry—their grandfather founded Ranbaxy Laboratories, India's largest maker of generic drugs. But they built Fortis almost from scratch, buying and building new hospitals until they controlled more than 50 in 2011. The brothers sold their stake in Ranbaxy to a Japanese firm in 2008 for $2.4 billion, and now concentrate mostly on Fortis.

Shivinder, a sprightly man in a bright turban, told me that he learned a lot from his time in the United States. "If you live only in India, you naturally measure yourself against Indian standards," he says. "If you have lived abroad, you measure yourself against the best in the world. That imparts a certain discipline."[25]

Tragically, the brothers' father, Parvinder Singh, died of cancer in 1999. But before that, while Shivinder was at Duke, his father sought treatment at the Memorial Sloan-Kettering Cancer Center in New York. Shivinder visited him there. Although it was a sad time, Shivinder was impressed by what he saw.

The best American hospitals, he realized, not only practiced outstanding medicine; they were also superbly organized. Doctors followed carefully documented procedures instead of relying solely on their instincts, as Indian doctors tend to. This no doubt cramped the style of one or two medical geniuses, but it also raised the corps of ordinary physicians to a consistently high standard. The Singh brothers decided to build a chain of hospitals that would combine Western technology with Indian parsimony.

The Singhs are not doctors; they are businessmen. Both are obsessed with getting not only the best out of their employees, but also the most. A top surgeon in America might perform 250 to 350 operations per year. A surgeon at a Fortis hospital will perform 1,200. The difference is partly due to regulation: American doctors are barred from doing much more, for fear that they will become exhausted and make mistakes. India can ill afford such tight rules—it has so few doctors that it must make the most of the ones it has.

Fortis does this by ensuring that its surgeons waste as little time as possible. Unlike doctors in rich countries, they spend almost no time wrestling with paperwork or administration. Surgeons in America sometimes even make their own coffee, marvels Shivinder. Not in a Fortis hospital.

An army of helpers takes care of all the mundane tasks, leaving surgeons free to operate—often. The economic logic is compelling. Doctors are more expensive than support staff everywhere, of course, but in India the gap is gigantic. Doctors are scarce and therefore well paid; cleaners and form-fillers are plentiful and cheap. The average wage for a doctor at Fortis is about $60,000 a year—a small fortune in India. Star surgeons can make more than $1 million. That would be a tidy sum even in America. Yet Fortis's prices are much lower than those at American hospitals. A kidney operation that might cost $100,000 in America costs less than $10,000 at a Fortis hospital.

To keep pace with cutting-edge medicine, Fortis "very aggressively" recruits ethnic Indian doctors who have studied or worked abroad, says Shivinder. Most of the firm's top doctors have worked overseas, at least for a while. They bring back not only knowledge and experience but also contacts: when a tough problem arises, they often know whom to email for advice. They help plug Fortis into the global medical conversation.

Some have brought specialized skills that were not previously available in India, such as transapical procedures for heart patients and ballooning techniques in spinal surgery. (The former involves passing a valve through an incision between the ribs. The latter is a minimally invasive way of mending fractured spines.) Others have brought more general skills, such as a deep knowledge of which therapeutic protocols have been proven in America. Many of the diaspora doctors who come to Fortis are used to doing prospective—that is to say, forward-looking—research; whereas in India, most clinical research is retrospective, a Fortis executive told me.

Fortis could try to keep up with the latest surgical techniques by reading medical journals, and many of its doctors do just that. But as in so many endeavors, hands-on experience is often better than book learning. By recruiting surgeons who have actually practiced a new technique, Fortis buys a nuanced understanding of its potential and its pitfalls.

Efficient private hospitals like those in the Fortis group are no panacea for India's health problems. For the poor, they are still far too expensive. But they make a big difference to the Indian middle class, which is expanding rapidly. And they attract a growing stream of patients from abroad.

The "medical tourism" industry is growing fast. The number of Americans heading abroad for health care is set to double between 2007 and 2012, from 750,000 to 1.6 million.[26] Even when you include the cost of the airfare, it is often cheaper for an American to fly to India for an operation than to have it done near home. To make things easier for medical tourists, Fortis is building a gleaming new hospital close to Delhi's airport.

The United States, with its uniquely expensive health-care system, could benefit immensely from frugal health technology. In a few cases, it already has. Not far from the half-built hospital where I met Shivinder Singh are the offices of Genpact, a contractor that handles dull tasks cheaply and well for other companies.

Genpact's CEO, Pramod Bhasin, an Indian who spent much of his career in America and Europe, is an evangelist for outsourcing. Organizations should stick to what they do best, he told me; most other tasks should be parceled out to contractors. Personnel departments, for example, need a few people to handle employee gripes face-to-face, but form-filling and data entry can more efficiently be handled by workers who specialize in these tasks. "I've got 10,000 people doing this," he says. "They're good at it."

Mr. Bhasin's back-office specialists analyze the business processes of American hospitals and suggest ways to make them leaner. For example, surgeons in some hospitals used to twiddle their expensive thumbs for half an hour while the bed in the operating room was changed. Genpact helped the hospitals do such basic things faster, thereby allowing doctors to perform 25 percent more operations each day. Demand for such services is brisk: Mr. Bhasin boasted in 2010 that Genpact's sales will "easily" grow from $1.2 billion to $10 billion by 2020.[27]

Yet stories like Bhasin's are rarer than you might expect. GE sells its inexpensive Indian-designed heart scanners and other devices in several countries, but they have yet to catch on in the United States. How can this be? Americans love bargains: that is why Walmart is the world's most successful retailer. The snag is that the American health-care system is designed to prevent the consumer—the patient—from knowing the cost of anything.

US clinics are often paid according to how many medical procedures they carry out, regardless of whether those procedures are necessary. As a result, American doctors massively overprescribe every kind of test that an insurer will pay for. If they don't, they risk being sued. All these costs are passed on to ordinary Americans, as either higher taxes (to pay for Medicare, the government plan for the elderly, or Medicaid benefits for the poor) or lower wages (to make up for the soaring cost of employer-provided group health insurance).

The waste in the system is incredible. Paul Grundy, a doctor who is the head of health-care technology at IBM, told me a revealing anecdote a few years ago. A middle-aged IBM executive was having chest pains. He had excellent health insurance, so he went straight to a specialist. His cardiologist put him through a bunch of tests, including a computerized tomography scan. The radiologist conducting the scan noticed something odd in his neck, so the executive saw a neck surgeon, who checked him out and found nothing. He went back to the cardiologist, who ordered an angiogram, which caused dangerous complications and landed him in the hospital for a while. In all, he ran up more than $150,000 in medical expenses before the chest pains disappeared on their own.

When they reappeared several months later, he spoke to Dr. Grundy, a doctor of preventive medicine by training. Dr. Grundy asked him if his lifestyle had changed recently. The executive mentioned that he had taken up gardening again. Dr. Grundy quickly established that his chest pains sprang from a muscle he had strained through overzealous Weedwacking.[28]

Many Americans with employer-provided health insurance imagine that their employer foots the bill for their health insurance. This is not merely wrong; it is completely wrong. Though it never says so on your pay stub, the cost of corporate health insurance comes out of the pool of money for compensating employees. When premiums rise, there is less left over for wages. The proportion of the cost of employer-provided health insurance shouldered by employees is "at or close to 100 percent," says Jonathan Gruber, an MIT economist.[29]

The fact that premiums roughly doubled in the past decade is the main reason why middle-class wages have stagnated in the United States. Conversely, the healthy salary gains of the 1990s were made possible by the success of HMOs (health-maintenance organizations). By ruthlessly holding down health-care costs, HMOs freed up funds for firms to give regular pay hikes. Yet because almost no one saw the connection, HMOs were hugely unpopular, and most companies stopped using them.

At some point, America will come to its senses and devise a health-care system that emphasizes value-for-money as well as technological brilliance. President Barack Obama has made a stab in that direction, though it remains to be seen how his rather complicated health reforms will work when (and if) they are implemented in 2014.* Meanwhile, the United States, like every other rich country, would have a much better chance of fixing its health-care woes if it took note of the torrent of money-saving, care-improving ideas fermenting in the East. Asians are eager to learn from the West: it's time for Westerners to return the compliment.

---

* In March 2010 President Obama signed a health-care bill aimed at extending health insurance to the millions of Americans who lack it. Under it, Americans will be obliged to buy health insurance on pain of fines. Those who cannot afford it will receive subsidies. At the time of writing, half the states had joined a lawsuit to have the mandate at the heart of the health reform ruled unconstitutional. If successful, this lawsuit would send the United States back to the drawing board.

5

NETWORKS OF TRUST

HOW THE BRAIN DRAIN
REDUCES GLOBAL POVERTY

My first child was delivered by a Nigerian midwife at a hospital in London. It was an arduous labor. My wife, Emma, did not want to take a pain-soothing epidural injection until it was absolutely necessary. She toughed it out for several hours. Finally, when the contractions were excruciating, she asked for a numbing jab. "Sorry, too late," was the reply. The baby was almost out.

So Emma winced and gasped and gave birth without anesthetic. I was impressed. So was the midwife. "You did OK for a Caucasian," she conceded.

Britain, like many rich countries, imports a lot of medical talent from poor countries. This is good for people like me. Thanks to that Nigerian midwife, my wife was never in any real danger and my son was born healthy. (He grew up healthy, too—as I write this book, he is doing his best to prevent me from doing so.)

Without nurses and doctors from Asia and Africa, British hospitals could barely function. But is it fair for rich countries to poach talent from poor ones? Poor countries have far too few skilled workers to begin with, yet they are precisely the people that rich countries are mostly likely to lure away. African workers who emigrate are more than ten times as likely to have some kind of tertiary education as those who stay behind (35 percent versus 3 percent). The same is true of South Asians: 5 percent of the workforce have an advanced degree, but 51 percent of migrants do.[1]

It seems obvious that this "brain drain" hurts the poor. If all the best doctors and engineers move to the West, who will staff hospitals or build railways in Nigeria or Bangladesh? Simple justice requires that rich countries should stop recruiting doctors and engineers from poor ones. Or does it?

One of the most surprising findings in modern economics is that the brain drain reduces global poverty. On balance, the outflow of talent from poor countries to rich ones is actually good for poor countries—and even more so for poor *people,* an important distinction to which I shall return shortly.

Granted, the circumstances that cause talented people to flee are often vile. They flee from wars. They flee from miserable wages, intermittently paid. They flee from corrupt political systems that fail to recognize skill and hard work. These are all terrible problems, but migration seldom aggravates them. On the contrary, it makes poor countries better off in several ways:

First, the prospect of earning big bucks working abroad spurs more people to acquire marketable skills. Having trained as nurses or accountants, many then decide not to emigrate after all. Several studies have found that an increase in skilled emigration tends to lead to a net *increase* in the number of skilled workers who remain behind.

Second, migrants from poor countries who work in rich ones often send money home. Such remittances are a huge boon to many poor economies. Unlike foreign aid, the money nearly always reaches its intended recipients. It feeds the elderly, pays school fees and launches small businesses.

Third, poor countries have the most to gain from intimate ties with the rich world. As migrants shuttle back and forth, they open and widen channels for trade. They also bring home a firsthand understanding of how rich countries work: knowledge that can be adapted and applied at home.

Finally, and most importantly, migration is good for migrants. If they did not think so, they would not move. The benefits to those who move are colossal and underreported. By far the most effective way for rich countries to help the poor would be to let more of them in.

In this chapter, I will explain how the brain drain makes poor people less so. Most of the examples are from Africa, a continent I know well and love better, having covered it full-time between 1998 and 2005, roving from the skyscrapers of Johannesburg to the sweaty forests of Liberia. I have kept in touch with various African diasporas ever since and return when I can. A trip to Nigeria in early 2011 provided some of the most vivid material that follows.

WHEN YOU LEAVE, WHAT HAPPENS TO MY WAGES?

Poor countries seldom worry about unskilled emigration. Often they welcome it, because when many unskilled workers move away, this can raise wages for those who stay behind. The fields of the old country still need plowing. If labor suddenly becomes scarce, employers will bid up its price.

The mass exodus from Ireland to America in the second half of the nineteenth century (roughly one-third of the population sailed away) caused the average income back home to rise by something between 5 percent and 25 percent, estimates Kevin O'Rourke, an economist at Trinity College, Dublin.[2] Robert Lucas, another economist, found that the huge outflow of builders and factory workers from Pakistan and the Philippines in the late twentieth century caused wages for similarly skilled laborers who remained behind to jump by a third.[3] And George Borjas, an economist who is often skeptical of the benefits of migration, judges that the departure of 30 percent of Puerto Ricans to the United States may have increased wages for low-skilled workers in Puerto Rico by 10 percent.[4]

The emigration of skilled workers from poor countries is much more controversial, yet it can also benefit those who stay behind. The possibility of migration dramatically increases the incentives for people in poor countries to study difficult subjects. An engineering degree is suddenly the ticket not merely to a good job in Africa, but to a fantastic job in America. When the potential rewards for qualifying as an engineer are so lavishly increased, more people will scrape together college fees and stay late in the library.

Having qualified, many will promptly emigrate. But others will not. Some will fail to obtain a visa. Some will stay behind to look after their aging parents. Others will discover that they can't quite bring themselves to leave home. In a brilliant paper called "Rethinking the Brain Drain," Oded Stark, of the University of Bonn, shows that emigration should boost skills more than it depletes them in the country from which the emigrants migrate.[5]

There is new evidence that Mr. Stark is right. The Philippines, a poor country, is the world's largest exporter of nurses. Yet because so many eager students pack its private nursing schools, it still ends up with more nurses per head than Austria.[6] In a study of Cape Verde, an archipelago in the Atlantic, Oxford University's Catia Batista and others found that although nearly a quarter of the country's university graduates emigrate, it would have up to 35 percent *fewer* graduates if migration were banned.[7]

A study of 127 developing countries by Michel Beine, Frederic Docquier and Hilel Rapoport found that overall the loss of skills to migration was outweighed by the extra skills acquired by people contemplating a move.[8] Many developing countries, especially large ones such as China, India and Brazil, would benefit from a higher level of skilled emigration. However, the same authors found that you can have too much of a good thing. Once countries start to lose more than 20 percent of their college graduates, they estimate, it starts to act as a drag on economic growth.[9]

In some cases, the brain drain does cause serious harm. For several poor countries, it aggravates a dangerous shortage of medical personnel. More than 80 percent of nurses from the war-scorched west African state of Liberia have emigrated. Burundi, an equally violent state in central Africa, has lost more than 75 percent.[10] Jamaica needs to train five doctors to keep just one, concedes Philippe Legrain, a British economist (and former colleague of mine), in his excellent book *Immigrants: Your Country Needs Them.*[11]

There is no quick fix for the doctor shortage in poor countries. Governments in rich countries can promise to stop actively recruiting doctors from poor countries, as Britain's has. But it is hard to stop private clinics from hiring them, and the governments of poor countries cannot stop their people from leaving. To do so would be both unethical and impractical. Even a totalitarian state like the Soviet Union could not prevent its people from emigrating. What chance has Liberia?

The only plausible way to persuade medical personnel to work in tough places is to make the conditions there more attractive. Poor countries don't have to match rich-world wages to keep their doctors because, given the choice, people usually prefer to work near home. But they do need to narrow the wage gap, and that will only happen as poor countries grow richer. In other words, the long-term cure for the medical brain drain is economic growth. Since migration promotes growth, it will ultimately be part of the cure.

MONTHLY MONEY FOR MOM

Twenty soldiers strolled into Haddish Welday's biology class one day and dragged off his teacher. The next day, the teacher's body was found lying in the street, shot to death.

As a student in Ethiopia in the 1980s, Mr. Welday lived in fear. Many days, he told me, he had to walk for a mile between one part of the campus and another, through the streets of Addis Ababa, the Ethiopian capital. "In that mile, we'd see two or three bodies lying side by side," he recalls. Each corpse would have a paper warning pinned to its clothes. "Let red terror rain on me" was one slogan that stuck in Mr. Welday's memory.[12]

Facing a rebellion, Ethiopia's Marxist dictatorship made an example of anyone it thought might be disloyal. Members of rebellious ethnic groups, such as the Tigrayans, were automatically suspect. A Tigrayan, Mr. Welday decided to get out of Ethiopia.

There was no legal way for him to emigrate to the capitalist West, so he went to the Soviet Union instead. He studied agricultural economics in Gorky, in what is now Belarus. He liked the people but found that the politics were "the same as Ethiopia, only with not so much killing." After a year, he boarded a train for Germany and sought asylum in America.

He now works in Arlington, Virginia, an agreeable town outside Washington, DC. It is an easy place to be Ethiopian. Greater Washington is home to one of the largest Ethiopian clusters outside Africa. Local restaurants serve tempting *injera* (pancakes that resemble large facecloths) and spicy *kitfo* (raw beef). Local taxi drivers often know the backstreets of Addis Ababa but would get lost looking for my old house in Bethesda. (Not that I'm complaining—I rather enjoyed being able to chat about Ethiopian politics with them.)

While Mr. Welday was finding his feet as an accountant, he worked five days a week in an office and drove a taxi on weekends. Now he has a stable job and is raising a family in Fairfax, a nearby town known for its annual Chocolate Lovers Festival. His wife runs a childcare business from their home. In short, the Weldays have become American.

Yet they maintain close contact with their homeland. Mr. Welday went back in 1991, after the Soviet Union collapsed and its Ethiopian client regime fell with it. His family welcomed him home and introduced him to his future wife. Mr. Welday and his wife keep a house in Axum, a city that was once the capital of a great empire but has faded from prominence in the past 1,400 years.

His mother lives in a small town nearby, in a home her son bought for her. It cost less than $1,000—land is cheap in the arid vastness of northern Ethiopia. Mr. Welday sends money to his mother every month. Sometimes he wires it via Western Union. Sometimes he gives envelopes of cash to visiting Ethiopian friends to deliver. He calls his mother once or twice a week to make sure she is well. It is cheap: only $2 for ten minutes. When she is sick, he arranges for her to visit a clinic in Axum.

He visits every couple of years. He likes to show his American children "how other people live." They have seen kids their own age in Ethiopia working as shopkeepers and plowing the hard, dry soil with their fathers. Mr. Welday hopes this will make them think twice before complaining about their suburban chores.

The events that spurred Mr. Welday to leave Ethiopia were tragic. A band of thugs tried to tear down an ancient civilization and rebuild it by force. The Derg, as Ethiopia's Marxist regime was known, uprooted millions of peasants from the land they had tilled for generations, loaded them into trucks and forced them onto collective farms. This caused a famine so terrible that Western television audiences took notice and pop stars organized a concert to feed the starving. The Derg stole as much of the aid money as it could and spent it on bullets.[13]

Clearly Ethiopia would be better off had it never slid into tyranny. But Mr. Welday's departure inflicted no additional harm on his homeland. Ethiopia lost an intelligent and hardworking citizen. But if he had stayed, he would not have been able to make good use of his talents. He could have been a statistician, but the Derg routinely falsified statistics, so his precision would have been pointless. He could have found a job as an agricultural economist, but the obstacle to higher crop yields was not some technical issue; it was the regime's habit of herding farmers into collectives at gunpoint.

Since 1991 Ethiopia has been better governed, though it is hardly a model democracy. If Mr. Welday were to go back now, he could probably find a good job. But it would not pay nearly as well as his current job, and his children want to go to college in America. So he remains in America, and why not? Like any normal human being, his first priority is his family, which he supports regardless of where its members live. Even so, he might retire to Ethiopia some day, he told me. You can live well in a poor country on savings from a rich one. And Africa is not a bad place to be old. The young treat you with deference, the sun is always warm and the *injera* have that perfect flannel-like consistency that makes all the difference.

BIGGER THAN AID, LESS FLIGHTY THAN INVESTMENT

The money that migrants send home is a huge source of income for poor countries. Recorded remittances to developing countries surged tenfold between 1990 and 2009, from $31 billion to $316 billion. Unrecorded ones (those envelopes stuffed with cash) nudge the total higher.

All told, the World Bank's Dilip Ratha estimates that remittances are the biggest source of external funding for developing countries—larger than foreign direct investment and more than twice as large as foreign aid.[14] Mr. Legrain writes that it is common for an engineer who earns $5,000 a year in a poor country to move to a rich one, earn

$30,000 a year and send $5,000 of it back to the old country.[15] His homeland is thus substantially better off, since when he lived there, he spent much of that $5,000 on himself. Now, all of it goes to others.

Some countries depend heavily on remittances. In Tajikistan, they are a staggering 46 percent of the economy. In Tonga, they are 39 percent; in Lesotho, 28 percent, since this tiny country's menfolk flock to work in the gold mines of neighboring South Africa. Miners earn good wages: you can see them in bars back home on their weekends off, proudly wearing their hard hats to impress the ladies.[16]

Aid is often stolen. Western governments hand over planeloads of cash with instructions that it must be spent on, say, distributing nets to guard against malarial mosquitoes. African governments agree, but somehow the money goes missing. Western aid agencies have few reliable ways to track the cash they fork over. Corrupt officials pocket bundles of it with impunity. The peasants who don't receive the nets probably never realize that they were supposed to. And even if they knew, to whom would they complain?

By contrast, if Mr. Welday's mother does not receive her monthly remittance, or if there is so much as $1 missing, she will tell her son straight away. He will immediately get on the phone with Western Union, which will correct the error promptly for fear of losing a regular customer. With millions of sharp-eyed grandmothers watching, remittances seldom go astray. Remittances are also less volatile than other financial flows. Bad news can make investors drop a country like a wriggling porcupine. Families are not like that: Mr. Welday will not stop sending money to his mother just because Ethiopia has suffered a corruption scandal or a coup.

Investors deem poor countries risky because they often are. However, diaspora investors are unusually tolerant of such risks.[17] They worry less about short-term shocks because they have a long-term attachment to their homeland. For a typical foreign investor in Nigeria's domestic market, a collapse of the Nigerian currency could spell disaster, since he wants to convert his profits into dollars and take them home. But for a Nigerian American investor, the same currency crash offers a chance to buy up cheap land and build a mansion for retirement.

Remittances are not only more stable; they are also counter-cyclical—that is, they tend to rise when other flows fall, creating a useful cushion. When financial crises hit Mexico in 1995 and Indonesia in 1998, the inflow of remittances increased.[18] When times are hard in Ethiopia, Mr. Welday is even more anxious to ensure that his relatives are provided for.

Some people fret that remittances are frittered away on "ceremonies and luxuries," as one writer put it.[19] Sometimes this is true. Families of migrants like to party as much as anyone else. But mostly the money pays for essentials, such as food and medicine, or is invested in land, education or small businesses.

Of course, people do not always answer surveys honestly. They may exaggerate the share of remittances they spend on schooling and downplay the share they blow on beer and prostitutes. Nonetheless, survey results are so consistent that they are probably not far from the truth.

A study of 6,000 small businesses in Mexico found that 20 percent of their capital came from remittances, mostly from Mexicans working in the United States. A survey in Pakistan found that remittance recipients were most likely to invest the money in farmland. Nigerians who received money from relatives in rich countries invested 22 percent in businesses, 35 percent in land or housing and 22 percent in education. The other big spending areas were food (10 percent) and health care (5 percent). Marriages and funerals accounted for a modest 0.4 percent.[20]

Remittances ease poverty. In Bangladesh, a country that sends many construction workers to oil sheikhdoms, families that receive remittances typically rely on them for half their income. One study found that a 10 percent increase in remittances per head can lead to a 3.5 percent drop in the share of the population who are poor. Household surveys suggest that remittances have reduced the proportion of Ugandans who are poor by 11 percent and account for perhaps half of the poverty reduction in Nepal in recent years.[21]

Emigrants take their skills with them when they leave home, but the money they send back helps others learn. It does so directly, when it is spent on school fees, and it does so indirectly, when it puts food on a family's table.

Hungry children cannot concentrate in class—their growling bellies drown out the math teacher. Amply fed families not only breed more-studious children; they are also less likely to pull their daughters out of school and put them to work in the fields. A study of 82 countries by Christian Ebeke, of the Université d'Auvergne, found that remittances made child labor significantly less common. Another study, in rural Pakistan, found that families with a migrant member were 54 percent more likely to send their daughters to school.[22]

Remittances are so useful that governments often try to encourage them. There are smart ways and dumb ways of doing this. Mexico takes a smart approach. Under the 3 × 1 Program, groups of migrants band together to fund infrastructure projects in their hometowns, and the government chips in $3 for every $1 they invest. Thousands of projects around the country have been financed this way.[23] Other smart ideas include borrowing money by using future remittances as collateral. Some countries, notably Israel, have borrowed money directly from their diaspora members by issuing "patriotic" bonds.[24]

Robert Mugabe, Zimbabwe's leader since 1980, has opted for the dumb approach. Having wrecked his country's economy and driven legions of Zimbabweans to emigrate, he has tried to grab the money these migrants send home to feed their families. His methods are crude, yet ineffective. In 2004, the governor of Zimbabwe's central bank went on a world tour to persuade Zimbabweans abroad to wire money home using official channels, thus enabling the government to take a cut.[25]

There were two flaws in this plan. First, hardly any Zimbabweans wished to share their hard-earned cash with the thuggish regime that had driven them away in the first place. Many came from villages that Mr. Mugabe's ruffians had burned to the ground for failing to vote for him. That rankles.

Second, although the government promised to take only a small cut, no one believed it. Mr. Mugabe's regime has a long record of grabbing as much as it can. For many years, Zimbabwe had a rigged exchange rate. The government would decree that a Zimbabwe dollar (the local currency) was worth more than it really was. Zimbabweans who sent home hard currency via official channels would be forced to exchange it at the official rate, allowing the government to confiscate most of it. As Mr. Mugabe's printing presses whirred and Zimbabwean inflation accelerated from 70 percent in 2000 to

89,700,000,000,000,000,000,000,000 percent (yes, really) in November 2008, the local currency became completely worthless. For some reason, exiles were reluctant to swap their hard-earned hard currency for billion-dollar bills that even beggars rejected.[26]

Instead, they used informal channels to send money home. For example, a Zimbabwean teacher in London would pay money into a friendly businessman's offshore account. The businessman would then ask his cousin in Bulawayo to pay an equivalent amount, in bags of maize meal, to the teacher's sister. Zimbabweans in South Africa used a simpler dodge: they would simply give a wad of hard currency to a bus driver who was heading toward their home village. For a reasonable fee, he would deliver it to their family.

Zimbabwe is an extreme example.* But such informal channels for remitting money are common in the developing world. Nearly 80 percent of migrants in South Africa who send money to other African countries use informal means, as do more than 60 percent of those in Ghana, Senegal and Burkina Faso.

One reason is that banks overcharge. Migrant workers in the Gulf can send money home to India for as little as $1. Yet to send $200 from Burkina Faso to Ghana costs $32. From Nigeria to Benin it costs $25.[27] The obstacle is not distance—these countries share borders. The problem is the exclusive agreements that some African banks have with international money-transfer agencies. Several governments also rig their exchange rates, thereby taking a bite out of remittances before they reach grandma.[28]

The cleverest way to elude rapacious bankers and governments involves mobile phones. Few poor people in Africa have bank accounts, which are expensive to open and require traveling to town. But most people have access to a mobile phone. So in 2007 Safaricom, a Kenyan mobile phone company, started offering mobile banking. In effect, it created an electronic currency (equivalent to the Kenyan shilling) that can be pinged from one phone to another as easily as sending a text message. Shops accept these digital IOUs, and a network of 24,000

---

* And its monetary policy has grown saner since 2009, when the government abandoned the Zimbabwe dollar and allowed people to use American dollars or South African rand legally.

Safaricom agents exchange electronic cash for the paper variety. They are far more accessible than banks.

M-Pesa, as the service is known, caught on fast. It had 13.5 million users in December 2010—most of Kenya's adult population. Before M-Pesa, the most popular means of sending money within the country were: by hand (58 percent) and by bus (27 percent). Now M-Pesa dominates the market and has started to attract imitators.[29] In March 2011, the firm hooked up with Western Union to allow Kenyans in any of 45 countries to send money home.[30] If Barack Obama wants to send a few bucks to one of his cousins, it will take only a few seconds out of his busy schedule.

NETWORKS OF TRUST

In poor countries, people seldom trust strangers. They seldom trust institutions, either. When they see a policeman approaching, they do not feel safer; in many countries, they expect to be robbed. I found this out firsthand a few years ago when I hitched a ride on a beer truck in Cameroon. In the four days it took us to get from the coast to a small town in the jungle, we were stopped 47 times at police roadblocks. A plump officer would amble up and inspect our tires, axles or papers, searching for something we had done wrong so he could demand a bribe to overlook it.

The policeman at the thirty-first roadblock invented a rule about carrying passengers in beer trucks, which of course we had broken. When I suggested to him that the rule in question did not really exist, he slapped his holster and asked, in French: "Do you have a gun?" I had to admit that I did not. He replied triumphantly: "I have a gun, so I know the rules."[31]

Francis Fukuyama, a political theorist, argues that people in "high-trust" societies find it easier to do business with each other, and therefore tend to prosper, while low-trust societies tend to stagnate.[32] If so, much of Africa is in trouble.

Nigeria is the epitome of a low-trust society. People paint the words "This house is not for sale" on their walls. If they do not, someone may sell it while they are away. Nigerian voters expect politicians to be light-fingered: Sani Abacha, the country's military ruler from 1993 to 1998, is estimated to have stolen more than $1 million for every day he was in office, including weekends.[33] And Nigerian companies assume that at least some of their employees will embezzle.

Given these conditions, it is tricky to run a business in Nigeria, and even harder to run one that links Nigeria with another low-trust country, such as China. Yet it can be done. Chike Obidigbo, who runs a soap factory in Enugu, in southwestern Nigeria, told me how.

Dr. Obidigbo is a huge man with a soft voice and a courteous manner. He works in a big run-down building with uneven stairs and a giant mural in the foyer of Jesus Christ herding sheep. He welcomed me warmly, shaking my slim hand gently in his enormous one, and showed me around.

His factory is full of thumping, humming machines that turn palm oil and chemicals into soap, stamp it into bars and wrap it in plastic. The machines were mostly made in China. They are not as good as European ones, Dr. Obidigbo told me, but they are much cheaper. They are also easier to buy: you can show up with a bag of cash and a Chinese firm will ship you what you want straightaway. European firms, by contrast, require letters of credit and all kinds of paperwork that Nigerians find difficult and time-consuming to arrange.

Chinese machines are more appropriate for Nigeria's level of development, Dr. Obidigbo believes. Sophisticated European machines must be maintained by highly qualified engineers, he says. There are not enough such people in Nigeria, and the best-qualified tend to work for mobile-phone companies that pay far better wages than Dr. Obidigbo can afford. Also, Chinese machines are better at coping with an intermittent power supply, since the same problem sometimes afflicts China, too.

Dr. Obidigbo travels to China from time to time, but he does not speak the language and he cannot fly halfway round the world every time he wants to buy a new soap machine. So he relies on the Nigerian diaspora to connect him to Chinese suppliers. When he wants to inspect a product he has seen on the Internet, to make sure that it is exactly what he wants, he asks a Nigerian agent in China to go look at it. He has met several such people at trade fairs in China. They are all from Dr. Obidigbo's tribe, the Ibos.

"When you hear people speaking Ibo outside Nigeria, you must go and greet them," he laughs. He trusts them, partly because they are his ethnic kin, but mostly because he knows an Ibo middleman in

Guangdong depends on his reputation to stay in business. If he cheats one Ibo, all the others who buy machinery in Guangdong will soon know that he is a cheat.

The Ibos have long had a reputation as merchants and travelers, but these days they range more widely than ever before. So many African traders congregate in one area of Guangzhou that their Chinese neighbors call it *Qiao-ke-li Cheng* (Chocolate City).[34] The Nigerian manufacturing hub in Enugu and the nearby state of Anambra enjoys a symbiotic relationship with China, mediated by the two nations' diasporas.[35]

Dr. Obidigbo is one of a new breed of global Nigerians, straddling borders in his business and personal life. He wears the loose, cool robes of a traditional Ibo. He is devoutly Christian and treats his elders with an elaborate show of deference. Yet he is also at ease with other cultures, and has a soft spot for England, where he studied marketing at Salford and Lancaster universities. (He even praises the English weather: "Sometimes it's good to be cold," he told me.) And he has raised a cosmopolitan family. His two eldest children are living and working in London, while his twin daughters attended the University of Bradford in England together and were studying at a language school in Paris when I met him. His niece runs an oil consultancy and flits between London and Lagos.

As a child, Dr. Obidigbo loved the sound of machines at the palm-oil mills managed by his late father. As an adult, he was determined to set up a factory of his own. Raising capital was not easy. He started small in 1986, cranking out tubs of hair cream. Eager to grow, he told the traders who bought his hair cream that if they wanted more, they would have to pay him in advance. They agreed, and he used this cash to expand. He branched out into new areas, collaborating with the UK-based Coventry Chemicals to develop new lines of disinfectant. Before long he was making soap, shampoo, detergent, air fresheners and just about anything else that might clean a home, a shirt or a body.

His firm, Hardis and Dromedas, is not huge—when I visited in 2011, it was selling about 550 million *naira* ($4 million) worth of products each year. But in a place like Enugu, that is no trivial sum. Dr. Obidigbo employs 380 workers. Indirectly, he provides work for plenty more: the market traders who sell his soaps and moisturizers, the truck drivers who deliver them and the models who star in his advertisements.

Dr. Obidigbo's cosmopolitan outlook gives him a certain confidence. Manufacturing in Nigeria is hard. Interest rates are high. Roads are awful. Power comes in "periodic vengeful surges . . . as if the God of lightning has . . . taken personal charge," as Wole Soyinka, a Nigerian novelist, once put it.[36] (Hardis and Dromedas spends a fortune on generators.) Plus, security is precarious. "Lots of my friends have been kidnapped [for ransom]," he sighed to me. Everyone with any money in this part of Nigeria is nervous—except the politicians, who have bodyguards with submachine guns.

Despite the obstacles, Dr. Obidigbo thrives. His travels make him open-minded. He takes ideas from China, Britain or Nigeria and blends them into a business strategy. He competes against cheap imports which, though banned,* are ubiquitous. Although he operates in one of the toughest business climates on Earth, he still makes money. That is no small accomplishment.

Dr. Obidigbo's experiences mirror those of countless other entrepreneurs who use diaspora networks. As we have established, countries trade more with places from which they have received immigrants. When you are doing business with a distant land, there is no better guide than someone who lives there but speaks your language. This is especially important for businesses from poor countries, because they can seldom afford to hire expensive consultants to guide them.

Another reason why trade follows migration is that exiles hanker after products from their homeland. This is sometimes called the nostalgia trade. The average Honduran, Ethiopian or Filipino in the United States, for example, spends more than $1,000 a year on things he or she misses from back home, such as tasty Honduran *baleadas*

---

* Nigeria bans the import of many different types of goods. In principle, such bans are a bad idea—if they worked as planned, they would deprive consumers of choice. In practice in Nigeria, they are hardly enforced at all. Importers bribe border officials to allow trucks of Chinese-made soap and shampoo into the country. The bribes work out to be cheaper than paying tax or duty, so Chinese goods have a head start over locally produced ones.

or Filipino fish sauce.[37] And every British expat's home has a pot of Marmite in the larder.*

MIGRATION AS AN INSURANCE POLICY

People in poor countries have long used the extended family as a form of insurance. When everyone feels an obligation to help not only their immediate families but also their more-distant kin, fewer people starve. If your crop fails, you can ask your cousin for a bag of rice.

Migration allows families to spread their risks geographically. When one or two members of a family migrate, the whole family is effectively buying insurance against hard times in their homeland. This is especially useful if that homeland is unstable—as any Somali or Afghan can attest, putting all your nest eggs in one basket-case is a bad investment strategy.

Migration is a sound strategy for all kinds of families. Nnenne Ohabuiro, a civil servant in Enugu, explained to me how this can work. At 59, she has seen six violent changes of government in Nigeria and one horrific civil war. (Her tribe, the Ibos, tried to secede between 1967 and 1970.) She has watched her country's fortunes yo-yo with the price of oil. In boom times Nigeria's rulers built a magnificent new capital city, Abuja, in the middle of nowhere; in hard times they have struggled to service the national debt.[38] Living in Nigeria teaches one to prepare for the unexpected.

Mrs. Ohabuiro's family has done this by spreading itself across borders. One of her sons moved to the United States. Now a naturalized citizen with two children, he runs an export-import firm, buying spare parts for cars in Indiana and shipping them to Nigeria. When we spoke in February 2011, she also told me that another of her sons was about to marry a Nigerian-British woman who works as a pharmacist in the United Kingdom. The rest of the family remains in Nigeria, but

---

* Marmite looks like motor oil and tastes like congealed salt. Brits spread it on toast. If you didn't grow up eating it, you'd hate it. A Japanese caretaker once threw away a jar of Marmite I was storing in a communal fridge in Tokyo, on the grounds that whatever it was, it was clearly rotting. If you are not British, you will not understand how miffed I was.

not all in their hometown. Mrs. Ohabuiro's daughter, for example, works as a banker in Abuja.

A handsome woman with bright red lipstick, Mrs. Ohabuiro beamed with pride discussing what her children have achieved.[39] She told me she was thinking of retiring from her civil-service job—she investigates corruption—and trying her luck in the United States. She is not sure if she would ever settle in the United States permanently, but she thinks it's a good idea to acquire American citizenship, because you never know when it might come in handy.

The wider the family network, the greater the chance that some branches will prosper and be able to support their less-fortunate kin. The risks are spread most effectively if a family has one foot in the rich world and another in a fast-growing emerging market. A crisis in Nigeria will not affect the livelihood of a Nigerian pharmacist in London. Likewise, when America is reeling from a high oil price, Nigeria is reveling in it. Migration makes a family more resilient.

PEOPLE MATTER MORE THAN PLACES

People matter more than patches of earth.[40] We are so used to looking at the world through the prism of nation-states that we often forget this. It is natural to feel attached to one's own country, but it can prevent us from seeing the world as it really is.

For example, suppose that a Salvadoran who earns $10,000 a year moves to the United States and starts earning $20,000. He is suddenly much better off. But since his income of $10,000 was above average back home, his departure makes El Salvador slightly poorer. And since his new salary of $20,000 is below the American average, his arrival has made America poorer, too. This is just a snapshot—it does not take account of remittances, networks, and the speed with which immigrants rise within American society. But it captures a crucial anomaly in how we measure the world. By dividing it up into countries, we can make an increase in human prosperity look like the opposite.

A couple of years ago two economists, Michael Clemens and Lant Pritchett, devised a fresh way of measuring economies. Instead of calculating the average income of the people who currently live in El Salvador, they calculated the average income of those who were born there, regardless of where they now reside. And their new measure, which they call "income per natural," makes the world look very different.

Many poor countries suddenly look much better off. You would expect this to be true of small countries with lots of emigrants, such as Guyana, Liberia and Jamaica. But what is startling is how broadly the impact of migration is felt. Some 43 million people live in countries where "income per natural" is at least 50 percent higher than income per resident. A remarkable 235 million live in places where it is at least 20 percent higher. And an incredible 1.1 billion—more than the entire population of Africa—live in countries where the difference is 10 percent or more. For El Salvador, for example, the figure is 16.5 percent.

The first thing Clement and Pritchett's study shows is that in the battle against global poverty, the best weapon is a welcome mat. And yet rich countries' borders are far from open. If you come from a poor country, obtaining a visa to work in a rich one is extremely hard. Sneaking in illegally is no picnic, either, even if you hail from a place such as Mexico or Turkey that shares a border with the rich world.

Four out of five Haitians who have pulled themselves out of poverty (defined using a global poverty line of $10 per day) have done so by moving to the United States. Nearly half of the Mexicans who have achieved this modest standard of living have done so by crossing the Rio Grande. More than a quarter of non-poor Indians got that way by coming to the United States. And tens of thousands of infants are prevented from dying each year by the simple fact that their parents emigrated.[41]

When people try to think of ways to ease global poverty, they seldom mention migration. They tend to instead think of things like microcredit. There is nothing wrong with microcredit (the lending of small sums of money to poor entrepreneurs). It has lifted many people out of poverty, which is why Mohammed Yunus, whose Grameen Bank pioneered this approach in Bangladesh, won the Nobel Peace Prize in 2006. Yet, as Mr. Pritchett points out, the average gain from a lifetime of microcredit in Bangladesh is about the same as the gain from *eight weeks* working in the United States. After doing a quick calculation of the total benefit that Grameen Bank confers on its clients, he asks, mischievously: "If I get 3,000 Bangladeshi workers into the US, do I get the Nobel Peace Prize?"[42]

Governments, naturally, find it hard to look at people rather than places. A government that felt responsible for all the people born within its country's borders would not mind subsidizing education that prepares them for the global labor market, even if they subsequently take their skills elsewhere. A government that thinks its duties end at the water's edge would probably take a different view.

A government that looked beyond its own borders would try to keep its diaspora engaged, by allowing dual citizenship, for example. It costs nothing, and it makes it easier for migrants to move back and forth.[43] Yet only half the governments in Africa allow their people to hold two passports. (Attitudes are softening, but not fast enough.)

A rich country that measures the success of its aid policies by the effect they have on poor countries will hire armies of development experts to assess whether it is better to subsidize bed nets in Burundi or road-building in Nepal. (This is, roughly speaking, what happens today.)

A country that looked instead at the effect that its policies have on flesh-and-blood people might decide to forget about foreign aid and just open its borders a little wider. This seldom happens, because many voters in rich countries object strongly to immigration. I'll address this topic in more detail in Chapter 7.

Citizens of poor countries, by and large, would like their homelands to be rich. Countries that have already made the transition from widespread poverty to mass affluence offer a roadmap. It is only a rough roadmap, and there is no need to follow it precisely. But there are a number of things that virtually all rich countries have in common, such as peace, the rule of law and secure property rights.

Few Africans would want to copy wholesale the social arrangements of foreigners. But the more they interact with the rest of the world, the more they will learn about what works and what doesn't. Emigrants, returnees, border-straddling businessmen and families with feet in multiple countries all funnel the best ideas from elsewhere back to their homeland. They filter them, too; rejecting the ones they find unappealing and adapting the good ones so that they mesh with local customs. Furthermore, the brains that drain from poor countries are often the most constructive critics of the way things are done back home. Ponder, for example, the career of Mo Ibrahim.

THE BILL GATES OF GOOD GOVERNANCE

Mr. Ibrahim is a Sudanese-born engineer who moved to Britain as a young man. He studied in Bradford and Birmingham, worked for British Telecom and eventually founded a mobile-phone firm, Celtel, which connected millions of Africans and made him rich.

Mr. Ibrahim now devotes his life and much of his fortune to promoting good governance on the continent where he grew up. Having done business in the West and all over Africa, he believes that the steepest obstacle to African progress is the abysmal way the continent has been ruled since independence: "We have wasted 50 years," he fumes. "Enough is enough."[44]

He is right. Consider Botswana. At independence, in the 1960s, it was poorer than neighboring Zimbabwe. Now it is roughly 30 times richer.[45] The difference cannot be due to culture, since the two nations are culturally quite similar. It is surely because Botswana has been consistently well governed, whereas Zimbabwe suffers Robert Mugabe's incompetent tyranny.

Rather than despairing, Mr. Ibrahim decided to something. In 2007 he started publishing the Ibrahim Index, which ranks African governments on various measures of honesty and effectiveness. It is rigorously compiled and carefully consulted, for example by aid agencies wondering which African states to assist. Even more useful, potentially, is the Ibrahim Prize, which offers a fat dollop of cash ($5 million over ten years and then $200,000 a year for life) to an African head of government who has ruled honestly and—this is crucial—stepped down when his term of office expired. The idea is to reward good presidents, of whom Africa has had distressingly few. Joachim Chissano, the ex-president of Mozambique, won the prize in 2007. Festus Mogae of Botswana won it the next year. In 2009 and 2010, however, no outgoing African leader was deemed worthy.[46]

Given the feeble competition, even a moderately good African ruler can expect to earn a comfortable retirement courtesy of Mr. Ibrahim. If the prize prompts even one president to keep his fingers off the trigger and out of the till, it will be money well spent.

6

NETWORKS OF HATE

GENOCIDE, TERRORISM AND CRIME

Gunmen burst into Charlotte Nyamugali's hut one night and forced her to help them loot it. They made her carry all her possessions—"my clothes, my family's clothes, kitchen implements, everything," she told me—away to their camp. Charlotte argued with the gunmen as they herded her through the bush, so two of them raped her. They also beat her with a baton and broke her wrist. She somehow managed to escape back to her hut, where, two months later, another group of men with guns arrived and stole what little the first group had missed.[1]

I met Ms. Nyamugali in 2003 in Walungu, a small town in the Democratic Republic of Congo not far from the Rwandan border. She told me her story in a wavering voice barely louder than a whisper. It was horrible to listen to; I choked as she recounted the details. Yet the worst thing about her story is how utterly commonplace it is in eastern Congo. As I was talking to Ms. Nyamugali, another 20 or so women wearing extravagantly colored dresses and headscarves were sitting silently in a semicircle, patiently waiting their turn to tell their stories.

"Everyone here has been 'visited' more than once," said Eveline M'Bigohe, another villager. "Sometimes they violate both the wife and the husband." She went on: "We spend the nights outside. We hide by the edge of the river. As night falls, we put the children in the bush. We teach [them] to be silent."

Ms. M'Bigohe's ten children cry a lot. It rains on them when they hide outside—they live in a rainforest. "Most kids understand the situation," she said. "As evening falls, my three-year-old goes to hide [without being told to]. And he won't go on his own to the toilet."

No one knows how many people have died in Congo's war. No one is counting the graves, let alone putting names to them. Estimates of the carnage range from a horrific 900,000 deaths to an unthinkable 5.4 million.[2] Most of the victims die not of machete wounds but because the war makes them poorer, hungrier and more prone to disease.

Many of the villagers from around Walungu were so scared, they told me, that they'd walk 90 minutes every evening to the relative safety of the nearest garrison town. Every morning, they'd walk back to their fields. This three-hour hike over mountainous terrain burns up precious calories. It means that these people have neither the time nor the energy to tend their crops properly. Thanks to the war, "we can't possibly get enough to eat," lamented Zihalirwa Barnaba, a peasant in a faded, checked shirt.[3]

PART ONE: THE POLITICS OF HATE

This chapter looks at the dark side of tribalism. It examines how networks of trust can be infected with hatred or twisted for criminal ends. It uses three examples: ethnic slaughter in central Africa, terrorism in the name of Islam and Nigerian criminal networks. These problems are all very different from each other. What they have in common, however, is the abuse of group solidarity. Unscrupulous politicians whip up tribal hatred to cement their grip on power. Terrorists justify murder by selectively quoting a book that more than a billion people revere. Criminals use ethnic networks to boost their profits and dodge the law. All these problems spread copiously across borders.

I want to be clear: I am not saying that tribalism causes wars, or that Islam causes terrorism, or that being Nigerian makes you dishonest. What I am saying is that ethnic and religious ties are tremendously powerful, and just as they can be used to promote commerce and innovation, so can they be harnessed for malign purposes.

Let's start with the war in the Democratic Republic of Congo, which officially ended in 2003 but is still smoldering in the east of this vast central African nation. The war is staggeringly complex—at various times it has involved eight national armies and at least two dozen militias and rebel groups. I don't have the space here to explain its many causes.[4] What I'm going to do instead is discuss the role of tribalism in Congo's war, which is intimately entwined with the Rwandan genocide. The men who raped Charlotte Nyamugali were members of the *interahamwe*, the Hutu militia that tried to exterminate all the Tutsis in Rwanda in 1994. What were they doing in Congo? It's a twisted story.

To oversimplify: Rwanda and Burundi, Congo's tiny neighbors, are home to two groups, the Hutus and the Tutsis, both of which spill into Congo and other countries in central Africa. Hutus are a large majority in Burundi and Rwanda. Tutsis make up roughly 15 percent of the population in each country and 5 percent of the population of eastern Congo.

The stereotype is that Tutsis are tall and thin with long noses, while Hutus are shorter and have flat noses. Tutsis traditionally herd cows, while Hutus grow crops. In reality, the lines are blurred. There are short Tutsis, long-nosed Hutus and plenty of inter-marriage. Some anthropologists insist that the labels are meaningless. Perhaps so, but the people of central Africa certainly understand them to mean something. Hutus have massacred Tutsis—and vice versa—in 1959, 1963, 1970, 1972, 1988, 1993 and 1994.

The two groups have probably skirmished for centuries, but organized massacres are a modern evil. Much of the original blame lies with German and Belgian colonists, who decided that the Tutsis were a superior race to the Hutus, and ruled through them. As one writer puts it, "They made forced laborers of the Hutus, and whip-wielding overseers of the Tutsis. They even made everyone carry an ethnic identity card."[5]

After independence, many African politicians realized that appeals to tribal solidarity could win support for despotism. In Burundi, Tutsi officers led a coup and held onto power with the excuse that if they let go, the Hutus would kill all Tutsis. Juvenal Habyarimana, the dictator who ruled Rwanda from 1973 to 1994, persuaded many Hutus that his rule was somehow democratic because he was a member of the majority tribe.[6] When Hutus took power, they slaughtered thousands of Tutsis and imposed quotas on the number of civil-service jobs the living ones could hold.

The genocide that struck Rwanda in 1994 was not, as it is sometimes portrayed, a spontaneous outburst of tribal hatred. It was meticulously stoked, planned and executed by one of the most authoritarian states in Africa.

The Habyarimana regime was facing a threat. It had treated Tutsis so badly that 600,000 of them had fled the country. Some members of the Tutsi diaspora had organized an army and invaded Rwanda in 1990. Some of the Hutu elite decided that the only way to hang on to power was to exterminate all Tutsis. Ignoring a 1993 peace accord, they recruited and indoctrinated thousands of militiamen, and imported enough machetes to give one to every third adult Hutu male. They whipped up fear with bloodthirsty, conspiratorial radio broadcasts portraying the Tutsi rebels as demonic creatures with tails and glowing eyes. They convinced superstitious Hutu peasants that the time was coming when they would have to kill or be killed.

The spark came on April 6, 1994, when a plane carrying President Habyarimana and his Burundian counterpart was shot down by unknown assailants. Within hours, the massacres began. The dead president's most bigoted associates, led by a colonel named Theoneste Bagosora, seized control and started killing prominent Tutsis and moderate Hutus on preprepared lists.* They used all the apparatus of the state to orchestrate the slaughter. Militia units in every village rounded up Tutsis and urged their Hutu neighbors to kill them with farm tools. Those who refused to join in were killed. Between 500,000 and 800,000 people were murdered in 100 days, a faster rate of killing than any genocide before or since.[7]

Today, dozens of memorials dot the country. In a church at Ntarama, south of the capital, Kigali, the possessions of the dead have been left to rot where they were dropped between the wooden pews.

---

* Colonel Bagosora was convicted of crimes against humanity in 2008 by an international court, and sentenced to life imprisonment.

Some 5,000 Tutsis sought sanctuary in the church. The militia tossed in hand grenades—dots of sunlight still peep through little shrapnel holes in the corrugated iron roof. Then they finished the job with clubs and machetes.

Few escaped. Pacifique Rutaganda, a survivor, says he slipped out through a window, dodged the crowd of killers and ran into the bush. He crept back in the evening to see if anyone was still alive and found a few of his neighbors still murmuring, despite having had their arms or legs hacked off. An outbuilding, into which victims were crammed with their mattresses and burned alive, is still blackened with soot. Bones are scattered on the floor of the church; I had to take care not to crunch them underfoot. Many more have been gathered up in rough white sacks, or laid out on tables for display. The smallest skulls are mostly incomplete—infants' jawbones tend to shear off when clubbed.

The genocide continued until the Tutsi rebels won the war. Mr. Rutaganda recalls with clarity the moment when he first encountered them. He was hiding in the bush and he heard them firing in the air to attract the survivors' attention. "I was overjoyed," he says, "because I knew I was not going to die."[8]

In the popular imagination, that is where the story ends. Movies such as *Hotel Rwanda* (2004) leave off with the Tutsi rebels driving the genocidal Hutu militias out of the picture. But in truth, the horrors were far from over. The genocidal Hutu militiamen fled into the rainforests of what is now Congo (called Zaire between 1971 and 1997) and continued to launch attacks from there. So the new Tutsi-led Rwandan army invaded Congo to crush them. It did so with cold ferocity, killing perhaps 200,000 people, including many civilians.

The Rwandans also overthrew Mobutu Sese Seko, the Congolese tyrant, because he had supported the Hutu extremists. In his place they installed Laurent Kabila, a Congolese rebel who they thought would do their bidding.* The new president double-crossed them,

---

* The Rwandans pretended at the time that the army that overthrew Mobutu was an indigenous Congolese rebel force led by Kabila. Subsequent research has shown that the Congolese rebels were little more than window dressing, as Jason Stearns describes in his book *Dancing in the Glory of Monsters: The Collapse of the Congo and the Great War of Africa.*

however. Irked by Rwandan interference, Kabila started arming and supporting what was left of the genocidal Hutu army still hiding in the Congolese jungle. So Rwanda invaded Congo again in 1998, and nearly overthrew Kabila, too.

Militarily, it was a stunning operation, even if it ended in failure. Congo is 90 times larger than Rwanda, and its capital, Kinshasa, is 1,000 miles away, across a jungle with no roads. The first time the Rwandans invaded, they did so on foot, in gum boots. The second time, they flew a small elite force to capture an airport near Kinshasa, from which they planned to mount a surprise assault. Kabila was saved only by the intervention of two foreign powers: Angola, an ally, and Zimbabwe, a creditor. (He was later murdered, in 2001, by one of his own bodyguards.)

Paul Kagame, a Tutsi who is Rwanda's current president, has one all-consuming priority: to prevent another genocide. So long as Hutu extremists lurk in Congo's leafy vastness, he cannot rest easy.

President Kagame is an extraordinary man. Tall, thin and tough as an armor-piercing bullet, he is little known outside central Africa but arguably the most effective military leader on Earth. He is also one of the most ruthless. Born in Rwanda, he watched Hutu mobs torch Tutsi homes in his village when he was a toddler.[9] His family fled to Uganda, where he grew up in a refugee camp. When an appalling dictator called Milton Obote seized power in Uganda in 1981, Kagame joined the bush war to overthrow him. Back then, there were only 27 men in the rebel force, led by a young Ugandan officer named Yoweri Museveni. Five years later, they ruled Uganda. Kagame became President Museveni's chief of military intelligence before he was 30 years old.

Having overthrown Uganda's dictatorship, Kagame turned his attention to the equally brutal one in Rwanda. He and his friends formed a secret movement called the Rwandese Patriotic Front (RPF). At its core were the Rwandan exiles in the Ugandan army, who made up at least 20 percent of Museveni's forces.[10] RPF members quietly mobilized Rwanda's civilian diaspora. They held family gatherings and made lists of all the Rwandans they knew around the world, Tutsis and moderate Hutus, so they could beg them for money to overthrow the Habyarimana regime.

Then, in 1990, they invaded Rwanda. The Rwandans in the Ugandan army cast off their Ugandan uniforms en masse and joined the revolution, stealing all the guns and supplies they could carry. Their commander was killed on the second day of the invasion. Kagame, who had been training in the United States, flew home and took charge, turning the RPF into the most disciplined army in central Africa. When his men looted or raped, he had them executed. He drilled into them not only how to fight, but why they were fighting. He stopped the genocide on a negligible budget, with unreliable secondhand weapons. His campaign was "a work of plain genius," various military men told Philip Gourevitch, of the *New Yorker*.[11]

President Kagame's brilliance is beyond question. He started with nothing and overthrew (or helped to overthrow) despots in three countries (Uganda, Rwanda and Congo). What other commander, anywhere in the world, can boast as much? Yet morally, he is a profoundly troubling figure. His halting of the genocide was an act of incomparable good. But, some wonder, did he have to kill quite so many people in the process, and in the aftermath? His actions in Congo may have kept Rwanda safe, but at a horrific cost. Indeed, he has made it easy for demagogues there to stir up hatred of Tutsis in general.

I was in Kinshasa in August 1998, when Kagame's troops were approaching for the second time. A panic-stricken President Kabila was recruiting a militia to defend his regime. Voices on the radio were howling for blood. "Wherever you see a Rwandan Tutsi, regard him as your enemy," urged one broadcast, ordering loyal Congolese citizens to "bring a machete, a spear, an arrow, a hoe, spades, rakes, nails, truncheons, electric irons, barbed wire, stones and the like, in order, dear listeners, to kill the Rwandan Tutsis."[12] Drunken mobs who took up arms made little distinction between Rwandan Tutsis and Congolese ones. I saw charred bodies lying in the street, where they had been sloshed with gasoline and set ablaze.

After the Rwandans were beaten back from the city, the war degenerated into a vile scramble for loot.* A confusion of armies and

---

* In a letter, the novelist Joseph Conrad once described the colonial exploitation of Congo as "the vilest scramble for loot that ever disfigured the history of human conscience."

militia groups fought for the chance to plunder Congo's mineral wealth—the nation's soil is studded with diamonds, copper, gold, cobalt and coltan. Most of these groups claimed they were fighting to defend themselves or their people from aggression. Many believed it.

Tutsis sometimes liken themselves to Israelis: they are surrounded by people who want to exterminate them, but they survive because they are brainier and better disciplined than their enemies. In fact, their situation may be even more precarious than this analogy suggests. Many in the Tutsi minority who dominate Rwanda today were born abroad, or lived most of their lives in exile before 1994. Some, including President Kagame, arrived with only a basic knowledge of *kinyarwanda*, the local tongue. It is as if, in 1945, Germany were conquered by an army of German Jews who had lived all their lives in Britain and barely spoke German.

The chatter about Tutsis in central Africa is as venomous as the chatter about Jews on the Arab street. The word in the markets of eastern Congo is that Tutsis are cunning, untrustworthy and brutal. "They came here to dominate," a bar owner in Bukavu, a city near the border with Rwanda, complained to me, adding that "everyone here" wants to fight them.[13] A young mother in the same city says that 800,000 dead Tutsis is not enough: "There are still some left."[14]

Hateful rumors circulate. One says that beautiful Tutsi women have laced their breasts with poison to murder the Congolese politicians they seduce. Tutsis whose families have lived in Congo for more than a century are labeled invaders. One survey found that more than 80 percent of Congolese did not consider any Tutsis to be their countrymen. As a popular saying goes, "Even if a log lies in a river for 100 years, it doesn't become a crocodile."[15]

There is no good reason why the people of central Africa should not get along. Some people blame the killing on overpopulation.[16] Many of the killers are indeed desperately poor and eager to seize their victims' land or cows, but this cannot explain all the horror. Rwanda is no more crowded than the Netherlands, and Congo is not crowded at all.

In my view, the crucial element is leadership. Tribal solidarity is a useful and deep-seated trait. It prompts people to work together and to take care of one another. But because it is so powerful, it is also dangerous. The urge to defend one's kin against threats can be warped to justify preemptive attacks on outsiders.

This is a huge temptation for bad politicians, because people who feel threatened tend to rally around their leader. It is far easier to scream, "The Tutsis are planning to kill us!" than to fix a poor nation's schools. The best way to avoid ethnic strife is for leaders to avoid inflaming it in the first place. South Africa could have gone the same way as Congo or Rwanda, but because of leaders such as Nelson Mandela, who tirelessly preached reconciliation, it did not.

One of the worst things about leaders who stoke the fire of ethnic hatred is that once that fire is lit, it tends to keep burning. Even if it is doused for a while, it can reignite. The World Bank reports that more than 90 percent of the civil wars in the first decade of the twenty-first century occurred in countries that had already experienced a civil war in the previous 30 years.[17] The murderous feelings that thugs like Habyarimana and Bagosora incited between Hutus and Tutsis have now spread over a wide swath of Africa. The hate passes from cousin to cousin and from village to village. Before long, both sides just "know" that everyone from the other tribe is plotting against them.

At home, Rwanda's government is trying to soothe relations between Hutus and Tutsis. Considering the country's complete devastation in 1994, President Kagame has done a good job of restoring order. His regime is efficient, investor-friendly and relatively uncorrupt. Buoyed by ample foreign aid, it has rebuilt Rwanda's shattered school and health-care systems. Average incomes are now above their pre-genocide level, having fallen by half in 1994. Hundreds of thousands of refugees have returned, both Tutsis and Hutus. The ruling party stresses that it is not a tribal party. It has abolished ethnic identity cards and forbids the breakdown of official statistics by tribe. Rwandans are encouraged to think of themselves as one happy family, a courtesy that extends even to Hutu rebels in Congo who surrender and come home.

These rebels are sent to a reeducation camp below the hills of Ruhengeri, a scenic spot to which tourists trek to watch wild gorillas. The purpose of Camp Mutobo, says the boss, a Ugandan-bred Tutsi called Frank Musonera, is to teach ex-fighters how to lead productive lives in the new Rwanda. Having spent years in the bush, and having been taught by their commanders that Rwanda's Tutsi rulers kill Hutus on principle, they face a culture shock when they come home and realize that Rwanda is at peace, he explained to me in 2004.[18]

Over the course of their two-month stay at the camp, these Hutu ex-fighters are taught practical skills, such as how to open a bank account or start a carpentry business. They are also taught how to be what Mr. Musonera calls "good patriotic citizens." This includes imbibing the ruling party's view of history—that ethnicity was unimportant in Rwanda before the colonists arrived and that all subsequent tribal killings were the fault of bad governments.

The lessons contain much truth, but it is still striking how uncritically Camp Mutobo's inmates claim to swallow them. Innocent Habimana, a 21-year-old Hutu ex-guerrilla who had been in the Congolese bush for ten years before coming to the camp, recites what he has learned: "There are no Hutus and no Tutsis, we are all Rwandans and we have to live as brothers. Everyone in the camp accepts this." Asked whether the Tutsi-led army, against whom he fought several desperate battles, has ever done anything wrong, Mr. Habimana replies without hesitation: "No, nothing."[19]

The message is drummed into civilian ears, too. All young Rwandans are obliged to attend "solidarity camps" where they are taught to love one another. Some find it useful; others feel that they are being indoctrinated to love the ruling party, which claims to be democratic but which tolerates only token dissent.

On the evening before Rwanda's presidential election in 2003, I sat in the tiny apartment that served as the campaign headquarters of the main opposition candidate, Faustin Twagiramungu, a moderate Hutu. Mr. Twagiramungu admitted that he had no chance of winning. His party had been banned, his campaign leaflets seized and his supporters were terrified.

As he spoke, some of his provincial campaign managers, all 12 of whom had been arrested the previous day, were paraded on television, denouncing their former leader as a "divisionist," the government's term for someone who seeks to incite another genocide. It is an absurd charge to level at Mr. Twagiramungu. Because of his vocal opposition to violence, members of his own tribe put him on a death list in 1994, and he had to be smuggled out of his home in a rolled-up carpet. He also lost 32 relatives during the genocide. Mr. Twagiramungu showed me a letter, which he said was from one of his campaign managers who had just denounced him. The message, he said, was "I'm so sorry, but I have to stay alive."[20]

President Kagame won 95 percent of the vote; Mr. Twagiramungu managed only 3.7 percent.* The ballot was secret, in the sense that the government did not know how individuals voted. But it knew how small areas voted, and collective punishments are not unheard of in Rwanda. The voters I spoke to were visibly scared. One group of peasants I tried to interview by the side of a road refused to express any opinions about anything at all. And I suspect that as soon as I drove up, someone called the police, because two cops arrived within minutes and demanded to know what was going on. I told them I was interviewing voters. They ordered me to redirect my inquiries to the Bureau of Elections in the capital.

In another village near Kigali, in the shade of the banana trees, a villager told me, "There are no Hutus or Tutsis any more, only Rwandans. We live and work side by side. There are no problems." He added that everyone he knew felt the same way. But I couldn't help noticing that my driver, who was originally from the area, had put on sunglasses and pulled up his hood. He didn't want to be recognized, he said, by the people who had murdered his father and 4,500 of his neighbors.

I asked Alison Des Forges, of Human Rights Watch, perhaps the most respected chronicler of the genocide, what she thought Rwanda's future might hold. There will not be another genocide, she said. Genocide requires control of the state, and those who control the Rwandan state are unlikely to let go anytime soon. But given the instability of the region, and the unresolved frustrations stopped up within Rwandan hearts, "there could be a resumption of violence, and that could take an ethnic turn."[21]

---

* In 2010, President Kagame was again reelected, this time with only 93 percent of the vote.

PART TWO: NETWORKS OF TERROR

A tiny tropical fish sits in a glass vase on each table in a restaurant in the lobby of the Oberoi Hotel in Mumbai, India. A bright red piano fills the air with music. The passion fruit soufflé with bitter chocolate pavé and goats' milk ice cream is, frankly, delicious. The bill would cripple most Indians.

One day in the fall of 2008, gunmen walked into this restaurant and started killing. They shot diners and staff at close range, spattering blood over the walls. Some survivors say they smiled as they did it. In all, at least 175 people died in attacks that occurred across the city of Mumbai, which began on November 26 and lasted until November 29.

The terrorists targeted the most expensive hotels in India's commercial capital, the Oberoi and the Taj. "Everyone in my social class lost friends," says Cyrus Guzder, the owner of a transport firm. "We've all been to weddings and parties here," he told me over canapés in a members-only club at the Oberoi.[22]

The killers belonged to a Pakistani group, Lashkar-e-Taiba, that aims to wrest control of Kashmir, a mostly Muslim state, from India. Attacking posh hotels and murdering members of the Indian elite is a logical (though evil) way to pursue this goal. The same cannot be said of one of the attackers' other targets. Although Jews play no role in the Kashmir dispute, the terrorists sought out a small Jewish center in Mumbai and murdered its occupants.

Why? Jews have a special place in radical Islamist demonology. They occupy land that many Muslims consider holy. Their survival and success, despite the hostility of their far more numerous neighbors, fuels countless conspiracy theories. Some radical Muslims believe that Jews secretly control the American government. Since the United States is the world's hyperpower, that means Jews can be blamed for more or less anything. The Mumbai terrorists took their orders from handlers in Pakistan, who reportedly told them that the deaths of Jews were worth 50 times more than those of other victims.[23] That, presumably, is why they took such trouble to find and murder half a dozen harmless Jews, one of whom was pregnant.

The *ummah*, or global community of Muslims, is a wonderful thing. It spreads faith and charity and interest-free loans around every continent. Unfortunately, it also spreads violence of the sort seen in Mumbai that November day. Islam does not cause terrorism—the vast majority of Muslims are peaceful. But many terrorists cite the Koran to justify their actions.

Terrorism perpetrated in the name of Islam is alarming for several reasons. First, it is global in its ambitions. Nationalist terrorists, by contrast, typically have narrow aims—the Irish Republican Army poses no threat to Americans; Basque separatists have no quarrel with India. Islamist radicals often have local grievances, too: the Palestinian group Hamas wants to defeat Israel, Chechen rebels want to break free of Russia and so on. But many also see themselves as soldiers in a wider struggle.

Some Muslims believe that the non-Muslim world is waging war on them. The most extreme believe that all non-Muslims are their enemies. Some dream of restoring Islamic rule to every country that has ever had it, including Spain.

The greatest source of strength for Islamist radicals is that they can piggyback on a powerful, worldwide network of more than a billion Muslims. This network is as open as it is influential: anyone can become a Muslim, although in some countries it is not so easy to leave the faith. For many Muslims, their religion is the most important thing in their lives: a moral guide, a source of solace and a community. For many, a political message wrapped in a Koranic verse can be persuasive.

Islam stresses compassion toward fellow Muslims. Since many Muslims take this obligation seriously, they are outraged by injustice inflicted on Muslims anywhere. Since they make up one-sixth of the world's population and live largely in turbulent countries, there are plenty of examples of suffering. Iraqis were tortured in disgusting ways in Abu Ghraib. Uighurs are humiliated daily by the Han Chinese. Many Muslims live under cruel dictatorships propped up by American aid. And gory footage of abuses is easy to obtain. With a bit of editing, it can make convincing evidence of a (nonexistent) global conspiracy against Islam. For anyone with an Internet connection, such propaganda is only a click away.

The global Muslim network allows Osama bin Laden to wield global power even after his death. A team of American Navy SEALs put a stop to his plotting in May 2011, by bursting into his Pakistani hideout and shooting him. But his ideology lives on.

While he was alive, bin Laden was deeply involved in the practical planning of several terrorist outrages, but not nearly as many as he inspired. He never met Major Nidal Hasan, for example, but he gave him a convincing reason to walk into an army base in Texas in November 2009 and murder 13 people.* According to witnesses, Major Hasan began by bowing his head, as if in prayer. Then he shouted *Allahu akbar!* (God is great!) and started firing. He did not stop until a policeman shot and paralyzed him.[24]

Major Hasan planned his massacre alone, and carried it out alone. He bought the murder weapon with his own money, from a gun shop next to the strip club he frequented.[25] He needed no material help from any organization—terrorism is cheap.

He was motivated, however, by bin Laden's perversion of Islam. As a young man, he had attended a radical mosque in Virginia where two of the hijackers of September 11, 2001, had also worshipped. In the run-up to the massacre, he corresponded by email with the former imam of that mosque, Anwar al-Awlaki, one of the foremost propagandists of al-Qaeda, the group bin Laden founded.

Major Hasan reportedly sent 21 emails to Sheikh Awlaki and received two replies. Given that American forces were killing Muslims in Iraq and Afghanistan, he asked, was it lawful to kill American soldiers? Awlaki assured him that it was his Islamic duty.[26]

Some have argued that Major Hasan's motives were personal. As a military psychiatrist, he had treated soldiers who had returned traumatized from Iraq and Afghanistan. Some speculate that he acted as he did to avoid being sent into combat, where he might have to kill fellow Muslims or be killed himself. Carl Tobias, a law professor and terrorism expert at the University of Richmond, told Fox News, "[F]rom what I see in the news, this is just a person acting individually because he doesn't want to deploy overseas."[27] But surely there are easier ways of avoiding combat.

Major Hasan was not the only terrorist inspired by Sheikh Awlaki. This US-born Yemeni preacher is an important figure because he

---

* At the time of writing, Major Hasan had been charged with the killings, but not convicted.

speaks flawless colloquial English—he lived in the United States for much of his adult life. The FBI started investigating him after the 9/11 attacks but came up empty-handed. They reportedly discovered that he enjoyed the company of prostitutes, but they could not prove his connections to terrorism.[28]

He left the United States in 2002 and is now based in Yemen. From this refuge, he posts lectures online preaching holy war against the West. Previously, such messages were easily accessible only to Muslims who spoke Arabic. Sheikh Awlaki has spread them to a wider audience, including many angry young British and American Muslims. He excels at summarizing al-Qaeda's philosophy in clear English, says Katherine Zimmerman, of the American Enterprise Institute, a Washington, DC–based think tank. More than 5 million copies of his taped sermons have reportedly been distributed in the West.[29] Al-Qaeda's ability to recruit Western Muslims is a crucial weapon in its war against the West. It is quite hard to enter the United States using a Saudi or Pakistani passport, but easy if you have an American one.

Shortly after killing bin Laden, President Barack Obama ordered a missile strike on a car thought to be carrying Awlaki. He missed; Awlaki was no longer in the car.[30] Next time he may not be so lucky. But his lectures will live on in digital perpetuity. Accomplices of the suicide bombers who killed 52 people in London on July 7, 2005, were found to own copies. The "Toronto 18" arrested in June 2006 for plotting to storm Canada's parliament and behead its prime minister, watched Awlaki's lectures as part of their training. The five men who plotted an attack on Fort Dix in New Jersey in 2007 were avid fans. And Umar Farouk Abdulmutallab, a Nigerian who tried to blow up a Detroit-bound plane on Christmas Day 2009 with explosives in his underwear, met Awlaki in Yemen. In this last case, the imam appeared not merely to serve as an inspiration to murder but also to have put the bomber in touch with the al-Qaeda operatives who helped him with the practicalities.[31]

Bin Laden once said that 90 percent of al-Qaeda's battle is conducted in the media. It is more complicated than that. The mass media are important, but so are the conversations people have with friends about what they have read or seen. Ideas spread more easily when they come from people we trust. Lies, too, seem more credible when they reflect badly on people we already dislike.

This may be why so many Muslims believe conspiracy theories about the United States. For example, only 40 percent of American Muslims believe that the 9/11 attacks were carried out by Arabs, despite bin Laden's triumphant admission that he was responsible.[32] Many swallow the story that the American government itself was behind the attacks. This is manifestly ridiculous: it would have involved then-President George W. Bush persuading dozens of top-ranking military and intelligence officers to collaborate in a plot to murder thousands of American citizens in broad daylight. Yet variations on this conspiracy theory persist. Repeated from angry mouth to credulous ear, they grow in the telling. And they encourage some to view the United States as a kind of global supervillain.*

Propaganda spread through Islamist networks makes young radicals yearn to kill. But to become deadly, they often require face-to-face training. (Major Hasan, a professional soldier, was an exception.) "[E]ffective jihadist terrorists are generally the graduates of training camps or war zones, rather than the passive consumers of jihadist propaganda on the web," says Peter Bergen, a journalist best known for once having interviewed Osama bin Laden. "Hotheads in a coffeehouse are a dime a dozen," Michael Sheehan, the deputy police commissioner in New York responsible for counterterrorism, told him. "Al-Qaeda central is a critical element in turning the hotheads into an actual capable cell."[33]

Mohammed Sidique Khan, the leader of the London subway and bus bombers of 2005, trained with al-Qaeda in Pakistan. Faisal Shahzad, who narrowly failed to detonate a car bomb in New York's Times Square in 2010, was trained in bomb-making by the Taliban, also in Pakistan. David Headley, a Pakistani American, trained with Lashkar-e-Taiba in Pakistan and then gathered intelligence both for that

---

* Muslims are not the only ones who swallow conspiracy theories, of course, nor the only ones whose credulity is colored by their prejudices. Republicans are much more likely than Democrats to believe that Barack Obama's birth certificate was faked, and Democrats are much more likely than Republicans to believe that the Bush administration might have orchestrated the attacks of September 11, 2001. The former is provably false. The latter is deranged.

group and for al-Qaeda. He traveled to Mumbai to scout the hotels and the Jewish center that were attacked in 2008. He also went to Denmark to scout the offices of *Jyllands-Posten,* a newspaper that had published some cartoons of the Prophet Muhammad, and a nearby synagogue. He relayed his findings to an al-Qaeda operative in Pakistan but was arrested before any Danish journalists or Jews could be murdered.[34]

By the summer of 2010, some three dozen US citizens or residents had been arrested for going abroad to receive training as Islamist terrorists.[35] Bryant Vinas, a Hispanic American convert, went to Pakistan in 2008, learned how to fire rockets and then joined an attack on an American base in Afghanistan in September that year. "The fact that seven years after 9/11 a kid from Long Island managed to waltz into an al-Qaeda training camp, a feat that no American spy had done, despite the some $75 billion a year that the United States was spending on its intelligence agencies, says a great deal about how the US intelligence community actually works," grumbles Mr. Bergen.[36]

Perhaps, but it also says something about the power of affinity networks. The top al-Qaeda leaders may be deeply hidden, but the global jihadist network is adept at passing information back and forth between sympathetic ears. A would-be recruit from Long Island or Leeds starts by seeking out others with similar beliefs. One introduction leads to another, and before long, he is in the wilds of Pakistan being taught how to wire up a suicide vest.

Governments cannot hope to foil every terrorist plot. So a big part of any counterterrorism strategy must be to try to prevent people from feeling alienated in the first place. In majority-Muslim countries, the best medicine would be faster economic growth, argues Vali Nasr of the Council on Foreign Relations. "Commerce," he writes, "softens manners and makes a politics based on reason and deliberation, rather than fighting and romanticism, far more imaginable."[37] In countries where Muslims are a minority, the key is to promote better relations between Muslims and non-Muslims. In this area, the United States scores better than its critics allege.

BOOSTING THE *UMMAH*'S IMMUNE SYSTEM

Azhar Usman, a stand-up comic, says he is a "very patriotic" American Muslim. "I would die for this country," he declares. After a beat, he adds: "By blowing myself up." Another beat: "Inside a Dunkin' Donuts." His largely white, liberal audience guffaws. But not everyone gets the joke: one furious listener thought he was advocating the murder of police officers, who can often be found in donut shops.

I asked Mr. Usman what it was like being a Muslim in the United States. He said it depended on the headlines. A few days before we spoke, Abdulmutallab, the "underwear bomber," had almost succeeded in incinerating a planeload of passengers over the Eastern Seaboard. When he heard the news, Mr. Usman felt two things: disgust at the perversion of Islam that teaches that mass murder is sacred, and a sinking feeling of "here we go again." With his bushy beard and South Asian looks, Mr. Usman is exactly the kind of man who attracts fearful glances when terrorism is on people's minds.[38]

It was at its worst in the days after September 11, 2001. Hate crimes against Muslims soared. These were mostly nonviolent—the FBI reported no instances that year of an American Muslim being murdered for his faith—but threats and vandalism are nasty enough. And Muslims endured countless slights that, while not worth reporting to the police, were vexing.

Shabana Shakir-Ahmed, a suburban mother from Cincinnati, Ohio, recalls chatting with a shop assistant not long after the twin towers fell. She does not wear the hijab, so the assistant did not at first realize she was Muslim. But when she saw the name on her credit card, her attitude stiffened. Mrs. Shakir-Ahmed had bought enough cosmetics to qualify for a free bag, but when she asked for it, the assistant said they were all gone, though there was a heap of them clearly visible behind her.[39]

Many Americans view Muslims with suspicion. Irresponsible pundits pour diesel on the flames. "We should invade their countries, kill their leaders and convert them to Christianity," wrote Ann Coulter, a polemicist, two days after September 11.[40] Michael Savage, a talk-radio host, described the growth of America's Muslim population as "throat-slitters . . . clawing at the gate."[41] Provoking Muslims is an effective way to court publicity. Terry Jones, a Florida pastor whose entire congregation would fit into a medium-sized kitchen, shot to fame in 2011 by burning a Koran.[42] The blame for the murders that followed rests squarely with the mobs in Afghanistan that committed them, of course. And it would be wrong and unconstitutional for America to muzzle hatemongers such as Pastor Jones. But one wishes he would shut up, and it might help if the media did not reward his idiocy with airtime.

Being a religious minority rather than a racial one, Muslims are easier to stereotype. In theory, they all believe in the same book. By selectively quoting Koranic verses that sound bloodthirsty, Islamophobes can argue that Islam is a religion of war. (One could do something similar with Bible verses that, for example, endorse slavery, but few Americans worry that the Christians next door will enslave them.) In polls, only atheists and Scientologists are more disliked than Muslims. Some 40 percent of Americans think Islam is more likely to encourage violence than other religions.[43]

Yet while some Americans mistreat their Muslim compatriots, most try hard to be fair. Despite all the tension over terrorism, three-quarters of American Muslims say they cannot think of a single time when they have been discriminated against. Among immigrant Muslims, the figure is 82 percent.[44] When Mrs. Shakir-Ahmed complained about that shop assistant, for example, the manager apologized profusely and gave her two free bags. Many Americans are actually making an effort to learn more about Islam. Mrs. Shakir-Ahmed, who works as a volunteer tour guide at a local Islamic center, saw a surge in visitors after September 11. Their questions have gradually grown less ignorant. These days, no one asks her if she belongs to a harem, she says.

To an encouraging degree, America's Muslims are well off and well integrated. A 2009 Gallup poll found them slightly more likely than other Americans to have jobs, and slightly more likely to be professionals.[45] Only 15 percent feel isolated from American society, less than half the figure in Britain or Germany.[46] According to a Pew Research Center poll, 72 percent say their communities are good places to live and 71 percent believe that most people who want to get ahead in the United States can do so if they work hard.[47]

American Muslims are a diverse bunch. Asked about their race, a plurality (35 percent) describe themselves as African American. Another 28 percent say they are white, 18 percent say Asian and 18 percent tick "other." Racial disparities among Muslims roughly mirror those in the broader society. Asian American Muslims are better educated and earn more than African American ones, for example. And an immigrant Muslim dentist will have quite different experiences from a black American who converted while in jail.[48] (Quite a few African Americans converted to Islam while in prison, where Muslim groups proselytize energetically.)

Muslim Americans were pleased when Barack Obama, a man with Muslim roots, was elected president. But many remain furious about American foreign policy. They see that the United States (in their view) favors Israel over the Palestinians. Many abhorred the invasions of Iraq and Afghanistan. Many chafe at Obama's copious use of drone-fired missiles to assassinate suspected Taliban leaders in Pakistan, a tactic that kills hundreds of innocents.[49]

Dalia Mogahed, of Gallup's Center for Muslim Studies, argues that American Muslims strongly reject terrorism because they are so well integrated.[50] This is true, but not uniformly so. Among black Muslims, for example, only 36 percent say they have a "very unfavorable" view of al-Qaeda. Perhaps some of them have only a hazy notion of what al-Qaeda is. Nonetheless, the poll suggests a worrying degree of alienation.

African American Muslims tend not to be upwardly mobile immigrants from Africa. They are mostly native-born, and, as mentioned before, many converted to Islam while in prison. There is nothing wrong with Muslims seeking converts in American jails; many felons would benefit from a more spiritual worldview. The worry, however, is that some of these converts may be attracted to the most radical strains of Islam. Ex-convicts are often angry at the society that locked them up. If they browse jihadist websites, they learn that others share their anger—and that God wants them to act on it. For some, this is a seductive message.

Young Muslims of all races, meanwhile, are angrier than their parents.

American Muslims under 30 are twice as likely as their elders to believe that suicide attacks on civilians in defense of Islam are sometimes justified (15 percent versus 6 percent, according to Pew[51]). Azhar Usman, the comedian, says we should not read too much into this. It is part of American culture for the young to rebel, he says, so young

Muslims' anger is a sign that they have assimilated. I hope he's right, but I wonder.

Even among those who express alarming views, only a tiny fraction will do anything terrible. Most of those who speak approvingly of suicide bombing are no doubt thinking of wars in far-off lands rather than of blowing up the local mall. But it does not take many terrorists to cause mayhem, as Major Hasan showed at Fort Hood.

The key to curbing Islamist terror will be to delegitimize it: to persuade so many Muslims that it is wrong that the terrorists will have few places to hide. The only feasible way to do this is via the global Muslim network. Muslims are more likely to listen to other Muslims, so the more who speak out against al-Qaeda and its ilk, the harder it will be for them to operate. It is particularly helpful when radical Muslims denounce bin Ladenism, because such people are hard to dismiss as American stooges. Abdullah Anas, a former comrade-in-arms of Osama bin Laden during his days fighting against the Soviets in Afghanistan, denounced the suicide bombings in London 2005 as "criminal." Sayyid Imam al-Sharif, a man whose extremist writings profoundly influenced bin Laden himself, was so disgusted by al-Qaeda's habit of killing fellow Muslims that in 2007 he wrote a book from his Egyptian prison cell decrying it. He declared that blowing up Muslims was wrong, as was killing civilians in the West. He described bin Laden as "extremely immoral."[52]

There is only so much outsiders can do to encourage such epiphanies, but treating Muslims well when they visit the West would help. Several years ago, in the northern Nigerian city of Kaduna, I met an ex-terrorist called Muhammad Ashafa. As a young man, he led an Islamist gang that murdered Nigerian Christians during interfaith riots. He had repented, however, made peace with his enemies and started a joint charity to promote Muslim-Christian dialogue. I knew he had visited the United States recently and asked him what he thought of the place. He replied that he had been pleasantly shocked. He had assumed that it was a nation of materialists who believed in nothing. But when he started talking to Americans, he discovered that they were a deeply religious people. If more Muslims realized this, they would not be so hostile to America, he argued.[53]

Another encouraging sign in the war of ideas is the growing realization among Muslims that al-Qaeda offers no vision for the future besides bloodshed. Many Muslims cheered bin Laden in 2001, when they thought he was standing up to the United States. But then his followers started killing large numbers of Muslims, in Afghanistan, Iraq, Pakistan, Saudi Arabia, Indonesia and other places. Al-Qaeda preaches that anyone who disagrees even slightly with their worldview is an infidel, and therefore worthy of death. It is hard to build a broad-based movement around the slogan "Death to nearly everyone."

Al-Qaeda's popularity among Muslims has plummeted in all countries where the group has been active. Pew polls have found that, between 2003 and 2011, confidence in Osama bin Laden to do the right thing fell from 59 percent to 26 percent in Indonesia and from 19 percent to 1 percent in Lebanon. It also fell from 72 percent to 34 percent in Gaza and the West Bank, as Palestinians realized that bin Laden was not, in fact, helping their cause. (These polls were all conducted before he was killed.)[54]

None of the revolutions of the so-called Arab Spring in 2011 had anything to do with al-Qaeda, Peter Bergen observed in an op-ed:

> The Google executive* and Facebook revolutionaries who launched the revolt in Egypt represent everything that bin Laden and al-Qaeda hate: Secular, liberal and anti-authoritarian, they also include—gasp—women. Even the Muslim Brotherhood, the Islamist mass movement in Egypt, which joined the revolution as it was already in motion, is opposed by al-Qaeda. The Brotherhood participates in conventional politics and elections, which bin Laden and his followers believe are against Islam.[55]

Al-Qaeda was miffed enough to reply. Sheikh Awlaki derided Mr. Bergen as "a so-called terrorism expert" and predicted that Taliban-style regimes would take over Arab countries at some unspecified point in the future.[56]

That seems unlikely. As an ideology, bin Ladenism is ebbing. It is still highly dangerous—its believers will continue to carry out atroci-

---

* Wael Ghonim. See Chapter 8.

ties in many countries, including the United States. But there are encouraging signs that the *ummah* is growing resistant to the virus that lurks in its bloodstream. Most Muslims are acutely aware of the threat that terrorism poses, not only to the world in general but to themselves in particular. They have a strong interest in discouraging it, and in spotting the jihadists in their midst before they act on their beliefs. In November 2009, for example, five Virginian Muslims went to Pakistan to train as terrorists. They were caught and convicted because their fellow American Muslims alerted the FBI. In fact, it was their parents who turned them in.[57]

PART THREE: NETWORKS OF GREED

I once dialed a wrong number in Nigeria and, thinking I was talking to an expert on a particular subject, started asking how I might get hold of a piece of information I needed urgently. The Nigerian gentleman on the other end of the line had no idea what I was talking about. But, without missing a beat, he assured me that he would be able to get hold of this piece of information if I could first send him several hundred dollars to bribe a librarian.

Nigeria's reputation for quick-witted criminality may be unfair, but it is not wholly without foundation. The country's most ubiquitous cultural ambassadors, alas, are the scammers who send out billions of emails offering a share of a late dictator's loot to anyone gullible enough to reveal his bank details. Most Nigerians are honest, but ill-gotten wealth carries less stigma in Nigeria than in many other countries.

I once met a retired Nigerian blacksmith who had somehow saved enough money to start building a hotel—at least, that was what he told me. The hotel was real enough: four stories of solid masonry sprouting up amid the millet fields on the edge of a fast-growing city. I had heard, however, that the true owner was the blacksmith's son, who worked in the United States. I asked the blacksmith about him, as we relaxed on plastic chairs watching shirtless laborers shimmy up wooden scaffolding poles. He immediately grew defensive. Why was I asking such questions? Did I work for a government agency?

The blacksmith said he couldn't recall which American city his son lived in or what he did for a living. I gave up quizzing him and asked one of his neighbors instead. The neighbor said he was pretty sure the man's son was making hefty sums from some criminal enterprise. But if someone is rich in Nigeria, he added, no one asks where the money came from.

Criminals today make extensive use of international networks. Since the early 1990s, the lowering of barriers to legitimate trade has had the side effect of allowing an explosion of cross border crime. The huge increase in global shipping over the past two decades means there are far more containers in which to hide contraband. The spread of cheap, secure Internet connections and disposable phones makes it easier for international criminals to coordinate their operations. And the increase in global financial flows creates a vast, churning ocean in which to launder dirty money.

"National borders are a boon to criminals and a block to law enforcement agencies," laments Moises Naim in his fine book *Illicit: How Smugglers, Traffickers and Copycats Are Hijacking the Global Economy.* A Texan cop will nail you in El Paso but cannot touch you if you step across the frontier into Mexico. Mr. Naim argues that criminals have adapted to globalization in much the same way as terrorists have. Fixed hierarchies have given way to decentralized networks. Controlling leaders have been supplanted by multiple loosely linked agents and cells. The traditional model of the Sicilian mafia, in which gangsters join a criminal organization for life, is being swept aside by more flexible, ad hoc arrangements.[58]

Nigerian gangs fit comfortably into this new world. They speak English, so they can negotiate deals with anyone. They also speak their own languages, such as Ibo, so they can natter with each other without much fear that Interpol will understand.

They come from a country where the informal economy is larger than the legal one, so they are used to living outside the law. Most informal businesses involve activities that are not in themselves illegal, such as cutting hair or trading. But because they operate without permits and without paying tax, they cannot turn to the law to enforce contracts that go sour. So they learn how to use social networks to figure out whom they can trust and whom they cannot. Such skills are easily transferable to criminal businesses, such as drug smuggling.[59]

A typical Nigerian criminal network consists of small cells of between two and ten members, according to Aimar Alkholt, a researcher at the University of Bergen, in Norway. All or most will be from the same tribe. They are highly mobile and adapt readily to any new environment. They typically make a deal and then disperse, regrouping later. They are quick to bribe officials but slow to resort to violence, since they don't want to attract the attention of the police.[60]

Nigerian middlemen are big in the drug trade. Nigeria itself grows almost no narcotics, but that hardly matters, since the real money is in moving them across borders. This requires ingenuity, to stay one step ahead of the law, and flexibility, so that when the police choke off one supply route, the dealer can quickly find another. So, for example, Nigerian gangsters in Thailand buy raw opium smuggled in from Myanmar or Afghanistan. They then ship it to Nigeria, process it into heroin and smuggle it into America via Europe, hidden in the suitcases of European women. If one of these European "mules" is caught, little harm is done to the network, since she does not know the real names of the men who hired her, and they know only a little about the other cells in the network. If the police wise up to one smuggling corridor, the Nigerians will open another, using their contacts in South Africa or Ghana.[61]

Nigerians were virtually unknown in the drug trade before the 1980s. Now they are one of its most dynamic forces. They are less important than the Mexicans, since Nigeria lacks a long land border with the world's biggest drug market, but they are important wholesalers in several American cities. At the street level, where they would be conspicuous, "the Nigerians vanish," observes Mr. Naim.[62]

A management consultant evaluating a Nigerian criminal network might say that its core competence is not selling drugs but making connections. Once forged, such connections can be used for more than one type of crime. For example, if Nigerian gangsters are smuggling illegal immigrants into Europe, they may ask each migrant to swallow a condom full of heroin. Or they might do a deal with Chinese makers of counterfeit watches whereby they arrange for African migrants to hawk their products on the streets of Paris or Rome.[63]

Ethnic networks can be self-reinforcing. For example, more than 90 percent of the Nigerian prostitutes trafficked to Europe are thought to come from Edo, a small state in south central Nigeria.[64] Typically, a young woman is introduced to a madam in Nigeria by someone she knows. The madam pays for her passage to Europe, including forged documents, which can cost around $10,000. In return, the young woman takes on a debt of $40,000 to $100,000. She may not understand quite how large the sum is—it may be quoted in a currency with which she is not familiar—but she will understand that the debt is binding. A signed contract is often solemnified by a *juju* ritual, perhaps involving a bag of the young woman's hair and nail clippings.

When the young woman arrives in Europe—Italy is the most popular destination—she is handed over to another Nigerian madam, for whom she works until the debt is paid off. According to Jørgen Carling, a Swedish researcher, Nigerian sex traffickers are less violent than their Eastern European counterparts, not because they are soft-hearted, but because they have devised more subtle means of persuasion. The *juju* helps. So does the fact that the debt bondage they inflict on young women is usually temporary. The women typically clear their debts within one to three years. Some then become madams; others go home.[65]

Many end up destitute or diseased. But some return home rich, at least by Nigerian standards. The *Italos,* as they are known, "built proper houses. They sank private boreholes to supply running water day and night. They introduced shiny new four-wheel drives to the unpaved roads of Benin City [the capital of Edo state]," reports Somini Sengupta, of the *New York Times*.[66] The stories of women who made good money in Europe ensure a steady supply of new recruits. The traffickers, meanwhile, seldom lose. They use the same routes and safe houses to transport both sex workers and asylum seekers. Borders are profitable for those who ignore them.

THE DARK SIDE OF TRIBALISM

It is impossible to stop ethnic and religious networks from being used for evil purposes, at least some of the time. Conspirators work with people they trust, and the easiest way to find such people is through ancient bonds of tribe, family or faith. Since mass migration has made so many ethnic networks global, we will have to get used to globalized terrorism and crime. We must also expect many local conflicts to spread across borders, though few will be as bloody as the fight between Hutus and Tutsis in central Africa.

The question of how to solve these ills is beyond the scope of this book. In some cases, the network is both the problem and the solution. Violent preaching spreads through the global Islamic network, but so too does the lesson that terrorism only makes Muslims worse off. Tribal hatred can spread through tribal networks, but so can a message of tolerance, as Nelson Mandela and Mahatma Gandhi have shown. In other cases, the solutions have nothing to do with networks. The only plausible way to shut down the world's illegal drug barons would be to legalize drugs. I think such a radical policy shift would do more good than harm, but it is unlikely to happen anytime soon.[67]

It is easy, when contemplating the dark side of tribalism, to grow afraid of migration itself. For it is thanks to migration that we are brought daily into contact with people whose backgrounds and beliefs differ sharply from our own, and whose deepest loyalties may lie elsewhere.

Yet as I hope I have established in the first five chapters of this book, the benefits of migration vastly outweigh its costs. These benefits are especially visible in the United States, the land of immigrants that is the subject of my final three chapters.

"A PONZI SCHEME THAT WORKS"

WHY MIGRANTS CHOOSE AMERICA

In a field in Delaware, a hundred teams are vying to see whose machine can hurl a pumpkin farthest. Some have built medieval-looking trebuchets. Some have built pedal-powered doohickeys. No explosives are allowed at the annual Punkin Chunkin—a rule that galls some contestants. Yet the biggest air cannons, with barrels up to 150 feet long, can shoot their fruit projectiles most of a mile. "It's one heck of a peashooter," marvels a spectator.

Need I mention that virtually all the competitors are male? Dorothy Blades, a rare female chunker with a pink hard hat, pink gloves and a pink cannon, speculates that men crave that sense of power that only blasting a pumpkin into orbit in front of a large crowd can provide. "Plus, it's a drinkathon," she adds.

The Punkin Chunkin shows what can be achieved when hundreds of mechanically adept minds focus on one utterly pointless objective. The hydraulics on those air cannons must be engineered just so, as must the springs on the catapults. The machines' names—of course they have names—must be either macho ("Second Amendment") or crude ("Chunkin Up"). Distances must be measured with a handheld

GPS system that gives readings to the nearest hundredth of a foot. After each pumpkin lands, eager men on quad bikes zoom around looking for the crater, and then start triangulating.

All in all, the Punkin Chunkin is a perfect illustration of what makes the United States great. Only in the richest country on Earth could regular guys spend tens of thousands of dollars building a pumpkin gun. Only in a nation with such a fine tradition of inventiveness, not to mention martial prowess, would so many choose to do so. And only in a land of wide-open spaces would they be able to practice their "chunkin" without maiming their neighbors.[1]

If I sound flippant, it's to make a serious point. As I write, Americans are feeling pessimistic. Only a third of them think the country is on the right track.[2] Only about half expect their children to enjoy a better standard of living than they do.[3] The country is struggling to emerge from the worst recession since the 1930s. It is weighed down by debt, riven by political partisanship and seemingly incapable of addressing its long-term budget woes.

Fareed Zakaria, of CNN, talks of a "post-American world." The *Onion,* a satirical newspaper, reports that the last man who believed in the American dream, a bar worker in Pennington, Illinois, has finally given up.[4]

I find such pessimism overblown. America has profound economic problems, to be sure. But despite the decline of the past few years, my impression of the United States—after tramping around 44 of them— is one of spectacular material abundance. I'm not talking about the way the superrich live. An American billionaire's lifestyle is not so different from that of a billionaire anywhere else. What is conspicuous about America is that ordinary people—plumbers, police officers, middle managers and the like—enjoy a standard of living that foreigners can only marvel at.

America's greatest strength is that people want to live there. People cannot vote freely with their feet, but if one goes by their words, America is by far the most popular destination among would-be migrants. A worldwide Gallup poll in 2009, for example, found that nearly four times as many people said they wanted to move to the United States as to any other country.[5]

The reasons for this are complex, but I would emphasize two. First, America offers an unbeatable material standard of living. Second, it offers the widest variety of niches. Because it is so vast and diverse, virtually any immigrant can fit in, whether she is a socially conservative Arab or an ostentatiously gay Nicaraguan.

Let's start with America's material prosperity. Rather than plunging straight into cross border statistical comparisons, I'm going to tell you a story. I was researching an article about poverty in Appalachia in 2005. I flew to Kentucky, drove to a remote hamlet in the mountains and asked some local charity workers to introduce me to the poorest people they knew. I phrased it more tactfully than that, of course. I said I'd like to "see how people live around here." This fooled no one.

The people of Appalachia may not be rich, but they are not stupid, either. They knew exactly why a journalist might be nosing around their neighborhood. My guide introduced me to her Uncle Enos with the words: "This is Robert. He's writing an article about poor white trash." Uncle Enos smiled and said: "That's me."

Enos Banks is a loud, jovial fellow in late middle age. He lives in a trailer with half a dozen cars in varying states of disrepair parked outside and a pile of crushed Pepsi cans below the porch. He has no job—he used to work as a driver for a coal-mining firm, but left after a heart attack in his 40s. He wears a cowboy hat and talks with an accent that outsiders find nearly impenetrable.

He tells a cracking yarn about ketchup. One day, he spilled a splotch of it on his shirt. For fun, he persuaded his brother-in-law to shout angrily and shoot a gun through the window. When their two wives came rushing in, they saw Mr. Banks lying there covered in what looked like blood. "My wife passed out," he chuckles, "and my brother-in-law's wife shook him till his [false] teeth rattled."

Mr. Banks is clever with his hands. When the price of gasoline hit the sky, he grafted a chainsaw engine onto a bicycle to make a moped. He likes to be prepared. He walks with a walking-stick–cum–rifle, with a plastic cap on the end of the barrel to keep out the dirt. If someone tries to mug him for his painkillers, he says, he is ready to "shoot them plumb between the eyes." And if he runs out of bullets, he has a big knife strapped to the contraption with duct tape.

He "draws" $521 a month in Supplemental Security Income (a form of cash assistance for the elderly, poor and disabled). He laments that the authorities deduct $67 a month because he won $3,600 on the slot machines. Why, he asks, won't they take account of all the money he has lost while gambling? It is a fair question.[6]

No American would dispute that Mr. Banks is poor. But by global standards, he is not. Shortly before I met him, I interviewed another man with roughly the same income: Mbwebwe Kabamba, the chief trauma surgeon at the biggest hospital in the Democratic Republic of Congo. After 28 years as a doctor, his salary is only $250 a month, but by operating on private patients after hours, he stretches it to $600 or $700.[7]

Given the lower cost of living in Congo, one might guess that Dr. Kabamba is better off than Mr. Banks. But the doctor has to support an extended family of 12, whereas Mr. Banks's ex-wife and three sons all claim public assistance. Indeed, the reason Mr. Banks split up from his wife, he says, is because they can draw more benefits separately. She still lives in the trailer next door.

What do Dr. Kabamba's wages buy? He has a four-bedroom house with a kitchen and living room, which would be ample if there weren't a dozen people under his roof. His home would be deemed unacceptably overcrowded in America. Even among the 44 million Americans officially classified as poor, only 6 percent live in homes with more occupants than rooms.[8]

Dr. Kabamba would quite like running water and a steady power supply. His family fetches water in jars, and the electricity comes on maybe twice a week. Air-conditioning would be nice, but "that's only for VIPs," says Dr. Kabamba. In America, 84 percent of *poor* households have air-conditioning. Some 98 percent have a color television (two-thirds have two or more) and two-thirds have a car.[9]

Dr. Kabamba earns enough to feed his children, but not as well as he would like. The family eats meat about twice a month; he calls it "a great luxury." In America, poor children eat more meat than the well-to-do. In fact, they get twice as much protein as their government says is good for them, which is why the Walmart in Mr. Banks's neighborhood sells such enormous jeans.[10]

A Congolese doctor, a man most of his countrymen would consider wealthy, is worse off materially than most poor people in America. That puts America's prosperity into context. It also helps explain why so many of the world's huddled masses yearn to live there. But it is not only people from poor countries who seek a better standard of living in the United States. Americans are richer than people in other rich countries, too. Income per head in America is about 40 percent higher than the average among the members of the Organisation for Economic Co-operation and Development (OECD), a club for rich industrialized nations. Among OECD members, only Luxembourg (a tiny tax haven) and Norway (an orderly Scandinavian country sitting on a huge pool of oil) score higher. Compared with other reasonably large rich countries, America is substantially better off: 40 percent richer than France or Japan, 35 percent richer than Germany and 22 percent richer than Canada.[11]

One can quibble with these statistics. Americans work longer hours for their extra cash. Their health care costs more. And the American average is skewed by very high incomes at the top. It might be fairer to compare median household incomes, but this is tricky, since different countries define "household" differently.

Also, the figures I'm using are based on purchasing-power parity: a measure that tries to correct for the different cost of living in different countries. The OECD's number-crunchers are honest and meticulous, but this measure is still subjective. For example, $1 buys you more cheese in America than its equivalent in euros would in France. Does this justify tweaking downwards our estimate of a Frenchman's purchasing power? The Frenchman might say no, since the cheese he buys is tastier than the rubbery muck Americans wolf down. The cheesemakers of Wisconsin might retort that their cheese is much more flavorful than those snooty Frenchies will admit. Multiply these imponderables by the sum total of everything that anyone spends money on, and you have an idea of how difficult it is to compare living standards in different countries.

Despite these and other caveats, the statistics do support a broad-brush conclusion that Americans are materially better off than people in other rich countries. And it certainly chimes with my unscientific impressions, formed by visiting hundreds of American families and comparing their lot with those of hundreds more in dozens of other countries.

My observation is that a skilled blue-collar worker in America lives as well as an educated professional in Europe or Japan. To take one example of many, I once stayed with a family near New Orleans. The father was a mechanic; the mother a librarian. They lived in a spacious home by the bayou. I couldn't help noticing that it was bigger than the home of the vice president of a medium-sized software company that I used to work for in Tokyo. Granted, the VP's home was more elegant, with more antique woodblock prints and fewer pictures of his daughters riding quad bikes. But the mechanic had two cars, a recreational vehicle, a huge backyard and an above-ground swimming pool. In the American heartland, such luxuries are unremarkable.

Yet they are only part of America's allure.

NICHE NATION

Consider the story of Joshua Lee. He grew up poor: his father was a day laborer in South Korea. He did his compulsory military service on an American base in Seoul, where he polished his English and learned to like hot dogs. He moved to America in 1990, when he was 27, to study theology in Kentucky. He painted houses to support himself.

He met his wife, a Korean American, and moved to northern Virginia, where there is a hefty cluster of Korean Americans. Eventually, he found a job writing for a Korean-language newspaper about Korean American issues.

When he first came to America, Mr. Lee was astonished by how rich nearly everyone was. He recalls his first dinner with Americans: how huge the bowls were, how immense the portions. He was startled to see people leave lights on in empty rooms. He is still impressed: "The roads are so wide, the cars so big, the houses so large—everything is abundant," he says.[12]

Yet this is not why he came here, and it is not why he stayed and became a citizen. For Mr. Lee, America is a land that offers "the chance to be whatever you want to be." More prosaically, it is a place where nearly any immigrant can find a niche.

Mr. Lee's is an agreeable one. He lives in a suburb with safe streets, spacious backyards and good schools. He eats Korean food every day, but not for every meal. He attends a Baptist church where the services are in Korean, but the Sunday school classes for children are in English. He retains what he loves about his native culture—the work ethic, the language, the kimchi—while shrugging off the rest.

For example, he never liked the way his neighbors in Korea stuck their noses into each other's business. Everyone knew how you were doing in school. You could not get a good job without connections. There was constant social pressure not to lose face. When Mr. Lee went back to visit, he slipped right back into the old straitjacket. He wanted to pop out to the corner store, but realized he would have to put on a smart shirt and trousers to do so, despite the stifling humidity. If the neighbors saw him in shorts and flip-flops, what would they think? In America, no one cares.

In Korea, he says, to express an unusual opinion is to court isolation. In America, you can say what you think. To relax, Mr. Lee listens to Rush Limbaugh and Sean Hannity, two combatively conservative talk-show pundits. "Maybe you don't like these people, but I really [do]," he says.

Because America is so big and diverse, immigrants have an incredible array of choices. With more than 300 million people, the United States is nearly two and a half times more populous than Japan, the second-largest rich nation. The proportion of Americans who are foreign-born, 13.5 percent, is higher than the rich-country average of 10.3 percent. And in absolute terms, the gulf is much wider. America's foreign-born population of 43 million dwarfs that of any other country. Japan has only two million. Mainland China has fewer than a million—less than the foreign-born population of the tiny island-state of Singapore.[13]

Despite its staggering economic boom of the past three decades, China has not become a mecca for migrants. As discussed, it has begun to attract back ethnic Chinese who had previously emigrated, and it has attracted a fair number of expatriate businesspeople on temporary postings. But it has nothing like America's tradition of welcoming foreigners and encouraging them to become American. In China, such a transition is all but impossible. It is easier in India, but only slightly.

Americans, by contrast, are nearly all descended from people who came from somewhere else within the past couple of centuries. And the variety of countries from which immigrants come to the United States— roughly speaking, all of them, and usually in significant numbers—is unmatched. This means that, no matter where an immigrant hails from, he can find a cluster of his ethnic kin somewhere in America. In fact, he is probably spoiled for choice. Polish or Arab, gay or straight, Presbyterian or Buddhist, nearly anyone can find a welcoming niche. Of course, you can find clusters of ethnic minorities and religious denominations in other rich countries, but not nearly as many. For example, an immigrant to a European country who wants Filipino food and a Tagalog church might find them in the capital city. But he will struggle to recreate a familiar lifestyle anywhere else in that country.

Immigrants to America have a choice of weather and landscape, too, from snowy Alaska to baking Texas, from the mountains of Colorado to the forests of Maine. It is no coincidence that northern Virginia, where Mr. Lee lives, has roughly the same climate as his homeland: winter is freezing, summer is muggy, autumn is delightful and spring brings cascades of cherry blossoms.

Such noneconomic considerations are hugely important. Religious affiliation, for example, has a strong effect on who comes to the United States, observes Michael Fix, of the Migration Policy Institute. Although Muslims slightly outnumber Christians in Nigeria, Nigerian immigrants to America are 92 percent Christian and only 5 percent Muslim. Most South Koreans are not Christian, but four-fifths of Korean immigrants to America are. Migrants from the Middle East and North Africa are mostly Muslim, but 28 percent are Christian, and 10 percent are Jewish—far more than you would expect if faith played no role in the decision to migrate.[14]

One reason why religious affiliation affects migration is that information flows through religious networks. Nigerian evangelicals talk to other Nigerian evangelicals. If one of them has moved to America and found a good life there, he will tell his friends back home. Some may decide to join him. In all likelihood, they will move to the same neighborhood, to be near someone they know. The flow of like-minded migrants to the same destination quickly snowballs.

Additionally, America is an easy place to practice more or less any religion. It is not just that the country has an admirable tradition of religious tolerance, though that is important. It is also that the religious impulse itself is respected. In the more aggressively secular parts of Europe, the pious are sometimes treated with derision. Even Tony

Blair, Britain's former prime minister and a devout Christian, complains that his home country treats religious people as pariahs. If you talk about your faith, he grumbles, "People . . . think you're a nutter." That's British for "lunatic."[15]

THE ENGLISH FOXHUNTER

Consider another migrant's tale. Dennis Downing, an Englishman, moved to the United States for the foxhunting. He is a professional huntsman: he looks after the hounds that chase the fox during a traditional foxhunt. In 1997, Britain elected a government that threatened to ban the sport. A ponderous parliamentary report concluded that being torn apart by dogs "seriously compromises the welfare" of a fox.

Mr. Downing was then working in the county of Worcestershire. His local member of parliament was an outspoken hunt-banner. Kids at school taunted Mr. Downing's daughter. "They said the dogs should be shot and killed," he remembers. Elsewhere in England, saboteurs disrupted foxhunts, sometimes violently.[16]

Seeing the writing on the wall, Mr. Downing left Britain in 1998. (Foxhunting was finally banned in 2004.) After three years with a hunt in Alabama, he moved to Virginia, where English-style foxhunting has been popular since George Washington's day. He now works with the Blue Ridge Hunt and lives in the beautiful Shenandoah Valley. He likes the weather, the space and the freedom to do the job he has loved all his life.

That freedom is secure. Virginia will never ban hunting, but even if it did, there are plenty of other states that won't. America has 50 states with 50 sets of laws. Power is so decentralized that you can more or less choose which rules you want to live under. If you like low taxes and the death penalty, try Texas. For good public schools and bike paths, try Portland, Oregon. Even within states, the rules vary widely. Bath County, Kentucky, is dry; neighboring Bourbon County, as the name implies, is not. And nearby Montgomery County is somewhere in between: a "moist" county where the sale of alcohol is banned except in one city. Liberal students can let it all hang out at the University of California, Berkeley; those from traditional backgrounds may prefer a campus where there is no peer pressure to drink or fornicate, such as Brigham Young, in Utah, or Bob Jones, in South Carolina.

THE SOMALI DUTCH ATHEIST

People move for a variety of reasons. Alejandro Mayorkas, the head of the US Bureau of Citizenship and Immigration Services, says people come to the United States for one of two reasons: either because they yearn for freedom or because they are fleeing something.[17] That something could be a civil war or a culture that irks them. In Ayaan Hirsi Ali's case, it was both.

She was born in Somalia, one of the poorest and most chaotic places on Earth. As a young girl she was circumcised. "I heard it, like a butcher snipping the fat off a piece of meat," she recalls. Her grandmother taught her to expect men to be violent. If attacked, she advised her to duck behind the man, reach inside his sarong, grab his testicles and crush them until he fainted.[18]

Ms. Hirsi Ali grew up strong-willed. She fled from Somalia's civil war and then from an arranged marriage. She sought asylum in the Netherlands, a country she found shockingly nice. The policemen were polite and helpful instead of demanding bribes with menaces. The government gave refugees free room and board. "Where did they get the money from?" she wondered. "Why didn't it run out?"

She quickly learned Dutch and found work as an interpreter. In this job, she visited shelters for battered women, where she noticed that nearly all the victims were Muslim. These women seldom pressed charges against their violent husbands. The social workers would ask: "Do you have family here? Can they help you?" The women would reply: "But they support my husband, of course!" This infuriated Ms. Hirsi Ali: "I knew that many Dutch women were abused, too. But their community and their family didn't approve of it."

She began to campaign against domestic violence. She became a member of parliament, and won a dangerous kind of fame as an ex-Muslim apostate. In collaboration with a Dutch filmmaker, Theo van Gogh, she made a short film, *Submission,* about what she saw as the oppression of women under Islam. Soon after it was released, in 2004, an outraged fanatic murdered van Gogh and stabbed into his chest a letter to Ms. Hirsi Ali, promising to kill her, too. So she moved to America, where she is not so famous. She keeps sensibly quiet about exactly where she lives, but she can travel and shop without the constant fear of death. I caught up with her in Dallas in September 2009.

She praises the intellectual freedom in America. In the Netherlands, she says, think tanks are typically subsidized by the government and tied to a political party. This makes them timid, she says. If an idea is too controversial, they shy away from it. For example, she had a theory that the Dutch government-funded Muslim schools were fostering self-segregation, and asked whether they should be closed. No one wanted to even consider the question, she says; her colleagues were terrified of appearing racist.[19]

In America, by contrast, swarms of privately funded think tanks represent almost any view you can imagine. Their response to hard questions is more serious, she says. People ask if your hypothesis is true, and then suggest ways to raise the money to find out. After she arrived, Ms. Hirsi Ali started a foundation to study violence against Muslim women. No one knows how common this is in America. Ms. Hirsi Ali means to find out.[20]

Before she visited the United States, she admits, she had a negative view of the country. Listening to her Dutch friends, she assumed that Americans were fat, loutish, naïve and sexually repressed. "But then I came here and found it was all false," she smiles. Outsiders sometimes assume that it is hard to be an outspoken atheist in so devout a country as America, but Ms. Hirsi Ali finds it easy. When Christians ask her if she is a believer and she says no, "They don't try to kill me. They say they'll pray for me," she says.

Besides Somalia and the Netherlands, Ms. Hirsi Ali has also lived in Ethiopia, Kenya and Saudi Arabia. Of all these places, she thinks that America is the easiest place to assimilate. She has her niche, hanging out with "nerdy academics" and eating Japanese food. Unlike Mr. Lee, she is more or less divorced from her native culture. But that works just fine in America. "I'm surprised how fast complete strangers will invite you into their houses," she says. Asked what she dislikes about her new home, she concedes that the air-conditioning in public places is uncomfortably cold.

AMERICA'S DEMOGRAPHIC DIVIDEND

People often ignore demography because its effects are felt only gradually. In the short term, it makes little difference whether the United States welcomes a million immigrants each year or none. But in the long run, it is of paramount importance.

The fertility rate in the United States today is 2.1.[21] In other words, American women can expect to have on average 2.1 children each. This is almost exactly the "replacement rate," meaning that if there is no immigration, the population will neither grow nor shrink.

When you add immigration, however, the picture changes completely. With a few million newcomers each year—plus their children and their children's children—over time the population shoots up. According to the US Census Bureau, if immigration continues at a steady, moderate rate, the population will rise from 300 million today to 400 million in 2050, and 570 million in 2100. If the country sees a slight bump in the birthrate and slightly more immigrants arriving each year, the population will swell to 550 million in 2050 and 1.18 billion in 2100.[22] Since China's population will probably have fallen by then (it is currently 1.3 billion), there could actually be more Americans than Chinese in 2100—a possibility that few people imagine today.

Relatively small differences in growth rates yield wildly different outcomes in the long run. To reach a total of 570 million Americans by 2100, the population must grow by a mere 0.69 percent each year. To get to the colossal figure of 1.18 billion, it must grow only about a percentage point faster each year: a rate of 1.52 percent will do it. Relatively small differences in immigration policy, therefore, will have a huge effect over the long run.

The world is getting richer, and as people get richer, they tend to have fewer children. So the global population will stabilize and probably even start to shrink sometime this century. But there is no reason to suppose that migration will cease. As birthrates fall, *migration will become the primary determinant of how big each nation is*. The question of where people want to live will become more and more important.

Demography affects economic growth in a number of ways. For one thing, raw size matters: America's domestic market is currently the world's largest, and that makes the United States an attractive place to do business. The rewards of grabbing even a small slice of this market can be huge. For example, although most Americans believe in God and many view atheists as objectionable cranks, Richard Dawkins and Christopher Hitchens have grown rich selling antireligious books to American atheists.

Because America's market is so huge, it is the best place to test new products. If something you are selling is a hit in America, it is a hit, period. Amar Bhidé, a business professor at Columbia University, makes a more subtle point. American consumers not only spend more than those of other nations; they are also more "venturesome." That is, they are unusually willing to try new things. Their purchases reward innovators, and their feedback helps those innovators fine-tune their products.[23]

Innovation tends to come incrementally, Mr. Bhidé told me. *Eureka!* moments are rare. More often, inventors incorporate, at every stage, what their customers teach them about what works, what doesn't, and why. Apple's iPod, he points out, was not based on truly original technology. Rather, it skillfully integrated technology from multiple sources and countries. Millions of Americans bought the clunky, expensive first version. Apple used the cash and feedback from the first iPod to develop smarter and more user-friendly versions. Apple's iPods, iPhones and iPads have now swept the world.[24]

The age structure of a population also makes a big difference. The East Asian economic "miracle" was driven by a one-off bulge of working-age citizens. A postwar baby boom created an energetic generation that, in its prime years, did not have to support many old people. That demographic bonanza has now ended in Japan, where growth has slowed to a shuffle. It is fading in South Korea, too. In fact, rapid aging will make the whole of East Asia less dynamic.

The crunch will be most painful in China, which, thanks to the one-child policy, will be the first country ever to grow old before it gets rich. The generation that grew up surrounded by propaganda posters warning that "Mother Earth is too tired to sustain more children" will find that there are not enough children to look after them when they grow old and tired.[25] "No one has figured out how Beijing will care for a rapidly aging population with a quickly shrinking workforce," observes Gordon Chang, the author of a provocative book called *The Coming Collapse of China.*[26]

The United States must figure out how to cope with aging baby boomers, too. But it has two huge advantages. Smart and enterprising young foreigners want to move there, and the nation has a long and successful tradition of assimilating them. If America remains reasonably open to immigration—and that's a big if—it will age more slowly than any of its rivals.

In China, the number of working-age citizens supporting each old person—that is, the ratio of those aged 15 to 64 to those over 65—will tumble from 9:1 now to 3:1 in 2050, predicts the UN. In America the dependency ratio will fall more gently, from 5:1 to 3:1 over the same period. Europe and Japan will be spectacularly gray by then. Italy will be at 3:2; Japan's ratio will be 1:1.[27] (Japan is already using robots to look after the elderly and even keep them company. Needless to say, not everyone find this arrangement satisfactory.[28])

Countries, regions and cities are engaged in a global battle for talent. The most creative people can choose where to live. They tend to pick places that offer not only material comfort but also the stimulation of being surrounded by other creative people. This makes life more fun. It also fosters technological progress. When clever people cluster, they can bounce ideas off each other more easily. This is why rents are so high in Manhattan. Robert Lucas, a Nobel Prize–winning economist, argues that the clustering of talent is the primary driver of economic growth.[29]

So a country's economic prospects depend in large measure on whether it is a place where people want to live. Desirable destinations will attract talented and industrious migrants. Less desirable places will not.

How desirable is the United States, then? Pessimists point to its consistently less-than-world-beating scores on various global measures of well-being. On the UN's annual Human Development Index, for example, the United States comes in fourth, with Norway taking the crown.[30] On the Legatum Institute's Prosperity Index, it comes tenth, well behind Norway, Denmark and Finland.[31] These rankings often miss important nuances, however. They tend to measure the absence of problems rather than the presence of opportunity or excitement. Countries are (correctly) penalized for infants who die or homes that lack broadband. But what these indices fail to capture is the buzz that sets some countries apart.

The Nordic countries are nice places: polite, prosperous and orderly. But how many people, given the choice between living in Finland or America, would pick Finland? It's cold and dark and gloomy for half the year. The reason it has such high broadband penetration is because, during the long winter nights, there's not much else to do but sit indoors and update your Facebook page.

I once visited Finland in the dead of winter to give a speech. My hosts (from a Finnish aid agency) were delightful, and I was impressed by their ability to conduct an entire conference in English for the benefit of the one person who did not speak Finnish (me). But I did not get the impression that there was a whole lot going on in Helsinki that week. Compared to less perfect countries, Finland is a trifle dull. The vodka is intoxicating; the atmosphere, less so.

America, on the other hand, has huge social problems. It is more violent than other rich countries, it jails more of its people and its worst schools are truly appalling. But these ills are concentrated in a narrow swath of the population. If you are a young black male who has dropped out of high school, there is a 60 percent chance you will spend time in jail.[32] If you are a drug pusher, you are staggeringly likely to be murdered.* If you are middle class, by contrast, your local public school is probably pretty good and you are less likely to get mugged than you would be if you lived in London.[33]

That America's social ills are highly concentrated does not mean they don't matter. But they have surprisingly little impact on the daily lives of upwardly mobile immigrants. First-generation immigrants may run stores in rough neighborhoods, but their children go to college and become dentists.[34] And first-generation immigrants who arrive with marketable skills can skip the first stage entirely.

Richard Florida, an academic at the University of Toronto and the author of *The Rise of the Creative Class*, has compiled a Global

---

* Sudhir Venkatesh, a rather adventurous academic, spent a long time hanging out with inner-city crack gangs and found that, over a four-year period, the average dealer had a one in four chance of being killed.

Creativity Index, which is intended to measure countries' ability to harness talent. The index combines measures of skills, technology and tolerance. The United States comes in fourth, behind Sweden, Japan and Finland. But one could quarrel with his methodology. America comes top on certain measures, such as patents per head and college degrees, but it is deemed less tolerant than any other country in the top ten. This is because the index rewards "modern, secular" values and penalizes Americans for being religious and nationalistic.[35]

This is a mistake. Some religious countries are intolerant, but America is not one of them, as Ms. Hirsi Ali and others attest. A survey in 2009 by Gallup and the Coexist Foundation discovered that people of different religious backgrounds cohere markedly better with one another in the United States than in European countries.[36]

It is also a mistake to rate Americans as less tolerant because they are "nationalistic." Americans may have an annoyingly high opinion of their country, but theirs is an inclusive nationalism. Most believe that anyone can become American. Hardly anyone in Japan thinks that anyone can become Japanese, yet Japan is rated more "tolerant" than America. This is absurd. Japan is a terrific place. I lived there for five years, speak the language reasonably well and have nothing but admiration for the way so many people rub along with each other so peacefully on such a crowded archipelago. But it is hardly an open society.

Masayoshi Son, an ethnic Korean billionaire, once told me a little story that illustrates this point. He was born in Japan and lived there nearly his whole life. He founded a software firm, Softbank, which generates vast sums of money and employs thousands of Japanese people. He married a Japanese woman. But when he applied for Japanese citizenship, he was turned down. An immigration bureaucrat told him he could not become Japanese unless he adopted a Japanese surname. He refused, explaining that he was rather attached to his name. As a famous businessman, it was part of his brand. But the authorities retorted that no Japanese citizen had ever been called Son, and they weren't going to allow it now.

So Mr. Son went home, where his Japanese wife offered him a solution. She changed her surname to Son. When Mr. Son went back to the immigration authorities and they repeated that there was no precedent for a Japanese person being called Son, Mr. Son asked them to check the records. They found one Japanese Son—his wife. So they relented and gave him a passport.[37]

WHY SPACE IS THE FINAL FRONTIER

Another important American advantage is the country's physical size. Russia and Canada are more spacious, to be sure, but much of their territory is frozen and barely habitable. America is mostly temperate, and huge portions of the center of the country are wide open.

Consider Boise, Idaho. A 25-mile green belt runs through the city. The nearby foothills are latticed with biking trails. The sun shines 300 days a year. Crime is as rare as the colossal steaks.[38] And wherever you live or work, the great outdoors is only a few blocks away. "Life is easy here," says Jinye Huo, a Chinese software engineer in Boise. Her home is four times larger than her old flat in Beijing, and her commute is negligible.[39] She works at Balihoo, a firm that makes marketing software. Mountain bikes hang on hooks near her desk. Many of her colleagues fish or ski before coming to work.

At 3,000 people per square mile, the population density in Boise is less than a twentieth of Manhattan's.[40] Yet although Boise is remote—the nearest big city, Salt Lake City, is 340 miles away—it is no backwater. Since 1978 it has been home to Micron, a large semiconductor firm. (The local potato billionaire, J. R. Simplot, was an early investor, leading to inevitable jokes about the shift from potato chips to microchips.) A cluster of high-tech start-ups has sprouted. Surprisingly, between 2005 and 2007, Idaho generated more patents per worker than any other state.

The population of the Boise-Nampa metro area has nearly doubled in the past two decades, sparking a real-estate bubble. Yet housing is still laughably cheap: $150,000 buys you a spacious house with a garden. In London, $150,000 would not buy you a tiny flat above a pub.

The Internet lets people compare cities and neighborhoods by whatever criteria matter to them: house prices, commuting times, crime rates, the proximity of fly-fishing rivers and so forth. That gives a boost to remote but agreeable locales. Also thanks to the Internet, people can now live far from the madding crowd and yet remain abreast of its ignoble strife. "What Karl Marx called 'the idiocy of rural life' no longer applies," writes Joel Kotkin, a demographer.[41] A brain worker in Boise has the same access to technical and market information as her rival in San Francisco. In her leisure time, she can download the same books and films. She may not have the same choice of avant-garde theater, but that is a sacrifice she may be content to make.

America's hinterland is often mocked. Cosmopolitans dismiss it as "flyover country." Many assume that nothing interesting happens there. Yet as America's population expands, much of the growth will occur where there is space. Mr. Kotkin predicts a resurgence of the heartland as Americans move away from the coasts in search of more room. The same forces will attract immigrants to places that have traditionally been lily-white. The Boise metro area already has a population that is 17 percent ethnic minority, mostly Hispanic or Asian. Restaurants serve Japanese cuisine with an Idaho twist: huge portions.

America's sheer size means that Americans can keep reproducing and welcoming immigrants for the foreseeable future, without their country ever feeling crowded. If the population quadrupled, it would still be only half as crowded as Germany is today, and less than a fiftieth as crowded as Singapore.[42] David Bieter, the mayor of Boise, told me in May 2010 that his city could easily double in size again.[43]

America is not only vast; it is also far more decentralized than other rich countries. In Britain "there's London, London and London," scoffs Mr. Kotkin.[44] Paris, too, is the commercial, financial, political, media and entertainment capital of France. In America, no city dominates, regardless of what New Yorkers may tell you. Not everyone will want to live somewhere like Boise. Young single folk may prefer the dating scene in more crowded cities such as Atlanta or Seattle. When they get hitched and have children, however, they may decide to move elsewhere in search of space. America accommodates all life stages.

FEAR OF FOREIGNERS

Not all Americans think immigration makes their country stronger. Tom Tancredo, a Republican who ran for president in 2008, describes

America's porous borders as a "mortal danger."[45] Pat Buchanan, another former presidential candidate, talks of a "Third World invasion and conquest of America."[46]

Some fret about illegal immigration because they favor the rule of law. I watched President Barack Obama give a speech in New Orleans in October 2009, during which he said: "[W]hen there are people in Mexico City waiting in line and paying their fees and doing everything right, and they are having to wait for years, and then other folks are coming in without waiting in line—that's not fair."[47] But many Americans think their country admits too many legal immigrants, too.

Some fear that foreigners will compete with them for jobs or that they will swamp America's public services. Some worry that the immigrants themselves will be horribly exploited. The argument that stirs the hottest passions, however, is cultural. The late Samuel Huntington, a Harvard academic, argued that Hispanic immigrants, because they are so numerous, will not assimilate. Rather, they threaten to "divide the United States into two peoples, two cultures and two languages" and "[reject] the Anglo-Protestant values that built the American dream."[48]

Such gloom is misplaced. Unlike in Europe, it is extremely hard for an able-bodied adult to subsist on welfare in the United States. So immigrants in America work, which means they are seldom much of a drain on the public purse and have no choice but to assimilate. People who work together need to get on with each other, so they generally do.

Consider the story of Alberto Queiroz, a Mexican who crept across the border in 1994. After a stuffy ride in the trunk of a car, he found his first job in a Chinese-owned clothing factory in Los Angeles. Workers with papers were paid the minimum wage, he recalls. Having none, he had to make do with $2.50 an hour. Though unlawfully stingy, this was much more than he could have earned back home in Mexico.[49]

After two years he moved to North Carolina, a state that was then just starting to become a magnet for Mexicans. He picked blueberries for $5 a box, earning nearly $100, tax-free, for a 12-hour day. But this job lasted only until the harvest ended. So he sought more stable employment, which he eventually found at America's largest hog slaughterhouse.

Smithfield Foods' plant in Tar Heel, North Carolina, turns some 32,000 pigs a day into hams and loins. Its ruthless efficiency horrifies animal-rights activists, but it also makes meat cheaper for Americans. A century ago, food ate up half of Americans' take-home pay; it is now only about one-tenth, and no one gets trichinosis from pork anymore.

But is a slaughterhouse a nice place to work? Back in 2006, I asked the chairman of Smithfield, Joe Luter, to let me have a look around the Tar Heel plant, but he refused for reasons of "biosecurity."[50] In 2004 Human Rights Watch, a New York–based watchdog, issued a paper entitled "Blood, Sweat and Fear" that accused American meat and poultry producers of "systematic human-rights violations." Slaughterhouses are harsh and dangerous places, it said, and illegal immigrants, who form a large chunk of the workforce, find it hard to defy abusive employers. (If they kick up a fuss, they fear being deported.)[51]

Mr. Queiroz takes a more benign view. Yes, the work is hard, he acknowledges. The line goes fast and you have to keep cutting until your hands are exhausted. And yes, it is sometimes dangerous. He says he once saw a coworker lose a leg when he ducked under the disassembly line instead of walking round it. But many occupations are risky: taxi-drivers are 63 times more likely to die on the job than meatpackers.[52]

Mr. Queiroz does not think Smithfield was a bad employer. Wages of more than $10 an hour enabled him to buy a house back in Mexico. Cutting up pigs was easier than picking blueberries, he says, because he did not have to toil under the sun all day. And when he had had enough, he quit and set up a taco stand with his brother. That was in 2001. Now he owns a Mexican restaurant. America, he says, is "the land of opportunity."

Hispanics like Mr. Queiroz are by far the largest group of recent immigrants to the United States. One in five schoolchildren in America is Hispanic, as is one newborn baby in four. "Never before has a minority ethnic group made up so large a share of the youngest Americans," notes a report by the Pew Hispanic Center.[53] The Hispanic population has more than doubled in two decades, from 22.4 million in 1990 to 50.5 million in 2010. Hispanics have overtaken blacks as the largest minority, accounting for 16.3 percent of the population.[54]

These relative newcomers have a fistful of social problems. Young Hispanics are twice as likely as blacks to have dropped out of high school. They are also more likely to become teenage mothers. The Hispanic poverty rate, at 23 percent, is nearly twice as high as that of whites. And Hispanic neighborhoods are disturbingly prone to gang violence. According to the Pew Hispanic Center, 40 percent of Latinos aged 16 to 25 know someone in a gang, and 17 percent report getting into a fight in the past year.

In some states, the Hispanic influx has been sudden and socially destabilizing. North Carolina's Hispanic population has risen tenfold in two decades, from 77,000 in 1990 to 800,000 in 2010.[55] In some areas, the newcomers strain local services. Cindy Evans, director of a county children's clinic in Raleigh, North Carolina, told me that the proportion of her patients who are Hispanic has leapt from perhaps 2 percent in the early 1990s to about 65 percent.[56] The clinic is full of bilingual signs. Next to one, someone has scrawled: "Speak English!"

Many native-born North Carolinians are uneasy about the pace at which their state has become Latinized. Few of the newcomers arrived legally. Antipathy toward illegal immigrants, though widespread, is mostly mild and seldom violent. But it should not be dismissed, since it is politically influential.

It is possible that unskilled immigrants hurt the wages of unskilled locals. George Borjas, the Harvard economist, has estimated that native workers' wages decline by 3 to 4 percent for every 10 percent increase in immigrants with similar skills.[57] But others, such as David Card of the University of California, Berkeley, have found little or no impact.[58] Gianmarco Ottaviano, of the University of Bologna, and Giovanni Peri, of the University of California, Davis, find that nearly 90 percent of native-born American workers actually enjoy higher wages because of immigration.[59]

Even unskilled immigrants can make it easier for the native born to hold down jobs; for example, by looking after their children or elderly parents while they are out working. All immigrants spend money and most pay taxes. The benefits of immigration are often taken for granted. "Americans just assume they can have a pizza delivered for $9," says Federico van Gelderen, a Raleigh-based executive for Univision, a Spanish-language television station.[60]

Is the United States importing a Hispanic underclass, as some claim? I don't think so. Granted, foreign-born Hispanics are less educated and earn less than the average American, but that is hardly surprising, given that so many were until recently Mexican peasants. What matters is whether they are socially mobile, and the evidence suggests that they are. Although by some measures of income and education, the Hispanic average is not improving much, that average is dragged down by a steady influx of poor Mexicans. A better way of gauging progress is to look at intergenerational differences.

Hispanics who migrate to America swiftly become richer. Even the first generation's earnings are much closer to the American norm than to the Mexican one. The median household income for foreign-born Hispanics is $37,200, which is 74 percent of the median for all Americans. For native-born Hispanics, the figure is a more-than-respectable 88 percent.[61]

They tend to assimilate linguistically, too. Most Latino immigrants arrive with a poor grasp of English: among adults only 28 percent speak it fluently. But their children soon pick it up. Among native-born Hispanics, 88 percent are fluent and 38 percent speak nothing but English at home.[62] And Hispanics are steadily climbing the educational ladder. Whereas 51.7 percent of first-generation immigrants are high-school dropouts and only 24.6 percent have attended college, the figures among native-born Hispanics are 22.4 percent and 48.5 percent.[63]

Many Latino children help their less-fluent parents with form-filling, just as other children help their elders navigate the Internet. The parents, in turn, try to infuse their offspring with their work ethic and entrepreneurial spirit: Latinos open new businesses at a rate nearly twice the national norm.[64]

Miguel Lopez, who arrived from Mexico when he was 17, says his children will have a double advantage over him. Not only are they native-born Americans, but they are "native-born" to the information age. In 2006, when we spoke, Mr. Lopez was not doing badly himself: he owns a small window-cleaning company. He woos customers by giving them instant estimates, using satellite photos of their houses online. His business in Raleigh, North Carolina, grosses $150,000 in a good year. With only a high-school education, he says, there is no other country where he could live as well. But he hopes his children will go to college and do something better than washing windows.[65]

Because immigrants have to work, the United States does not have ghettos full of permanently jobless and alienated young immigrants, as does France, for example. This is perhaps why, although America is by some measures a violent country—its murder rate is three times higher than Britain's—its immigrants rarely riot. They are too busy earning a living. America has not in recent years seen anything like the immigrant riots that torched the Paris suburbs in 2005. The closest parallel, the Los Angeles riots of 1992, sprang from the unique grievances of the one large ethnic group whose ancestors did not voluntarily migrate to America: African Americans.

American talk-show hosts sometimes say odious things about illegal immigrants, but no openly xenophobic politician can attract the kind of support that France's Jean-Marie Le Pen did in 2002, or that Austria's Jörg Haider did before he got drunk and killed himself in a car crash. Political rhetoric in America is often heated but almost never leads to actual violence. Ms. Hirsi Ali recalls watching the 2008 vice-presidential debates on television with friends in New York. Her Democratic friends thought Sarah Palin was ghastly. Her Republican chums were nearly as appalled by Joe Biden. Tempers rose so high during the campaign that Ms. Hirsi Ali thought the country might come to blows. But then polling day passed, and it was over. She saw her Republican and Democratic friends eating cupcakes together. Americans get passionate about politics, she observes, but the next day they get on with their lives.

The fear that new immigrants are disagreeably different is hardly new. Mark Krikorian, a scholar who generally opposes immigration, notes that in seventeenth-century Massachusetts, one group of English Protestants (the Puritans) banished another group of English Protestants (the Quakers) and even hanged some of those who returned. Benjamin Franklin doubted that German immigrants would ever assimilate. "Why should the Palatine Boors be suffered to swarm into our settlements?" he asked, adding that they "will never adopt our Language or Customs."[66]

Today, there are 50 million Americans of German descent, few of whom still speak German. Indeed, they have intermingled and intermarried so much that they are barely noticeable as a separate group. They have assimilated. America has changed them and, just as crucially, they have changed America. Americans have adopted some of their more agreeable customs, such as drinking clear beer and watching sports on the weekend. German Americans have also helped introduce to America a wealth of ideas about medicine, engineering and philosophy. Call it the melting pot, the salad bowl or what you will—it still tastes good.

The doomsayers about immigration have always been wrong. It is a fair bet that they are wrong now. The United States has lost none of its capacity to absorb newcomers. A recent survey by Public Agenda asked immigrants in America how long it took them to feel comfortable and "part of the community." Some 77 percent said it took less than five years. Only 5 percent said they never felt like they fit in.[67] Contrast that with the 58 percent of people of Turkish descent in Germany who say they feel unwelcome.[68]

Immigration keeps America young, strong and dynamic. The country will continue to grow and thrive for the simple reason that people want to live there. "The populations of Europe, Russia and Japan are declining, and those of China and India are leveling off. The United States alone among great powers will be increasing its share of world population over time," predicts Michael Lind of the New America Foundation. That means the United States could remain the preeminent nation for longer than many people expect. "Relying on the import of money, workers, and brains," writes Mr. Lind, America is "a Ponzi scheme that works."[69]

8

THE HUB OF
THE WORLD

WHY AMERICA WILL REMAIN
NUMBER ONE

America's global network is unlike any other. The United States does not have much of a diaspora, since native-born Americans seldom emigrate permanently. But since the country has the world's largest stock of immigrants, it can plug into all the world's tribal and religious networks.

In the old days, European royal families cemented alliances by marrying, say, an Austrian princess to the French dauphin. Americans today do something similar but far more democratic and wonderful. Thanks to immigration, America enjoys intimate ties with every other culture. America is polygamously "married" to every other nation.

Mass immigration places the United States at the center of a global web of interconnection. It provides the country with legions of unofficial ambassadors, deal brokers, recruiters and boosters. Immigrants not only bring the best ideas from around the world to American shores; they also serve as a conduit for spreading American ideas and ideals back to their homelands, thus increasing the United States' soft power.

In earlier chapters, I described how ethnic networks speed the flow of ideas. Clever thoughts speed in and out of China when Chinese geeks in Beijing chat with Chinese geeks overseas. Insights flow back and forth between São Paulo and Pasadena when Brazilian scientists email their pals at Caltech. Since America is plugged into all these networks, a disproportionate share of the world's good ideas flow through it.

The process by which ideas are formed is mysterious, at least to me. So I asked Nathan Myhrvold, a former chief technology officer of Microsoft, to have a crack at explaining it. He is a playful, bearded fellow with the manner of an overgrown schoolboy who giggles when he describes "really cool" ideas. He went to college at the age of 14, finished a PhD in theoretical and mathematical physics in his early 20s and studied under the superstar cosmologist Stephen Hawking at Cambridge. He now runs a firm called Intellectual Ventures (IV) that seeks to profit from inventions.

"Invention is the closest thing to magic we have," he gushes. When trying to generate new ideas, "you have to make sure people feel OK about saying crazy things."[1]

Mr. Myhrvold convenes "invention sessions" with thinkers from a variety of fields. He puts them in a room with gallons of coffee and lets them bounce ideas around. Assistants record the conversation and help it along by projecting relevant scientific papers onto a screen. Mr. Myhrvold takes part with gusto. His company has pioneered technologies both varied and ambitious, from a hospital bed that changes shape to fit the patient's body to a new type of nuclear power station.

No idea is too outrageous to receive a hearing. One scientist suggested building a laser beam to kill malarial mosquitoes. Everyone laughed and said that it would cost too much. But when they thought about it, they realized that it might not. Lasers are much cheaper than they used to be, thanks to Blu-ray disc players. Image sensors to spot the mosquito are cheaper, too, thanks to digital cameras. Signal processors to relay that information are cheaper, thanks to mobile phones. And cheap technology to hit tiny targets with a laser beam already exists in laser printers. "We put all these pieces together, and realized we could do it," says Mr. Myhrvold. A working prototype was built in

2008. When I spoke to him in late 2010, IV was looking for a partner to manufacture it.

Mr. Myhrvold's firm is based near Seattle but flies in scientists from far and wide for invention sessions. It has also set up offices in emerging technology hotspots, such as Bangalore, Beijing, Seoul and Singapore. I was intrigued to know how ideas flowed from these spokes to the American hub, so in January 2011 I paid a visit to the Bangalore office.

I was shown around by Monish Suvarna, the president of IV India. He told me about the wide range of exciting projects the firm was working on in India. For example, Dr. Yamuna Krishnan, of India's National Centre for Biological Sciences, had invented a DNA nanomachine to deliver drugs to precisely the right spot in a patient's body. IV had partnered with her to develop it.

To staff its Bangalore office, IV drew heavily on the Indian diaspora. Mr. Suvarna, a software engineer, had worked for a number of high-tech firms in America, including the one that designed the voice synthesizer that Stephen Hawking (who has motor neuron disease) uses to talk. In 2007, however, Mr. Suvarna wanted to go home to India, because his father was ill. IV found him through the grapevine—someone there knew Mr. Suvarna's brother, a senior staffer at Google. When they offered Mr. Suvarna the chance to start an outpost in Bangalore, he seized it with both hands.

The IV team in Bangalore is small: around 20 people, including a dozen scientists. Most of the scientists are Indians who have worked or studied in the United States, or worked for an American firm in India. They are an impressive bunch—a former Intel technologist who now looks at ideas related to semiconductors and material sciences, a biotech expert who used to work for Morgan Stanley in Singapore, a patent lawyer who used to practice in the United States and so on.

India has a huge reservoir of scientific expertise, but tapping into it requires a feel for the local culture. "It's more about relationships than money in India," says Mr. Suvarna. "People will work with you because they know and trust you, not just because you are offering to pay them. They are more concerned that you will nurture their idea properly than that you will pay them well. So IV India had to build a web of relationships from scratch. That would have been very hard if we weren't run by Indians."[2]

Mr. Myhrvold's signature invention sessions are different in India. In the United States, experts are happy to get together and throw out crazy ideas until something sticks, but in India, they are more cautious. America is unusually tolerant of failure—people assume that you learn from your mistakes. In India, professors at prestigious universities worry that if they advance an idea that turns out to be no good, it will harm their reputation. So they like to test their ideas for a while before they approach IV.

"When we came here, people doubted we'd find [many] ideas," says Mr. Suvarna. Nathan Myhrvold guessed, however, that if IV gave Indian innovators the same legal and technical support they could find in America, they would achieve similar results. He was right—IV India helped Indian inventors file more than 200 patents in three years.[3]

One arresting example involves lasers (again!) and food. IV was looking for a way to preserve food without using packaging that includes bisphenol A (BPA), a chemical that may have side effects. (Some countries have banned its use in baby bottles.) IV posed the question "Can you preserve food without using BPA?" to some 5,000 scientists and inventors worldwide, including 1,200 in India. The staff at IV India activated their personal networks and their relationships with Indian universities to make sure that as many clever ears as possible heard the challenge. A promising answer came from a professor at Calcutta University, Dr. Anjan DasGupta, and a student of his.

Dr. DasGupta's idea was that radiation from low-intensity red lasers could prolong the shelf life of foods and vaccines. "We said 'OK, but to get a good patent on this idea, you need to do the following extra experiments,'" recalls Mr. Suvarna. Dr. DasGupta did as he was advised, and IV then helped him patent the idea.

During the collaboration, it emerged that red lasers could also be used to preserve unpasteurized milk, an unexpected bonus. Indians love milk—in rural areas, they will bring the cow to your house and milk it in front of you. But this is not practical in cities. And India's "cold chain" is unreliable—that is, you can never be sure that the milk you buy has been refrigerated all the way from farm to shop—so urbanites struggle to get fresh, safe milk. Many Indians think that pasteurizing milk spoils the taste, so the fact that red lasers can preserve milk without altering the flavor at all means the invention could be lucrative. IV certainly hopes so.

AMERICA'S WORLD WIDE WEB OF INVENTION

Until recently, America's technological preeminence was based on a simple formula: the world's best brains came to the United States. Some came because their own governments were wicked and stupid enough to persecute them: think of the Jewish physicists who fled Nazi Germany. More came because America was such a congenial place to conduct their research. Debate is free. Academics are well paid. And the process by which science is turned into new technologies— the country's scientific "ecosystem," if you will—is the world's most sophisticated. Universities work hand in glove with industry. Students and professors often set up companies to commercialize their ideas. Venture capitalists provide investment and advice.

This model still works pretty well. Migrants make up about half of the workers in the United States with science or engineering qualifications, and accounted for two-thirds of the growth in that talent pool between 1995 and 2006. Half of the bosses of Silicon Valley start-ups in 2005 were migrants, and foreign-born workers at America's most innovative firms file most of the patents: 72 percent at Qualcomm, 65 percent at Merck, 64 percent at General Electric and 60 percent at Cisco.[4]

On its own, however, the old model is no longer good enough. Other countries that were once scientific backwaters—such as China and India—are at last shaping up. In 1990 the "old" rich countries— North America, Europe and Japan—accounted for more than 95 percent of the world's scientific research, according to the United Nations. By 2007 that had fallen to 76 percent. China probably has more scientists than America now—both had about 1.5 million that same year.[5]

American scientists, however, are more productive. They wrote 28 percent of the published scientific papers in the world in 2007, against China's 10 percent, though the Chinese share had doubled since 2002. The quality of American papers is also higher: the best crude measure of this is the number of times a paper is cited by other scientists, and the average American paper is cited three times more often than the average Chinese one.[6]

Some reports of China's scientific rise are misleading. For example, according to Thomson Reuters, the number of patents filed in China grew by a staggering 26 percent a year between 2003 and 2009, against America's more modest 6 percent.[7] Thomson predicted that China would overtake America as the world's most prolific patent-generator in 2011.

That will be hailed as a triumph for China. But not every patent filed there represents an original or useful idea. Bureaucrats in Chinese patent offices are paid more if they register more patents. "That must tempt them to say yes to ideas of dubious originality," suggests my colleague Tom Easton. The Chinese government offers generous financial incentives to companies that file patents, making it worthwhile to patent worthless ideas. "Patents are easy to file, but gems are hard to find in a mountain of junk," says Tony Chen, a patent attorney in Shanghai.[8]

China really is becoming more innovative, but the picture is more nuanced than the headlines imply. The best Chinese ideas are the ones that travel. These are disproportionately generated through collaboration with scientists in other countries. For example, a Chinese study done in collaboration with American scientists is cited more than three times as often as the average domestically produced study.[9]

Cross border scientific collaboration is growing rapidly more common. A 2011 study by the Royal Society, a British scientific club once led by Sir Isaac Newton, found that the proportion of papers published in scientific journals that were the result of such collaboration has risen from 25 percent to 35 percent since the mid-1990s. And collaborative papers are far more likely to be cited by other scientists.[10]

America is well placed to exploit the trend toward greater collaboration—a high proportion of the best scientists of every ethnicity live in or have spent time there. Those who reside in America stay in touch with their brightest peers back home. Those who work in America for a while and then return home keep in touch with their peers in America. As migrants move in and out of American universities and technology firms, they create a web of ties that puts the United States at the center of the global scientific conversation.

The Royal Society's findings bear this out. The report notes that collaboration is often driven by linguistic or historical ties—scientists from Francophone Africa are especially likely to work with scientists in France, for example. Collaboration among developing countries is growing fast, but it is still dwarfed by the links between developing countries and rich ones—only 5 percent of African biomedical research papers are the result of partnerships between African countries, while 77 percent are the result of collaboration with a rich country.[11]

Scientists continue to collaborate even when their governments are at each other's throats. The number of papers coauthored by American and Iranian scientists, for example, rose 472 percent between 1996 and 2002 and 2004 and 2008.[12]

Overall, "the dominant role of the USA is striking," the Royal Society's authors observe. It accounts for 17 percent of internationally collaborative papers, far more than any other nation. It collaborates with nearly everyone—so much so that no country gets more than a 5 percent share of the United States' total output.[13]

Some Americans worry that when brainy immigrants flock to America, they grab tech jobs that might otherwise have gone to Americans. This is unlikely. The number of tech jobs is not fixed. And in fact, researchers William Kerr and William Lincoln have found that a rise in the number of skilled immigrants may actually stimulate native-born scientists to be more productive. When an American city attracts more foreigners with H-1B visas (which are given only to those with skills that are in short supply), the number of patents filed by locals rises.[14]

AMERICA'S WORLD WIDE WEB OF TRUST

As the world's favorite destination for migrants, the United States is also plugged into networks that link businesspeople to one another. America's ability to tap into all these networks gives it a competitive advantage. A good example is the story of Andres Ruzo, an entrepreneur who describes himself as "Peruvian by birth; Texan by choice." He moved to America when he was 19 to study engineering. He then founded a telecommunication business near Dallas. One company he started, Link America, builds mobile networks for police, firefighters and emergency services; another, ITS Infocom, manages communications networks for large companies. A network is like a baby, he told me: "It needs to be monitored. It needs to be fed. It needs to be cleaned. If not, it breaks down."[15]

Several years ago, Mr. Ruzo was looking to expand into Latin America. He needed a partner. He stumbled upon one through a religious network. Mr. Ruzo is a devout member of the Christian Life Movement, a lay Catholic organization. A friend of his, a priest in Costa Rica, introduced him to another IT entrepreneur and fellow Catholic, Vladimir Vargas Esquivel, who was based in Costa Rica and looking to expand northward. It was a perfect fit. And because of the way they were introduced—by a priest they both respected—both men felt they could trust the other. ITS Infocom now operates in ten countries and generates tens of millions of dollars in annual sales.

According to Mr. Ruzo, "Relationships are critical." In America, he says, you do business first, then become friends. In Peru, you become friends first and then you do business. "I can Google any CEO and find his contact information," he points out, "but that won't lead to a relationship. It's about trust. You will not buy a car from someone you don't trust."

Mr. Ruzo is bullish about the opportunities for expanding business between Latin America and the United States. The two places are in the same time zone. American firms can benefit from the lower cost of labor in Latin America. Latin American firms can benefit from the wealth and technology of their northern neighbor. Mr. Ruzo is trying to build a company that draws on the best of both traditions. In a way, he explains, "we're trying to Americanize South and Central America: to bring the culture of performance and results and speed and punctuality and quality and reliability to Latin America." At the same time, he thinks American firms can use Costa Rica as a base from which to serve Latin American markets. Costa Ricans have one of the most easily understood accents in Latin America, he says, so it makes sense to locate Spanish-language call centers there. Both Mr. Ruzo and Mr. Vargas Esquivel want their business to go global. So although they natter to each other in Spanish, they insist that the firm's official language must be English.

Immigrant networks promote business within the United States, too. For example, Sanjaya Kumar, an Indian doctor, arrived in America in 1992. He had grown up in Nigeria as part of the sizable Indian diaspora in the former British colony, and had gone to work in the United Kingdom for a while. But he found the horizons too narrow there, so he moved to the United States.

He studied public health at the University of Massachusetts Amherst and worked for a while for IBM, where he specialized in clinical informatics. He was shocked by how poorly and slowly information moves through the health-care system. He was also shocked by how many Americans die from preventable medical mistakes—perhaps 100,000 a year.[16]

In 1997, Dr. Kumar founded a software firm called Quantros, in Louisiana, to develop ways to help prevent such mistakes. He needed cash and advice to commercialize his ideas, so he turned to a network of ethnic Indian businesspeople called the Indus Entrepreneurs (TiE). He met an Indian American venture capitalist, Vish Mishra, at a TiE conference in California. Mr. Mishra advised him to move to Silicon Valley, where it would be easier to recruit bright people. "His contribution was invaluable. He groomed our team," recalls Dr. Kumar.

Today Quantros sells its services to nearly 2,000 American hospitals. The firm's engineers are mostly ethnic Indian, but the rest of the staff are mostly not. The company is now starting to expand into India, too. Again, Dr. Kumar found a way in via a personal introduction—one of his Indian American executives had attended college in Australia with another ethnic Indian who now runs a small outsourcing firm in India.[17]

Ethnic networks have drawbacks. If they are a means of excluding outsiders, they can be stultifying. The most successful ones are the most open. AnnaLee Saxenian, the Berkeley professor who has spent decades studying the immigrant networks in Silicon Valley, observes that immigrants manage to be part both of the Valley's social networks and also of their own ethnic networks that link them back to the countries where they or their parents were born.[18]

TiE, the organization that brought Mr. Mishra and Dr. Kumar together, is one of several US-based groups that successfully turn ethnic links into business networks. It started in Silicon Valley and now has a global membership of 13,000 in 13 countries. It has helped to set up firms worth an impressive $200 billion.[19] The combination of immigrant get-up-and-go with immigrant network-building helps to explain why immigrants in America tend to be more entrepreneurial than the native born. And the proportion of American entrepreneurs who are immigrants is rising: from 13.4 percent of the total in 1996 to 29.5 percent in 2010.[20]

Immigrants perform another essential role as employees of American companies. Their skills, contacts and knowledge are especially useful for multinational firms planning to expand overseas. This matters—multinationals are the most dynamic part of the American economy. Even though only 1 percent of American companies are multinational, these firms generated 27 percent of private-sector economic output in 2007. They account for 31 percent of America's economic growth since 1990 and 41 percent of the improvement in labor productivity.[21]

A WORLD WIDE WEB OF INFLUENCE

Currently, America's defense budget is not merely the biggest in the world; it is bigger than the next 45 biggest-spending countries combined.[22] The United States is also the only nation that can project significant military power anywhere on Earth. But its military hegemony won't last forever. China is catching up fast. North Korea has the bomb, and Iran may soon follow suit. In the future America's global sway will depend less on the threat of force and more on soft power. Fortunately, its charms are more potent than its arms. "Conventional wisdom holds that the state with the largest army prevails, but in the information age, the state (or the nonstate actor) with the best story may sometimes win," argues Joseph Nye, the Harvard professor who coined the phrase "soft power."[23]

America's story is an inspiring one: people from anywhere can roll up, become American and pursue happiness in any way they choose. Granted, Americans often fail to live up to their ideals. Immigrants are sometimes mistreated at the border. Neighborhoods are sometimes less than welcoming. Liberty is compromised when the United States holds prisoners in legal limbo in Guantanamo Bay. Nonetheless, America's story retains immense power because it is essentially true.

Many Americans fret that their nation is losing soft power, especially given the huge blow dealt to the reputation of American-style capitalism by the financial crisis of 2008. A newly confident China is pumping money into a global propaganda machine: $8.9 billion in 2009–10 alone. Since 2004 China has built hundreds of cultural centers, called Confucius Institutes, in foreign cities to promote Chinese culture and to encourage foreigners to learn Chinese. Beijing also funds a 24-hour English-language radio station and a cable TV news channel that aims to promote the Chinese government's view of world affairs.[24]

The Chinese government is anxious to amass soft power. It is "an important indicator of comprehensive national strength," says the *People's Daily*, a Communist Party mouthpiece. For this reason, "China needs to take all kinds of measures to educate the world about China so they can love it."[25]

American pundits reacted with alarm when Xinhua, the Chinese state news agency, broke ground on a gleaming new American headquarters in New York's Times Square, even as Voice of America, the nearest American equivalent, broached the idea of cutting its Chinese-language news service. "We are in an information war, and we are losing that war," lamented Hillary Clinton, US Secretary of State.[26]

Really?

People admire China's ancient culture. They are also keen to learn how the country has managed to grow so fast in recent years. Politicians in some countries have swallowed the line that the key to China's boom is authoritarianism. African autocrats make pilgrimages to Beijing to find justifications for their own love of state controls and their own disinclination to honor their people's civil rights. China's story is undoubtedly appealing to elites who distrust democracy.

But does it appeal to ordinary folk? Stripped of polite evasions, China's story goes something like this: "We're the world's biggest country. After a few unfortunate centuries of backwardness, we're reclaiming our rightful position as the world's most powerful nation, too. You can do business with us, but you can't join us. If you don't like it, tough."

We must not dismiss the rise of China's soft power, but authoritarian states are seldom much good at gentle persuasion. Consider how Xinhua presents the news. Here are the top English-language foreign stories on its website on April 18, 2011. From Nigeria, where an election had just taken place, the main news was that a riot had broken out in Kaduna state and at least two churches had been burned. In Afghanistan, a suicide bomber attacked the defense ministry. And in Iran, "President Mahmoud Ahmadinejad hailed the performance and achievements of the country's army in the past years as the country celebrated the national Army Day on Monday . . . Ahmadinejad also criticized the Western powers for what he called an interference in the domestic affairs of the regional countries."

The top three stories about China that day were, in order of prominence, "Chinese Premier, Ukrainian PM, Hold Talks on Bilateral Ties"; "China, New Zealand Vow to Foster Ties, Step Up Trade Cooperation"; and "Chinese Premier Meets Singapore's Senior Minister on Bilateral Ties."[27]

All these stories were obviously written by people for whom English is a distant second language. None contains vivid reportage, wit or even much information. Few make much effort to disguise their propagandizing purpose. The Nigerian dispatch does not explicitly say that democracy means having your house burned down, but Xinhua would clearly like you to draw that conclusion. Meanwhile, the top stories about China are so boring that even the participants in those bilateral talks probably did not read them.

That day, the most-searched subject on the Xinhua website was a week-old story about the US Department of State's annual report on human rights around the world, which Xinhua describes as an attempt to defame China. Without mentioning any of the specific abuses catalogued in the report, the story said only that the United States has human-rights problems of its own (though it does not say what they are) and that it criticizes China for (unspecified) political reasons.[28]

It is obvious to any adult that this "news" report is aimed at suppressing information, not disseminating it. Indeed, it is obvious to a child. I ran it past my nine-year-old son and he immediately spotted what was missing. "They haven't said anything about what they [the Chinese government] have done," he said. "You know, the torture and prisons and stuff."

Journalists in China have to please the party, not their audience. Until that is no longer true, Xinhua cannot hope to be trusted like CNN or Al-Jazeera. Chinese artists, too, are free only to express themselves in ways that don't annoy the government. Ai Weiwei, an artist who frequently annoys the government by speaking up for human rights, was arrested and held for three months in 2011 for "tax evasion."[29] Geoff Dyer of the *Financial Times* reported that when Zhang Yimou, an acclaimed Chinese film director, was asked why his films were always set in the past, "he said that films about contemporary China would be neutered by the censors. And this is from the artist who is the favorite of the authorities."[30]

For the record, I don't think Congress should cut funding for the Voice of America. But it is hardly the linchpin of American soft power; the private media matter far more. Foreigners devour American cultural offerings from the *Harvard Business Review* to *Kung Fu Panda*. Hollywood movies and television programs are powerful shapers of global opinion about America precisely because they are not trying to convince anyone of anything. Consider the propaganda value of a single episode of *The Simpsons*, a cartoon by Matt Groening about life in a fictional American town called Springfield. "Two Cars in Every Garage and Three Eyes on Every Fish" (which originally aired in 1990 and has been repeated ever since) lampoons both the greed of American capitalism and the corruption of American politics. Montgomery Burns, the owner of a poorly maintained nuclear power station, tries to bribe a safety inspector.

> Burns: Oh look! Some careless person has left thousands and thousands of dollars just lying here on my coffee table. [*Talking to his assistant*] Uh, Smithers, why don't we leave the room and hopefully, when we return, the pile of money will be gone. [*He leaves and returns a few moments later.*] D'oh, look Smithers, the money and a very stupid man are still here.
> Inspector: Burns, if I didn't know better, I'd think you were trying to bribe me.
> Burns: Is there some confusion about this? Take it! Take it! Take it, you poor schmo!

Having failed to bribe his way around the rules, Mr. Burns decides to run for governor so he can change them. He hires a muckraker, a character assassin and a "garbologist" to smear his opponent. To create the illusion that he is in touch with the common man, he arranges to be filmed having dinner with a lowly employee, Homer Simpson, who accepts because he doesn't want to lose his job. Mr. Burns takes scripted questions from the family over dinner, including this one from Homer's eight-year-old daughter:

> Lisa Simpson: Mr. Burns, your campaign seems to have the momentum of a runaway freight train. Why are you so popular?
> Burns: Ooh, a tough question, but a fair one. Lisa, there's no single answer. Some voters respond to my integrity, others are more impressed by my incorruptibility.

And so on. For a moment, it seems that this odious man will win the election. But Homer's wife, Marge, who despises Mr. Burns, saves the day by serving him a three-eyed fish from the polluted river by his power plant. Mr. Burns is filmed spitting it out. His campaign collapses.

This cartoon makes all the criticisms of America that its worst enemies might, yet the impression it creates is of a country where working-class families live in spacious homes with big backyards, where good eventually triumphs over evil and where witty scriptwriters from anywhere on Earth can say what they like about anyone. The show repeatedly mocks even the giant TV corporation that broadcasts it: Rupert Murdoch's Fox.

Not everyone likes *The Simpsons*. (My beloved English mother-in-law finds it grotesque.) But tens of millions of people watch it, and it is only one show among many. Americans churn out movies, television series, books, blogs, magazines, newspapers, cartoons, video games and music to suit nearly every taste. Big movies make more money abroad than at home these days, so Hollywood studios strain every creative muscle to please foreign audiences. Since it is a competitive industry with no agenda besides making money, it consistently produces hits.[31]

The media require freedom and openness to thrive, and the United States has both. If you don't like the liberal slant of the *New York Times,* you can read the more conservative *Wall Street Journal.* If you think both papers too sober, you can try the Drudge Report, the Huffington Post, or any of thousands of other uncensored sources of news.

By and large, the American media are meritocratic. It helps if your daddy owns a movie studio, of course. But in most cases, a talented foreigner has as much chance of breaking in as a native-born American. Hollywood studios have no compunction about casting foreigners even as all-American superheroes, such as Batman (Christian Bale, a Welshman) or Superman (Henry Cavill, an Englishman).[32] Legions of wannabes flock to Los Angeles and New York from every part of the world in the hope of making it. From Charlie Chaplin and Alfred Hitchcock to Arnold Schwarzenegger and M. Night Shyamalan, immigrants have always been an essential part of Hollywood's dynamism. Historically, they have won a disproportionate share of best-director Oscars.[33]

In some ways, the American media paint too rosy a picture of life in America. Most Americans are less rich and less beautiful than the characters in such TV shows as *Desperate Housewives* or *Sex and the City*. But by devouring its popular culture, foreigners do gain some accurate insights into American society. They see a country where, despite periodic flare-ups, people of different races get along reasonably well.

The 2004 movie *Harold and Kumar Go to White Castle*, for example, can be seen as a crass glorification of drug use, foul language and sexual promiscuity. Or it can be seen as a hilarious buddy movie wherein the fact that one buddy is Korean American and the other is Indian American barely matters. Kal Penn, the actor who plays Kumar, surely promotes America more effectively in his movies than he does as an associate director in the Office of Public Engagement in the White House, a job he took because he is a fervent fan of Barack Obama.[34]

American culture is not universal. People from the most puritanical parts of the world may find *Sex and the City* repulsive; never mind the output of America's porn industry. Many foreigners are also strangely immune to the charms of country music.* But at its best, American culture exemplifies values that are as close to universal as

---

* A countryphobic Australian friend of mine tells this joke: Why is a banjo better than a ukulele? Answer: because it burns quicker.

you can get in a world that includes both the Dalai Lama and Vladimir Putin. Most people in most countries would like to live their lives as they please.

Notions of freedom and possibility run deep in American pop culture. Martha Bayles, a cultural critic at Boston College, explained to me that young people from traditional societies watch *Friends* and see the possibility of greater independence, of living without constant oversight by older relatives.[35] American-style musical talent shows, meanwhile, spread the meritocratic ideal. Free competition is "an intoxicating idea," says Ms. Bayles, and in some countries may be subversive. *Super Girls,* a Chinese knockoff of *Pop Idol,** was cancelled because the Chinese government didn't like to see its subjects getting so excited about voting. (The official excuse was that the show was "poison" for young people: "*Super Girls* is certainly the choice of the market," admitted a cultural commissar, "but we can't have working people reveling all day in low culture."[36])

Nothing an authoritarian regime can produce is remotely as attractive as what comes out of Hollywood. Granted, Beijing hosted a flawless Olympic Games in 2008, and the opening ceremony was visually impressive. But mostly what it proved was that the Chinese government can make people march, dance and set off fireworks with military precision—and that its security forces were prepared to lock up truckloads of dissidents to prevent them from spoiling the show.

Perhaps America's most impregnable cultural advantage springs from sheer luck. The fact that English was the most widely spoken language when the information age began makes it likely that it will remain the global lingua franca. In business, science, politics, pop culture and social networking, no other language opens so many doors. The more people speak it, the greater the benefits of understanding it, so the more people will learn it. This feedback loop is unlikely to break anytime soon. And that will enhance America's influence, because it will ensure that its culture remains more accessible than any other.

---

* An American show adapted from a British one that is itself an adaptation of an old American format.

Soft power, of course, can be wielded for good or ill. Stalin had plenty of it; so does al-Qaeda. "It is not necessarily better to twist minds than to twist arms," observes Mr. Nye.[37]

Some foreigners fear that American voices foster empty materialism or tempt children to subsist on junk food. To me, the most disquieting strain in American popular culture is the glorification of violence in some American movies and songs. Some people defend misogynistic American rap as "social commentary," but some fans clearly think it cool to copy rappers who refer to women as "bitches." And some people take mindless action films literally, as I discovered while covering a doomed rebellion in Namibia in 1999, in which the rebels had fired themselves up by watching *Rambo* videos.[38]

Another worrying example is the improbable drama series *24*, in which secret agent Jack Bauer (played by Kiefer Sutherland) repeatedly saves America from terrorist attacks by torturing information out of terrorists. I confess I enjoyed the show. But, as Ms. Bayles points out, it popularizes the notion that American presidents just pick up the phone and have people murdered.[39] It also presents torture as a nearly foolproof way to extract life-saving information. Being a fictional character, Jack Bauer never tortures the wrong guy or extracts a false clue. This is a dangerous message, to put it mildly.

On balance, however, the United States exports more enlightened ideas than vicious ones, as the millions of foreigners who attend American universities can attest.

A WORLD WIDE WEB OF LEARNING

By a popular Chinese ranking, compiled by Shanghai's Jiao Tong University, 17 of the world's leading 20 universities are American.[40] Harvard alone has won more science Nobels than all but three countries (the United States, Germany and the United Kingdom).

Immigration constantly reinvigorates the American academe. American universities are the world's greatest largely because they attract the best minds from all over the world. And they attract the best minds because they are the best.

Many world leaders were educated in the United States. By one recent count, 46 current heads of government and 165 former heads of government attended American universities.[41] Alumni of Harvard's Kennedy School of Government alone include the secretary-general of the United Nations, the president of the World Bank, the head of China's Organization Department (China's top civil servant), the prime minister of Singapore and the current presidents of Mexico, Mongolia, Liberia and Colombia, not to mention the founder of the World Economic Forum.*

Nearly half of the students at the Kennedy School are foreign. They are never told what to think. Instead, they hear a range of views on the appropriate relationship between governments, markets and citizens, says Dean David Ellwood. Students are exposed to arguments for and against democracy. They see the problems associated with short election cycles and extreme partisanship, Mr. Ellwood told me, but also the benefits of accountability.[42]

It is hard to spend time at an American university without learning something about America. Qian Ning, the son of China's former foreign minister, was educated at the University of Michigan. He wrote afterward that his experiences in America made him "see that there are alternative ways for China to develop and for us to lead our personal lives. Being in the United States made us realize that things in China can be different."[43]

Carol Atkinson, of Vanderbilt University, concurs. "Research has consistently shown that exchange students return home with a more positive view of the country in which they studied and the people with whom they interacted. Frequently after returning home, they try to use the knowledge gained during their time abroad to improve the situation in their home country," she observes.[44]

This is probably also true of foreigners who attend American universities in their home countries or work for American employers. For example, Wael Ghonim, a young Egyptian Google executive who attended the American University in Cairo, played an influential role in the peaceful overthrow of Egypt's longtime despot, Hosni Mubarak, in February 2011.[45]

---

* Ban Ki-Moon, Robert Zoellick, Li Yuanchao, Lee Hsien Loong, Felipe Calderon, Tsakhiagiin Elbegdorj, Ellen Johnson-Sirleaf, Juan Manuel Santos and Klaus Schwab, respectively.

All told, the United States hosts 20 percent of the world's overseas students, more than any other country. Its lead is slipping (the figure was 28 percent in 2001[46]), but it remains huge at the top. Two-thirds of postgraduates who study abroad choose America. The majority of fellows and PhD candidates in the hard sciences are foreign: 65 percent in computing and economics, 56 percent in physics and 55 percent in math, notes Ben Wildavsky in *The Great Brain Race: How Global Universities Are Shaping the World.*[47]

French universities are also a popular destination for foreign students, but they are not nearly as global as their American rivals. Most of the foreign students they attract come either from Europe or from former French colonies.[48] The best American universities have more global alumni networks. A graduate of the prestigious École nationale d'administration in Paris will find fellow *énarques* in every part of the French establishment. A Stanford graduate can find other influential Stanford alums all over the world.

Great universities enhance American soft power. The Massachusetts Institute of Technology (MIT), for example, was founded in 1861 in Cambridge to accelerate the country's industrialization, but now promotes both pure science and entrepreneurial capitalism worldwide. Its staff and students come from far and wide. They attract funding from, and conduct research with, companies from more or less everywhere. They have also set up a prodigious number of their own firms. A 2009 study by the Kauffman Foundation estimated that MIT alumni had founded 25,800 companies that were still active, employing 3.3 million people and generating annual sales of $2 trillion.[49] "It's a very entrepreneurial culture," Susan Hockfield, MIT's president, told me.[50]

About 30 percent of MIT's foreign students go on to found companies, slightly more than half of which are based stateside. (The rest are usually in the student's home country.) In either case, these foreign students are contributing to the American economy or spreading American-style enterprise to their homelands.[51]

As well as generating knowledge, MIT disseminates it. Nearly all of the university's course materials, from texts to videos to lectures, are available online for free. You can read the simplified "Highlights for High School" or walk yourself through a whole course. Since the service began in 2002, some 70 million people have used it—roughly

7,000 times the number of students currently attending MIT. Half of the users are outside the United States. (The teenage children of Srikanth Nadhamuni, the Indian software whiz we met in Chapter 4, swear by it.) Where Internet speeds are slow, as in Africa, MIT sends memory sticks containing course materials via post to local servers.

The university operates a raft of projects and joint ventures abroad. Two foreign-born MIT economists—Esther Duflo, arguably the best of her generation from France, and the brilliant Abhijit Banerjee, of India—run a "poverty action lab" that tries to figure out what works and what doesn't in the fight against poverty. Their insight was that randomized controlled trials are the best way of assessing antipoverty programs. Their experiments in India and Africa have shown, among other things, that schools can combat the problem of teachers who go AWOL by giving each one a camera and making his pay depend on photographic proof that he showed up to work every day.[52]

In November 2010 I visited some of MIT's joint ventures with Tsinghua University in Beijing. Tsinghua is probably China's best university—both Hu Jintao and Xi Jinping went there—but its administrators know it has plenty to learn. It runs a joint MBA program, where up-and-coming Chinese entrepreneurs learn how to use data and evaluate the ethics of a business decision. "The MIT collaboration is very influential," says Pearl Mao, the program's director. Many students, she observes, "have never before thought systematically about dynamic, changing systems," such as companies or industries in flux.[53]

SOFT POWER AND DIPLOMACY

It is not easy for a superpower to be loved. Many people envy wealth and power. If you act as the world's policeman, you will inevitably kill innocents, thereby incurring the wrath of their friends, relatives and coreligionists. If you fail to solve the world's problems, you will be blamed for that, too. The United States is routinely castigated, for example, for failing to make peace between the Israelis and Palestinians, as if this were a simple task.

Given that starting point, America does pretty well. A poll of 29,000 people for the BBC World Service in 2010 found that American influence was viewed positively by 20 of 28 countries. This was a big improvement on the result from 2008, for which the BBC gave President Obama the credit.[54] This is probably correct. Whatever you think of Mr. Obama's policies, his election showed that Americans are willing to pick as their leader the son of a black African Muslim who grew up partly in Indonesia. This has done wonders for America's image abroad.

After the president's first year in office, Simon Anholt, an analyst, estimated the value of the "Obama effect" on America's global "brand" at $2.1 trillion. Each year, Mr. Anholt commissions a poll of 20,000 to 40,000 people to find out how much they admire various countries' citizens, culture, exports, governance, human-rights record and so on. He finds that admiration in one area often translates (illogically) into admiration in others. When George W. Bush was president, foreigners expressed less positive views of American goods, services and even the landscape.

Under President Obama, he found, America is once again the most admired country in the world, after slipping to seventh place in 2008. Employing the same tools that consultants use to value brands such as Coca-Cola or Sony, he guesses that the value of "Brand America" has risen from $9.7 trillion to $11.8 trillion. Writing in *Foreign Policy* magazine, Mr. Anholt called this "a pretty good first year."[55]

Immigration ensures that the picture America presents to the world includes at least some faces that resemble more or less everyone. Indians look at America and see two things. First, they see that legions of their compatriots have gone there and made good. Second, they see that Indian Americans are accepted without a murmur by the rest of American society. Two states in the supposedly racist South have elected Indian American governors: Bobby Jindal (in Louisiana, where Asians are 1.4 percent of the population) and Nikki Haley (in South Carolina, where the Asian population is only 1.2 percent).[56]

Chinese people see something similar: the cofounders of Yahoo and YouTube are Chinese American, as are a number of cabinet ministers and the cellist who played at Barack Obama's inauguration. No matter where you are from, there are at least some prominent Americans whose families hail from the same place. The Czech Republic is tiny, but still sired the founder of McDonald's (Ray Kroc), a former US secretary of state (Madeleine Albright) and some nifty tennis players (Martina Navratilova, Ivan Lendl).

To smooth relations with difficult countries, the United States can often send envoys who understand the local culture. Zalmay Khalilzad, an Afghan American, served as George W. Bush's ambassador to Afghanistan and helped his old homeland draft a democratic constitution. Recall that Gary Locke, a Chinese American, was made ambassador to China in 2011. Sometimes exiles give terrible advice. Ahmed Chalabi, an Iraqi who lived much of his life in America, assured the Bush administration that the reviled dictator Saddam Hussein had weapons of mass destruction (and also that American invaders would be greeted as liberators).[57] But on balance, it is immensely useful for the nation to be able to draw on the knowledge of its hyphenated citizens.

Migrant scholars lend depth to the foreign-policy debate. Consider some of the brains at just one American think tank, the Carnegie Endowment for International Peace. Marwan Muasher, a former foreign minister of Jordan, oversees Middle Eastern studies there. Dmitri Trenin, a former Soviet military officer with experience in nuclear diplomacy, heads Carnegie's Moscow office. An ex–finance minister of Chile (Alejandro Foxley) and an ex–trade minister from Venezuela (Moisés Naím) beef up its Latin American coverage.

Jessica Mathews, Carnegie's president, tells me the key to wielding influence is "very simple: you hire the best people." In countries where think tanks are subservient to the state, such as China and Russia, foreign outfits such as Carnegie enjoy a reputation for independence. If they can back this up with useful knowledge, they can sway policy. Carnegie scholars advised the authors of Russia's post-Soviet constitution. And when relations between the United States and Russia grew frosty under the younger President Bush, Carnegie's Moscow office helped keep a line of communication open between the two governments.

THE SIREN SONG OF ISOLATION

Some Americans think immigrant networks make America weaker. Mark Krikorian, the author of *The New Case Against Immigration: Both Legal and Illegal,* frets that modern immigrants' ability to call home every day makes them less likely to give up their old ties, and therefore less likely to become truly American. It is a coherent argument, but wrong.[58] Nationality need not be an either/or choice. Just as a man can be both a son and a husband, he can also be both Indian and American. His loyalties may sometimes be divided, just as a man may feel torn if his wife and mother are at loggerheads. But most such problems can be resolved or papered over. It is rare for relations to degenerate so badly that the man must sever ties with one of the women he loves.

Nations are not exactly like families, but the analogy holds. When the United States invaded Iraq, many American Muslims were furious. But it is quite possible to be furious with a particular American government and still loyal to the country itself. Democrats and Republicans manage this trick roughly half the time each.

When America admits migrants, it is not diluting its own culture, but spreading its ideals across the world. No other country has such influence. The closest contender, the European Union, wields tremendous soft power by letting neighboring countries join, as fifteen (mostly Eastern European) states have since the end of the cold war. To join the club, a country must accept market economics, abolish the death penalty and uphold a long list of human rights. But this power only works on countries in the same region—no one is considering letting East Asian or Latin American nations into the European Union.

Many things undermine American soft power. Well-publicized abuses, such as the torture of prisoners at Abu Ghraib prison in Iraq in 2003, spur some foreigners to hate Americans in general. Well-publicized insults, as when an attention-seeking Florida pastor burns a Koran, fuel anti-Americanism far and wide. Some aspects of American culture will always repel some people.

But the biggest threat to American soft power is the backlash against immigration. Thanks to the networks created by immigration, America is richer, more innovative and far more influential than it would otherwise be. Yet these advantages could all be frittered away if the nation were to close its borders.

CONCLUSION

A MOBILE WORLD

onfusion reigns on the border. I'm somewhere near Nogales, Arizona, racing around in a powerful four-wheel drive car with a US Border Patrol agent named Jim Hawkins. The radio hisses: another patrolman needs backup. We speed toward the scene but we're too late. The patrolman who called for help has already caught the coyotes (people-smugglers) he was chasing—and been assaulted by one of them.

Agent Hawkins decides to go looking for a suspicious pickup truck he saw earlier. There was someone in it using what looked like a Border Patrol radio, he explains, which could mean that it was a coyote. His instincts are shrewd, but wrong. The pickup's driver is using a Border Patrol radio because he is, in fact, another Border Patrol agent, who had impounded the vehicle after finding two dozen illegal immigrants squeezed in the back.

Their disguise was averagely cunning. They came in a convoy: two pickups, each with a sheet of plywood over the bed, painted the same color as the truck itself to make it look empty, when in fact it was packed with Mexicans. About 40 of them—men, women and children—sit glumly beneath a mesquite tree, waiting to be processed. Most of the coyotes fled into the roadside bushes. Only one was too slow to escape. He stands glowering in the shade, chafing against his handcuffs.

The border between Mexico and the United States is a good place to watch the struggle between the coercive power of a high-tech state and the human desire to feed one's children. Michael Nicely, the Border Patrol chief for the Tucson sector, is trying to convince me that the state has a chance.[1]

The Border Patrol's unmanned spy planes can hover over the border for 10 to 12 hours, he brags. (These are the same drones that the US army uses to vaporize terrorists, though of course in Arizona they are equipped with cameras, not Hellfire missiles.) Mr. Nicely's men have all manner of gizmos, from "stop sticks" that slowly deflate the tires of fleeing cars to PepperBall launching systems—glorified paintball guns that immobilize rowdy smugglers.

Captured migrants sometimes have no idea how they were spotted. I chat with a few in a holding pen in Nogales. Carmen Vasquez, a diminutive Mexican lady, tells me she was tiptoeing through the mountains with her family after dark when she was suddenly surrounded by Border Patrol agents on roaring quad bikes. Agent Hawkins explains to me (but not to Ms. Vasquez) that she was seen through an infrared camera on a distant hilltop.

"Don't let anyone tell you we can't control our borders," admonishes Mr. Nicely. "We just need more resources." He mentions lights, fences, infrared cameras and helicopters, of which he already has 53.[2]

The budget for the Border Patrol rose ninefold between 1993 and 2010, and the number of agents stationed on the southwestern border increased nearly fivefold, to 17,000, with no discernible effect.[3] The estimated number of illegal immigrants in the United States roughly tripled between 1990 and 2010, to 11 million. The only proven way to reverse the flow is to have a recession. Between 2007 and 2009, the number of illegals in the United States fell by 1 million, as construction firms went bust and their Mexican laborers went home.[4]

It is theoretically possible to seal a 2,000-mile land border between a rich country and a poor one, but wildly impractical. When America builds a 20-foot fence, Mexicans bring 21-foot ladders. In good economic times, a million people a year are arrested crossing the border.[5] Since the penalty for capture is "voluntary repatriation," the only deterrent to trying again is the $1,500 a head the coyotes charge.

If you don't use coyotes, it's free—but you'll be beaten up or worse if they catch you crossing "their" territory.

As she waits to be repatriated to Mexico, Ms. Vasquez assures me that she will be back soon. Her sister, she says, makes $1,000 a month cleaning hotel rooms in Florida, ten times what she could earn back home. A recent study found that the likelihood of success for a Mexican who keeps trying to sneak into the United States is approximately 100 percent.[6]

American immigration policy is a mess. The number of visas issued to foreign workers bears no relation to the demand for their services. For unskilled foreigners without relatives in the United States, it is virtually impossible to enter the country legally. This rule is popular with unskilled American workers, who fear that immigrants will displace them or drag down their wages. "Keep them fools out," says Alvin Pablo, an unemployed landscaper in Tucson, who says that Mexicans took his job.[7]

Yet the government's refusal to grant more visas does not keep unskilled workers out; it merely keeps them illegal. And that is actually worse for people like Mr. Pablo, argues Raul Hinojosa-Ojeda, of the Center for American Progress. The fear of deportation makes illegal workers accept worse conditions. Once legal, they demand higher wages and no longer depress those of the native born.[8]

Unskilled immigrants fill a valuable niche. In 1960 half of the native-born men in the American workforce were high-school dropouts performing unskilled tasks; today that proportion is only 10 percent, notes Tamar Jacoby of ImmigrationWorks USA.[9] Unskilled immigrants really do perform the jobs that locals don't want, from slaughtering pigs to emptying bedpans in nursing homes. And on balance, that creates jobs for locals. Mothers who can hire cheap nannies find it easier to go out and work. Firms that can hire immigrants to sweep the floors and mend the roof are less likely to move offshore in search of cost savings.[10]

Unskilled Mexicans cannot be kept out, but highly skilled workers from other parts of the world can. These people have choices. They are not so desperate that they will crawl through the desert in the dead of night to get into America. By making the legal immigration process long, arduous and unpredictable, America drives many skilled immigrants away.

According to a report by the Council on Foreign Relations, only 85,000 H-1B visas—temporary work permits for the highly skilled—are issued each year. In 2007 the number of applicants exceeded that limit on the opening day for applications. About a million green cards (which allow permanent residency) are issued each year, but these are allocated mostly to family members of those who already live in America. In a typical year, only 15 percent are awarded on the basis of skills. No other rich nation puts such a low priority on work-based immigration.[11]

Many immigrants are stuck in limbo. There are more than 500,000 doctors, scientists, researchers and engineers in America who entered legally but have yet to acquire green cards. "These workers can't start companies, justify buying houses or grow deep roots in their communities. Once they get in line for a visa, they can't even accept a promotion or change jobs. They could be required to leave the United States immediately—without notice—if their employer lays them off," observes Vivek Wadhwa, of Duke University. "Rather than live in constant fear and stagnate in their careers, many are returning home."[12]

The system is about as easy to understand as the American tax code. Surojit Sarkar, an Indian-born scientist working at Emory University, told me of his ordeal. In late 2008, his father fell sick and he hurried back to India to be with him, leaving behind his wife and infant daughter in Atlanta.[13]

To renew his visa to return to the United States, he had to undergo security screening. There was a problem. Dr. Sarkar does vaccine research, trying to figure out what imparts protective immunity to viruses, such as HIV. His line of work sends an automatic red flag to the screeners, since someone who knows about viruses could, in theory, use that knowledge for nefarious purposes, such as making biological weapons.

Dr. Sarkar was told to submit documentary proof of more or less everything he had done as an academic in the previous 12 years; every research paper, "the whole of my life," he says. He was told that the screening process would take a couple of weeks. But a few minutes' research on the Internet suggested that it would probably take much longer—waits of two years are not unheard of.

He ended up sitting around at his parents' home in New Delhi for three and a half months. "It was dreadful," he says. He missed his daughter's first birthday. He was lucky not to lose his job, as many people caught in this trap do. The US embassy would never give him any useful information. All they could tell him about his case was that it was "pending."

Eventually he was cleared to return. By the time he got back, however, his work was out of date. Vaccine research is a very competitive field. "I was getting scooped left, right and center," he says. "All the experiments that I had ongoing in the lab needed restarting from scratch."

The number of immigrant scientists like Dr. Sarkar subjected to such security checks has risen sixtyfold since September 11, 2001.[14] "I understand why you are screening us," he says. "But it has to be quicker."

For such a polite nation, America's border controls are surprisingly unpleasant. In a survey commissioned by the travel industry, more than half of visitors found American border officials rude and disagreeable. By a two-to-one margin, the country's entry process was rated the world's worst.[15] An immigration official lives in fear of admitting the next Muhammad Atta, but there is no penalty for excluding the next Einstein or humiliating a tourist who subsequently summers in France. Organizers of international scientific conferences are reluctant to hold them in the United States because not everyone they invite will be able to attend.[16]

The World Economic Forum talks of a "talent crisis," and predicts that the United States will have to add 26 million workers to its talent pool by 2030 to sustain the economic growth rates of the past two decades. Yet the government subsidizes foreigners to acquire PhDs at American universities and then kicks them out of the country. Michael Bloomberg, the mayor of New York City, describes America's immigration policy as "national suicide."[17]

When you treat every Hindu doctor and Chinese accountant as a potential terrorist, they eventually get fed up. Dr. Wadhwa surveyed 1,000 foreign students at American universities in 2008. A full 75 percent said they feared they would not be able to obtain a visa, and only 6 percent of the Indians and 10 percent of the Chinese said they would remain in the United States after graduation.[18]

President George W. Bush, who comes from the border state of Texas, tried hard to fix immigration. In 2005 and 2006 he pushed a two-pronged plan to tighten controls at the border while simultaneously relieving the pressure on it by creating a new temporary worker program for laborers. He also pushed for more visas for skilled workers and a "path to citizenship" for illegal immigrants who came out of the shadows, paid a fine, stayed out of trouble and paid their taxes. It was a good plan which earned him the enmity of millions of talk-radio listeners. His own party, the Republicans, defeated it in Congress.

President Barack Obama, a Democrat, has a more mixed record. He promised to push for something similar in his first year in office, but at the time of writing he had made little effort to do so, aside from the occasional speech. This is a shame, and a misreading of national sentiment to boot. Opinion polls suggest that American voters are more welcoming than their leaders imagine. Most respect immigrants for their drive and hard work, and 63 percent favor a path to citizenship for the illegal ones already in the country, so long as they prove themselves worthy.[19]

Most also favor tougher border controls and limits on the number of newcomers, but only 13 percent think it practical or ethical to deport all the illegal aliens currently in America.[20] This is hardly surprising. By one estimate it would cost $285 billion to round up and expel 11 million people—$922 in new taxes for every man, woman and child in the country.[21] By contrast, Mr. Hinojosa-Ojeda estimates that comprehensive immigration reform of the sort backed by Mr. Bush and Mr. Obama would add $1.5 trillion to the economy over ten years and raise wages for the native born as well as the newly legalized.[22]

Even the most ardent American opponents of immigration are not particularly extreme by global standards. In late 2005 I chatted with Chris Simcox, the head of the Minutemen, a volunteer group that watches the border and organizes protests against illegal immigration. He fumed at the "hypocrisy" of "a federal government that will not enforce the rule of law." He added: "That's going to lead to anarchy [and] out-of-control cultural change in this country."[23]

The Minutemen are often depicted as dangerous vigilantes, but mostly they just sit by the border with beer and binoculars, phoning the Border Patrol when they see a Mexican trying to slip by. Some are armed, but that is hardly unusual in Arizona. They have strict rules against brandishing those weapons and against trying to arrest immigrants themselves. One of them humiliated a migrant by photographing him with a T-shirt bearing the slogan: "Bryan Barton caught me crossing the border and all I got was this lousy T-shirt." For that, Mr. Barton was expelled from the Minutemen.[24]

As angry nationalists go, the Minutemen could be a lot worse. In South Africa, another country that shares a long land border with much poorer nations, and therefore attracts many illegal immigrants, xenophobic violence is routine and sometimes deadly. Blameless immigrants have been thrown off moving trains. In May 2008 anti-immigrant riots swept seven of South Africa's nine provinces and led to 62 deaths.[25] America's vigilantes are not in the same league.

With unemployment hovering around 10 percent,[26] now is not the easiest time for any American politician to push for a friendlier immigration policy. Yet the best way to restore order to the border would be to issue a number of visas that bore some relation to economic reality. In theory, one could lower the barriers to skilled workers without tackling the more controversial issue of unskilled migration. But politically, you have to do both together, explains Bart Gordon, a Democratic congressman from Tennessee.[27] The reason, he says, is that Hispanic voters want a path to citizenship for their undocumented cousins. An immigration bill needs a broad coalition of supporters to pass, so it will need to offer something for everyone.

If the broken system is not fixed, America's allure may fade. Migration is what academics call "path-dependent": that is, people are much more likely to move to a country where someone they know has already moved. A 2010 Gallup poll in 103 countries found that people with a family member abroad were more than twice as likely as others to wish to migrate permanently. And among those who said they had a friend or a relative they could count on in another country, 29 percent said they wished to emigrate. Among those without such a contact, only 13 percent did.[28]

Unskilled Mexicans will keep coming, regardless. But if the United States stops the flow of skilled immigrants from other parts of the world, "we may not have the option to turn it back on again," William Kerr, of Harvard Business School, told me. America today is well-connected to every other country, but those connections could grow stale. The world's brightest and most dynamic people could start going elsewhere, and that flow could become self-reinforcing.[29]

In plain English: America's immigration system is a disgrace. In the long term, it poses a serious threat to the United States' status as top nation.[30] But in the short term, it could be fixed.

NOT ALL BORDERS ARE INTERNATIONAL

I'm walking through the streets of Thurber, Texas, with Lindsay Baker, a historian with a hoe. The hoe is handy for killing rattlesnakes, which lurk in the long grass that has all but swallowed the town. Mr. Baker also uses it to scrape in the dirt for what the people who once lived here left behind. He finds some shards of an old medicine bottle, the cap of a salt shaker and a half-brick with markings that date it sometime between 1904 and 1936. If a brush fire clears the grass, you'll see artifacts like this everywhere, explains Mr. Baker, a man whose passion can be guessed from the titles of his books: *Ghost Towns of Texas* and *More Ghost Towns of Texas*.[31]

America has a lot of ghost towns. There are 1,000 in Texas alone.[32] Thurber was once home to 10,000 people. Now there are only five—not five thousand; just five people. In its heyday, in the late nineteenth and early twentieth centuries, Thurber was a coal town. Immigrants flocked there from Italy, Poland and Mexico to dig up fuel for steam trains. The coal was also used to fire bricks made from local clay. The town boasted churches, baseball teams and even an opera house.

But then someone found oil in Texas. Before long, the trains started burning oil instead of coal. Thurber's mine closed in 1926. And since cheap oil prompted Texans to start using asphalt instead of bricks to pave their roads, Thurber's brick kiln closed, too.

The workers left. Their homes were sold for $50 to anyone who could carry them off. You can still spot them in the surrounding countryside, serving as barns or storehouses. Little is left in Thurber itself but a smokestack, the graveyard (divided into Catholic, Protestant and black areas) and a few company buildings.

The story is not all wretched, however. Many workers found jobs in the oil business. The company that built Thurber struck oil and prospered. The old boss's daughter-in-law donated money for a museum to preserve Thurber's memory, which Mr. Baker runs.

Ghost towns are sad places, but also monuments to American dynamism. Throughout history, Americans have dealt with economic shocks by picking themselves up and moving on. The United States is not only a land of immigrants; it is also a land of great internal migrations. The pioneers headed west to find land and farm it. The Mormons trekked to Utah pulling handcarts. Southern blacks migrated northward in the 1930s to escape Jim Crow (the old system of racial segregation). Two generations later, many of their grandchildren are heading back to the South in search of jobs.

Mobility underpins America's surprising ability to adapt and reinvent itself. But worryingly, Americans are growing less mobile. In the 1960s about 20 percent of Americans moved every year. By 1980–1 that figure had fallen slightly, to 17.2 percent. In 2007–8 only 11.9 percent moved home—the most sluggish pace since records began in the 1940s. The number perked up a little in 2009, to 12.5 percent, but the long-term trend is toward staying put.[33]

There are two main reasons for this. One is the cult of home ownership. Many countries subsidize home buying; America does so lavishly. Owner-occupiers typically pay no tax on capital gains and can deduct mortgage interest from their income-tax bills. Fannie Mae and Freddie Mac, two government-backed mortgage firms, have squandered a fortune promoting home ownership among the uncreditworthy.[34] This contributed to the financial crash of 2008. It also makes Americans less mobile.

Renters can move easily; homeowners often cannot. When housing prices collapsed in 2008, many people were trapped by negative equity. By 2011, more than a quarter of American homeowners owed more than their homes were worth.[35] Such people are one-third less likely to move than those whose homes are above water.[36] Some cannot sell their homes at all. Others could, but don't want to take a big loss on an investment they thought was—how can I put this?—safe as houses. Either way, they are stuck. If a good job comes up in another town, they cannot take it.

Consider the story of Neely Whites, who bought a former crack house in New Orleans and fixed it up. It was looking really nice when, in 2005, Hurricane Katrina struck. In the storm's aftermath the neighborhood where she lived turned even rougher than before. Weary of drive-by shootings, Ms. Whites moved to Long Beach, Mississippi, and bought a house there in September 2006.

It was not the best timing. The property market promptly crashed. After fleeing a city that was literally underwater, Ms. Whites found herself stuck in a home that was figuratively so. She wanted to move closer to her new job as a financial consultant, cutting her daily commute from an hour each way to something less onerous. But she could not sell her home, and she owed the bank more than it was worth. To make matters worse, she was in the middle of a divorce. "I would have liked to split up a while ago. But not being able to sell the house means we can't [afford to]," she told me.[37]

Excessive home-ownership kills jobs, argues Andrew Oswald, of the University of Warwick, in Britain. European nations with high rates of home ownership, such as Spain, have much higher unemployment rates than those where more people rent, such as Switzerland. Mr. Oswald finds this effect to be stronger than tax rates or employment law.[38] If there are few homes to rent, he writes, jobless youngsters living with their parents find it harder to move out and get work. Immobile workers become stuck in jobs for which they are ill-suited. Areas with high home ownership often have a strong "not in my backyard" ethos, with residents objecting to new development. Finally, homeowners commute farther than renters, which causes congestion and makes getting to work more time-consuming and costly for everyone.

Home ownership has many advantages; I own one myself. But there is no good reason why renters should subsidize owners, as they do in many countries. Besides throwing sawdust in the national economic engine, such subsidies are unfair: owners are typically richer than renters. Alas, middle-class handouts, once granted, are politically almost impossible to take away.

The other threat to American mobility is health insurance. A company can buy health insurance for its employees with pretax dollars; an individual can buy it only with after-tax dollars. So although soaring premiums are prompting many firms to drop or restrict coverage, most Americans still get their health insurance from their jobs. This makes it hard for anyone with a sick child to quit and start a new business. It also makes it harder to switch jobs. Scott Adams, of the University of Wisconsin–Milwaukee, found that married men with no alternative source of insurance were 22 percent less likely to switch jobs than those who, for example, could obtain coverage through their wife's employer.[39]

Tying health care to a job can tie people to jobs they hate. Gerry Stover, who now runs a doctors' group in West Virginia, recalls a time when his wife was pregnant and he couldn't get a job at a private firm with health insurance. He became a prison guard. As a public employee, his family was covered. But the job was neither pleasant nor a good use of his talents. "You have a radio and you're put in a room with 70 criminals and told: 'If they get you round the neck, press the [panic] button,'" he shudders.[40]

Some people even get stuck in bad marriages because they need their spouse's health insurance, giving new meaning to the word "wedlock," notes Alain Enthoven, of Stanford University.[41] Whether Barack Obama's health reforms will improve matters remains to be seen.

Other factors also make Americans less mobile. People are living longer, and the elderly are less restless than the young. Most people have cars these days, so they don't have to move houses just because their job moved ten miles away. Nonetheless, a halving of American mobility since the 1960s is significant and potentially alarming. Is America losing its frontier spirit?

I don't know what the optimum level of mobility is. But I do know who is best placed to make that judgment: the millions of individuals and families who have to decide each year whether to stay or to go.

The central message of this book is that individuals should be allowed more freedom to choose where they live and work. When we make our own choices, we have a better shot at happiness. Such freedom is about far more than economics.

Consider the dilemma that faced Shoba Narayan, an Indian-born writer who moved to America as a student in the 1980s but asked herself, after 20 years, whether she and her family should move back to India. She drew up a list of pros and cons.

Her reasons to stay in America included: meritocracy in the workplace, a multicultural society and great material comfort. She wanted her kids to grow up with American values of "independence, self-reliance, and go-getting drive." She concluded that "America is the least imperfect society." It has its problems, "but at least I don't have to worry about traffic, pollution, bribery and petty corruption, trains running on time, etc." Plus, the kids can learn to ski in America.

Her reasons for moving back to India included: her parents were getting older and she wanted to take care of them. She hoped to instill in her kids Eastern values such as respect for their elders. She didn't want her daughters to become Britney Spears clones. She hoped to give something back to the country that nurtured her. And she "viscerally miss[ed] living in India—the food, [the] smell of jasmine, the autorickshaws, [the] music concerts, [the] cows on the streets, haggling at bazaars, wearing silk saris."*

Finally, there was family. "You can buy anything in America," writes Ms. Narayan, but you "can't buy family."[42]

After weighing all these imponderables, she moved back to India in 2005.

I can empathize. In 2010 my wife and I had to choose whether to stay in America or move back to England. It was not an easy decision. I had been covering America for five years for *The Economist*. Every minute had been a thrill, but I felt it was time to move on, and my wife, Emma, agreed. I had applied for—and been offered—the job of running *The Economist*'s business coverage from our head office in London. The Guest family was all set to move back.

But then, out of nowhere, I was offered a job that would have required me to stay in America indefinitely. David Bradley, a Washington media baron with disarmingly perfect manners, asked me edit one of his magazines: the *National Journal,* a highbrow political weekly. The challenge tickled me, as did the handsome salary he was offering. Had I been single, I would have said yes.

---

* Presumably she's talking about herself haggling and wearing silk saris, not the cows.

But career moves are more complicated when you have a family. Together Emma and I made a list of the pros and cons of staying or going. The reasons for staying went something like this. We both loved America. Everything works, more or less. The cost of living is much lower than in England, so you feel richer. The neighborhood we lived in is safe and has excellent schools. And Americans are open and friendly—when Emma had a baby in 2006, our neighbors took turns delivering home-cooked meals to ease our burden during the first few sleep-deprived weeks.

Professionally, too, there were good reasons to stay. I thought it would be fun to run a magazine. America is a terrific place to be a journalist. Information flows easily, officials are accessible and people you meet randomly in the street are usually happy to share their thoughts. Also, America's intellectual life is second to none. Britain has two or three world-class universities; America has dozens, plus a whole ecosystem of foundations and think tanks whose ideas actually influence government.

On the other side of the ledger, we had good reasons to return to Britain. Emma and I both missed the familiarity of our native culture. We love the caustic humor that bubbles through English conversation—the fact that you can be rude to your friends without upsetting them. We love how easy it is to chat with people who share the same childhood memories and cultural reference points—not many Americans know who the Clangers were.* Most important, we both have large families in England. Our children have ten first cousins of approximately the same age, and we want them to grow up playing together. We want them to know their grandparents, aunts and uncles, too. America has many virtues, but it's not home.

So we moved back. I was sorry to do so, as I've been sorry to leave every place where I've ever lived. There have been quite a few: I count 25 flats or houses in 15 cities in 6 countries, and I may have missed a

---

* *The Clangers* was a British children's TV show in the 1970s, which told harmless stories about gentle aliens on a distant planet. It was notable for its miserly budgets and primitive special effects: the Clangers themselves appeared to have been made out of old socks. Unless you are my age and British, there is no reason why you should care about this.

couple. My wife tells me it's time to stop moving about. We recently bought a house by a wood in the county of Buckinghamshire. (And yes, we took advantage of all the tax breaks.) The neighbors are nice. The kids have made friends. My wife is planning to plant hydrangeas in the garden.

So I understand the arguments for putting down roots. I don't for a moment imagine that a nomadic life is for everyone. Even the same person will often have different priorities at different life stages: a thirst for adventure at 25, perhaps, followed by the urge at 40 to find a quiet suburb with good schools.

All these decisions are best made by individuals. A world with freer movement is a world where people have more say in how they live their lives. Perhaps this is an impossible dream, but there are some steps that rich governments could take straightaway.

First, get rid of all the barriers that prevent the citizens of one rich country from working in another.
Americans are routinely refused permission to work in Europe, and vice versa. This serves no purpose. Neither continent will be suddenly flooded with foreigners if barriers fall, but millions of people will suddenly have more options.

We already know what free movement among rich countries looks like because it exists within the European Union. Roughly speaking, any citizen of any EU country can live and work in any other member state. You might assume that such freedom would be hugely disruptive. Some European countries are much richer than others—Germans, for example, are twice as wealthy as Poles—so you might expect to see a stampede of migrants from the poorer European countries to the richer ones.

In fact, only about 1.4 million EU citizens move to another EU country each year.[43] Out of a total population of 500 million, that is more of a trickle than a stampede.[44] Even if they could earn more by moving, most people prefer to stay put. And Europe's mobile minority respond quickly to changing economic conditions. The number of Poles moving to Britain fell by 47 percent between late 2007 and late 2008, when the recession struck and jobs dried up.[45] People move when there is a demand for their labor and stop when there is not.

A similar experiment has been running for some time in the United States. Fifty states, many as large as European countries, all allow any American from any other state to settle and work within their borders. In a world where economics was all that mattered, everyone in Mississippi would move to Connecticut. Last time I checked, that had not happened.

So it seems likely that completely opening borders within the rich world would lead to a modest extra flow of migrants, causing minimal social disruption. Since the people who move would be the ones who particularly want to move, it would increase the sum of human happiness. Those who regret moving would simply move back.

Second, rich countries should devise more rational policies for admitting migrants from the developing world, starting by welcoming people with skills.
Anyone who earns a science degree at a reputable Western university should be allowed to stay and work. Anyone who invests more than a certain amount in a business should be allowed to stay, too. Canada grants passports to investors; other countries would be foolish not to follow its example.

The precise formula for deciding whom to admit will vary from country to country. Some will award points for youth, education or wealth. Others could grant visas freely to foreigners with firm job offers. My personal preference would be to auction a large batch of visas, so that they go to those who value them the most. But the more countries experiment with different systems, the more they can learn from each other.

Rich countries should also bite the bullet and start letting in more unskilled workers from poor countries.
They bring youth and energy and there is ample demand for their services. As we saw in Chapter 5, allowing poor people to work in rich countries is the simplest and most effective aid program yet devised.

To cope with increased migration, governments will have to rethink certain domestic policies, especially those that concern social welfare and race. Rich nations can absorb a large influx of foreigners who come to work, but they cannot afford to welcome large numbers of foreigners who come to live on public handouts. Welfare states will have to be calibrated accordingly. Overgenerous welfare payments and mass immigration are not compatible.

Also, for the sake of social harmony, countries should avoid making rights dependent on ethnicity or skin color.

It makes sense to differentiate between citizens and noncitizens. But among citizens, everyone should be equal before the law. The American government enforces a wide array of racial preferences aimed at giving members of disadvantaged groups a leg up. In the unique case of African Americans, whose ancestors were enslaved and who until the 1960s were subjected to segregation in the South, there may be a moral case for affirmative action.[46] But it is too much to ask native-born Americans to accept special privileges for those who came to America voluntarily. Mass immigration is not politically sustainable unless the native born are treated fairly.

Someday, I would like to see a world where people can move as freely from one country to another as they currently do from one American state to another. That is extremely unlikely for many years to come, however. In the short-to-medium term, the best that we can hope for is a gradual shift to a world that is more welcoming to strangers.

My fervent hope is that America will lead the way. Its whole history is a testament to the invigorating power of migration. Had the United States never welcomed immigrants, it would be a backwater today—a paradise for buffalo, perhaps, but a midget on the global stage. I am glad that that is not how history unfolded. And I hope that America's leaders will pay heed, in the years to come, to the ideals etched on a certain statue overlooking New York harbor.

BECOMING AMERICAN

I'm standing at the back of a hall in Miami where 1,200 people are taking the oath of American citizenship. They come from 75 different countries, most of them poor. They stand and cheer when their motherland is called out. There are 417 Cubans, 95 Haitians, 9 Brits and 1 Somali. Helpful Spanish-speaking staff assure the old folks in wheelchairs that they need not stand, but are free to wave little flags ecstatically.

I'm here because I'm covering a presidential election. Barack Obama and John McCain's campaigns are poised to pounce on these newly minted Americans and sign them up to vote. They have erected stalls outside the building with signs in Spanish and Haitian Creole. The Cuban Americans tend to gravitate toward the McCain booth. Having fled a communist dictatorship, they are drawn to Republican ideals such as free enterprise and bashing the Castro regime. The Haitians seem to prefer Mr. Obama, not least because he is black. (Although, confusingly, he would probably be considered white in Haiti.)

The best case for migration comes from the mouths of the migrants themselves. I chat with one whose father was imprisoned by Fidel Castro for 14 years for no good reason, and another whose Nicaraguan father won American citizenship on the beaches of Normandy.

I meet Olga Willis, a lady from Russia with a fabulous gold handbag, as she struts up to the McCain booth and loudly asks where she can register to vote. Stalin murdered her great-grandfather, she says. Several of her relatives were sent to Siberia and dumped off the train in the snow. She studied English, married an American, moved to Florida and now works as a mortgage broker in Miami Beach. The McCain volunteers offer her a bumper sticker. She demands two, because "we have two cars."[47]

The climax of the citizenship ceremony is a song called "God Bless the USA," which includes the lines: "I'm proud to be an American/ Where at least I know I'm free." I've never liked this couplet. Like many Europeans, I'm a little queasy about loud declarations of patriotism. Where we come from, memories of patriotism warping into something terrible remain vivid. But as I look around the hall full of cheering, hugging new Cuban, Venezuelan, Haitian and Russian Americans, I am suddenly swept away by the crowd's happy frenzy. To my surprise, I feel a tear rolling down my cheek.

NOTES

INTRODUCTION: THE CURSE OF ISOLATION

1. Eric Ellis, "Keeping Dear Leader's Score," *International Herald Tribune*, October 19, 1994, http://www.nytimes.com/1994/10/19/opinion/19iht-ederic.html.
2. "International Migration 2009," United Nations, Department of Economic and Social Affairs, Population Division, http://www.un.org/esa/population/publications/2009 Migration_Chart/ittmig_wallchart09.pdf.
3. For a more detailed discussion of these numbers, see Chapter 1.
4. "Korea, North," *The World Factbook* (Washington, DC: Central Intelligence Agency, 2011), https://www.cia.gov/library/publications/the-world-factbook/geos/kn.html. The figures cited are for GDP per head at purchasing-power parity. North Korea publishes few accurate statistics, so the CIA's numbers are extrapolated from an estimate by Angus Maddison, an economic historian, in *The World Economy: A Millennial Perspective* (Paris: OECD, 2001), 149. These numbers are unreliable, but no more so than any other statistics about North Korea.
5. Christopher Hitchens, "A Nation of Racist Dwarfs," *Slate*, February 1, 2010, http://www.slate.com/id/2243112/pagenum/all/#p2.
6. For a brilliant account of the racial supremacist propaganda the Kim regime uses to distract attention from its own failings, see B. R. Myers, *The Cleanest Race: How North Koreans See Themselves and Why It Matters* (New York: Melville House, 2010).
7. Matt Ridley, *The Rational Optimist: How Prosperity Evolves* (New York: HarperCollins, 2010), 34–5.
8. *I, Pencil: My Family Tree as Told to Leonard E. Read* (Irvington-on-Hudson, NY: The Foundation for Economic Education, Inc., 1958). Available online from the Library of Economics and Liberty: http://www.econlib.org/library/Essays/rdPncl1.html.
9. Ridley, *The Rational Optimist*, 78–84.
10. David S. Landes, *The Wealth and Poverty of Nations: Why Some Are Rich and Some So Poor* (New York: W. W. Norton, 1998; London: Abacus, 1999), 179. Citations refer to the Abacus edition.
11. Landes, *The Wealth and Poverty of Nations*, 180–1.
12. Hugh Trevor-Roper, *Religion, the Reformation and Social Change and Other Essays*. Cited in Landes, *The Wealth and Poverty of Nations*, 181.
13. Ridley, *The Rational Optimist*, 82.
14. Ibid., 1–10.

CHAPTER 1: MIGRATIONOMICS

1. "Yan Cheung," profile, Forbes.com, updated March 2011, http://www.forbes.com/profile/yan-cheung.

2. "The World's Billionaires," *Forbes,* March 2011, http://www.forbes.com/wealth/billionaires/list. The magazine put Mr. Brin's net worth at $19.8 billion.
3. "Milestones in AT&T Network History," AT&T, accessed June 23, 2011, http://www.corp.att.com/history/nethistory/milestones.html.
4. International Air Transportation Association fact sheet, updated April 2011, http://www.iata.org/pressroom/facts_figures/fact_sheets/Pages/iata.aspx.
5. Brad Stone and Bruce Einhorn, "Be Evil: How Baidu Won China," *Bloomberg Business Week,* November 15, 2010, http://www.businessweek.com/magazine/content/10_47/b4204060242597.htm?chan=magazine+channel_top+stories.
6. Ibid.
7. "The World's Billionaires," *Forbes,* March 2011, http://www.forbes.com/wealth/billionaires/list?country=99&industry=-1&state.
8. Stone and Einhorn, "Be Evil: How Baidu Won China."
9. Niall Ferguson, *The Ascent of Money: A Financial History of the World* (New York: Penguin, 2008).
10. Ethan Zuckerman, "Listening to Global Voices." Filmed July 2010. TED video, 19:45. Posted July 2010, http://www.ted.com/talks/ethan_zuckerman.html.
11. Marcia Stepanek, "The New Digital Divide," June 4, 2010, Stanford Social Innovation Review blog, http://www.ssireview.org/opinion/entry/the_new_digital_divide.
12. "A Cyber-house Divided," *The Economist,* September 2, 2010, http://www.economist.com/node/16943885?story_id=16943885.
13. "International Migration 2009," UN Department of Economic and Social Affairs, http://www.un.org/esa/population/publications/2009Migration_Chart/ittmig_wallchart09.pdf.
14. Lant Pritchett, *Let Their People Come: Breaking the Gridlock on Global Labor Mobility* (Washington, DC: Center for Global Development, 2006), 17–20.
15. Neli Esipova and Julie Ray, "700 Million Worldwide Desire to Migrate Permanently," Gallup, November 2, 2009, http://www.gallup.com/poll/124028/700-million-worldwide-desire-migrate-permanently.aspx.
16. Pritchett, *Let Their People Come,* 21.
17. Ibid., 22.
18. "Global Economic Prospects: Economic Implications of Remittances and Migration" (Washington, DC: World Bank, 2005). Cited in Pritchett, *Let Their People Come,* 3–4.
19. Pritchett, *Let Their People Come,* 4.
20. Ibid., 33. At the time that study was done, $40 trillion was equivalent to 100 percent of the world's entire annual output. By way of comparison, foreign aid is typically a mere 0.3 percent of a rich country's gross domestic product.
21. Vivek Wadhwa, "Immigrants and Returnees," Cambridge, MA, November 7, 2007, http://www.law.harvard.edu/programs/lwp/people/staffPapers/vivek/Vivek%20Wadhwa%20Immigrants%20and%20Returnees.pdf.
22. Angela Ka-yee Leung, et al., "Multicultural Experience Enhances Creativity: The When and How," *American Psychologist,* April 2008, http://www.augsburg.edu/home/education/edc210/Leung_et_al_2008.pdf.
23. Robert Guest, *The Shackled Continent* (Washington, DC: Smithsonian Books, 2010), 1.
24. Jessica Pressler, "Charities, Old People, Jews Hit Hardest by Madoff Fraud," *New York,* December 15, 2008, http://nymag.com/daily/intel/2008/12/charities_old_people_jews_hit.html.
25. Author interview, April 13, 2010.
26. AnnaLee Saxenian, et al., "Local and Global Networks of Immigrant Professionals in Silicon Valley," Public Policy Institute of California, 2002, 27. See http://www.ppic.org/content/pubs/report/R_502ASR.pdf. Further information obtained via author interview, June 17, 2010.
27. Vivek Wadhwa et al., "The Grass Is Indeed Greener in India and China for Returnee Entrepreneurs," Kauffman Foundation, April 28, 2011, http://www.kauffman.org/uploadedfiles/grass-is-greener-for-returnee-entrepreneurs.pdf.

28. AnnaLee Saxenian, *The New Argonauts: Regional Advantage in a Global Economy* (Cambridge, MA: Harvard University Press, 2006), 5.

29. Ibid., 74–5.

30. Carlo Dade, "Transnationalism, Foreign Assistance, Domestic Communities: New Opportunities and New Challenges for Canada and the United States," special issue, *Focal Point,* Canadian Foundation for the Americas, March 2004, http://www.focal.ca/pdf/focalpoint_se_march2004.pdf.

31. Graeme Hugo, *In and Out of Australia: Rethinking Chinese and Indian Skilled Migration to Australia* (draft paper supplied to author).

32. Ibid.

33. Author interview, February 18, 2011.

34. Lynn Pan, *Sons of the Yellow Emperor: A History of the Chinese Diaspora* (New York: Kodansha, 1994), 381.

35. For a full account of this, see Deborah Brautigam, *The Dragon's Gift: The Real Story of China in Africa* (Oxford: Oxford University Press, 2009). For a shorter account, see "The Chinese in Africa: Trying to Pull Together," *The Economist,* April 20, 2011, http://www.economist.com/node/18586448?story_id=18586448.

36. See, for example, Robert D. Kaplan, "The Geography of Chinese Power," *Foreign Affairs,* May/June 2010, http://www.foreignaffairs.com/articles/66205/robert-d-kaplan/the-geography-of-chinese-power.

37. Agnes Winarti, "Chinese-Indonesians Can't Be Put in Boxes," *Jakarta Post,* May 26, 2008, http://www.thejakartapost.com/news/2008/05/26/chinese-indonesians-can039t-be-put-boxes.html.

38. "Overseas Compatriot Population Distribution," Overseas Compatriot Affairs Commission, Republic of China (Taiwan), http://www.ocac.gov.tw/english/public/public.asp?selno=8889&no=8889&level=B.

39. "Taiwan's Commonsense Consensus," *The Economist,* February 24, 2011, http://www.economist.com/node/18229208.

40. "Foreign Direct Investment in China," US-China Business Council, accessed June 23 2011, http://www.uschina.org/statistics/fdi_cumulative.html.

41. Fritz Foley and William Kerr, "Ethnic Innovation and US Multinational Firm Activity," Harvard Business School and NBER, August 2011, http://www.hbs.edu/research/pdf/12-006.pdf.

42. Pankaj Ghemawat, *World 3.0: Global Prosperity and How to Achieve It* (Cambridge, MA: Harvard Business Publishing, 2011), 58.

43. "Locals First," *The Economist,* March 5, 2011, http://www.economist.com/node/18277181. Further information obtained via author interview, June 16, 2010.

44. Wang Huiyao, "China's National Talent Plan: Key Measures and Objectives," Brookings Institution, 2010, http://www.brookings.edu/~/media/Files/rc/papers/2010/1123_china_talent_wang/1123_china_talent_wang.pdf.

45. Ibid.

46. "Table 3. The Indian Diaspora: Places with More Than 100,000 Members," Migration Policy Institute, http://www.migrationinformation.org/Profiles/display.cfm?ID=745#8. This is an Indian government estimate for 2005. The true total may be larger.

47. For a very short history of Indian emigration, see Daniel Naujoks, "Emigration, Immigration, and Diaspora Relation in India," Migration Policy Institute, October 2009, http://www.migrationinformation.org/Profiles/display.cfm?ID=745.

48. Hamish McDonald, "Lessons from the Souk," Chapter 3 in *Ambani and Sons* (New Delhi: Roli Books, 2010).

49. "Mukesh Ambani," profile, Forbes.com, updated March 2011, http://www.forbes.com/profile/mukesh-ambani.

50. Nandan Nilekani, *Imagining India: The Idea of a Renewed Nation* (London: Penguin, 2010), 58.

51. Ibid., 67.

52. Ibid., 62–3.

53. Ibid., 63.

54. Devesh Kapur, "International Migration and the Paradox of India's Democracy," Chapter 6 in *Diaspora, Development and Democracy: The Domestic Impact of International Migration from India* (Princeton, NJ: Princeton University Press, 2010).
55. Nilekani, *Imagining India,* 178.
56. Kapur, *Diaspora, Development and Democracy,* 183.
57. Ibid., 189.
58. Ibid., 190.
59. Ibid., 190.
60. Fareed Zakaria, *The Future of Freedom: Illiberal Democracy at Home and Abroad* (New York: Norton, 2003), 53.
61. 2000 US census, cited in Kapur, *Diaspora, Development and Democracy,* 195.
62. Scott Adams, *Dilbert,* September 16, 2003.
63. Elizabeth Grieco and Edward Trevelyan, "Place of Birth of the Foreign-Born Population," American Community Survey Brief, US Census Bureau, October 2010, http://www.census.gov/prod/2010pubs/acsbr09-15.pdf.
64. Anjli Raval, "The Professional Family Business," *Financial Times,* January 25, 2011, http://www.ft.com/cms/s/0/0b270eb8-2807-11e0-8abc-00144feab49a.html#ax zz1Q7VWgxtO.
65. "Lakshmi Mittal," profile, Forbes.com, updated March 2011, http://www.forbes.com/profile/lakshmi-mittal.
66. Palaniappan Chidambaram, interview on PBS documentary *Commanding Heights,* February 6, 2001, http://www.pbs.org/wgbh/commandingheights/shared/minitext/int_pchidambaram.html.
67. Kapur, *Diaspora, Development and Democracy,* Chapter 5.
68. See "India's Surprising Economic Miracle," *The Economist,* September 30, 2010, http://www.economist.com/node/17147648.

CHAPTER 2: BRIDGES TO CHINA

1. Lynn Pan, *Sons of the Yellow Emperor: A History of the Chinese Diaspora* (New York: Kodansha, 1994), 140–1.
2. Ibid., 8–9.
3. For a short account of the Taiping rebellion, see "Taiping Rebellion," *Encyclopedia Britannica Online,* Encyclopedia Britannica, 2011, http://www.britannica.com/EB checked/topic/580815/Taiping-Rebellion. For a rip-roaring novel based around it, try George MacDonald Fraser, *Flashman and the Dragon* (London: HarperCollins, 1985).
4. Stephane Courtois et al., *The Black Book of Communism: Crimes, Terror, Repression* (Cambridge, MA: Harvard University Press, 1999).
5. Pan, *Sons of the Yellow Emperor,* 364–7.
6. Jung Chang, *Wild Swans: Three Daughters of China* (London: Harper Perennial, 2004).
7. Pan, *Sons of the Yellow Emperor,* 43–83.
8. Rudyard Kipling, *From Sea to Sea and Other Sketches* (London: Macmillan, 1900). Quoted in Pan, *Sons of the Yellow Emperor,* 131.
9. Pan, *Sons of the Yellow Emperor,* 95.
10. "Advantages for the Advantaged," *The Economist,* June 17, 2004, http://www.economist.com/node/2765848.
11. Author interview, January 15, 2011. The full title of Dawis's book is *The Chinese of Indonesia and Their Search for Identity: The Relationship Between Collective Memory and the Media* (New York: Cambria Press, 2009).
12. Author interview, January 15, 2011.
13. Author interview, January 14, 2011.
14. Author interview and email correspondence, 2010.
15. Richard Behar, "The Year of Laying Cable Dangerously," *Fortune,* July 23, 2001, http://money.cnn.com/magazines/fortune/fortune_archive/2001/07/23/307376/index.htm.

16. Rosabeth Moss Kanter, "Using Networking for Competitive Advantage: The Lippo Group of Indonesia and Hong Kong," case study, Harvard Business School, 1996, 2–3, http://www.strategy-business.com/article/17609?gko=17096.

17. Ibid.

18. Ibid.

19. "James Riady Pleads Guilty Will Pay Largest Fine in Campaign Finance History for Violating Federal Election Law," press release, US Department of Justice, January 11, 2001, http://www.justice.gov/opa/pr/2001/January/017crm.htm.

20. James Riady, interview, *Knowledge@Wharton,* Wharton Business School, October 28, 2009, http://knowledge.wharton.upenn.edu/article.cfm?articleid=2365.

21. See, for example, Andrew Higgins, "How the Disgraced James Riady, Barred from Travel to the US, Made It Back," *Washington Post,* January 5, 2010, http://www .washingtonpost.com/wp-dyn/content/article/2010/01/04/AR2010010403106.html.

22. Author interview, January 14, 2011.

23. Corporate profile, the Lippo Group, accessed June 24, 2011, http://www.lipporealty .com/CORPORATEPROFILE/tabid/55/Default.aspx.

24. Author interview, September 24, 2010, and subsequent communication by email.

25. "A Tale of Two Expats," *The Economist,* December 29, 2010, http://www.economist .com/node/17797134?story_id=17797134.

26. Shiying Liu and Martha Avery, *Alibaba: The Inside Story Behind Jack Ma and the Creation of the World's Biggest Online Marketplace* (New York: HarperCollins, 2009), 3.

27. Ibid., 7.

28. Ibid., 19.

29. Ibid., 23.

30. Author interview, July 20, 2010.

31. Author interview, November 1, 2010.

32. Company overview, Alibaba Group, accessed June 24, 2011, http://news.alibaba.com/ specials/aboutalibaba/aligroup/index.html.

33. Author interview, November 2, 2010.

34. "Alibaba and the 2,236 Thieves," *The Economist,* February 24, 2011, http://www .economist.com/node/18233750?story_id=18233750.

35. Company overview, Alibaba Group, accessed June 24, 2011, http://news.alibaba.com /specials/aboutalibaba/aligroup/index.html.

36. All the numbers in this paragraph were cited in Tom Easton's terrific cover story for *The Economist,* "Let a Million Flowers Bloom," March 10, 2011, http://www .economist.com/node/18330120.

CHAPTER 3: DIASPORA POLITICS

1. James Bell, "Upbeat Chinese May Not Be Primed for a Jasmine Revolution," Pew Global Attitudes Project, Pew Research Center, March 31, 2011, http://pewresearch .org/pubs/1945/chinese-may-not-be-ready-for-revolution.

2. For example: Anthony Saich, "Citizens' Perceptions of Adequate Governance: Satisfaction Levels Among Rural and Urban Chinese," in Everett Zhang, Arthur Kleinman and Weiming Tu, *Governance of Life in Chinese Moral Experience: The Quest for an Adequate Life* (New York: Routledge Taylor & Francis Group, 2011), 199–214.

3. Kathrin Hille, "The Big Screening," *Financial Times,* November 18, 2010, http://cachef .ft.com/cms/s/0/2af0086a-f285-11df-a2f3-00144feab49a.html#axzz1Rt7RY5iU.

4. Owen Fletcher, "Hit-and-Run Sentence Sparks More Outrage," *Wall Street Journal,* January 30, 2011, http://online.wsj.com/article/SB10001424052748704832704576113873869112398.html.

5. In another joke, God tells Mubarak that the world will end in two days. Mubarak announces to his people: "I have excellent news. I will be your president until the end of time." See Isandr el Amrani, "Three Decades of a Joke That Just Won't Die," *Foreign Policy,* January/February 2011, http://www.foreignpolicy.com/articles/2011/01/02/three _decades_of_a_joke_that_just_wont_die.

6. See *Revolution in the Arab World: Tunisia, Egypt and the Unmaking of an Era* (Washington, DC: Foreign Policy, 2011).

7. For more on Mao's legacy, see Jasper Becker, *Hungry Ghosts: Mao's Secret Famine* (London: John Murray, 1996); Jung Chang and Jon Halliday, *Mao: The Untold Story* (New York: Anchor, 2006); and Stéphane Courtois et al., *The Black Book of Communism,* trans. Jonathan Murphy and Mark Kramer (Cambridge, MA: Harvard University Press, 1999).

8. Perry Link, "The Anaconda in the Chandelier," *New York Review of Books,* April 11, 2002, http://www.nybooks.com/articles/archives/2002/apr/11/china-the-anaconda-in-the-chandelier.

9. "The Communist Party of China (CPC, CCP)," ChinaToday.com, http://www.chinatoday.com/org/cpc, accessed July 12, 2011.

10. Guy Sorman, *The Empire of Lies: The Truth About China in the Twenty-First Century* (New York: Encounter Books, 2008), 76.

11. Organisation for Economic Co-operation and Development, "China's Emergence as a Market Economy: Achievements and Challenges" (presented at the China Development Forum, March 20–21, 2011), http://www.oecd.org/dataoecd/27/17/47408845.pdf, 14.

12. "Asia's New Aristocracy," *The Economist,* January 20, 2011, http://www.economist.com/node/17929037. How many poor people there are in China depends on how you measure it. The official poverty line is set so low (barely 50 US cents a day) that less than 3 percent of Chinese people fall below it. Using a less stringent $2-a-day measure, the World Bank estimated that 36 percent of the Chinese population was poor in 2005, nearly 480 million people. That number should have fallen considerably since then, since China has grown richer. http://data.worldbank.org/country/china.

13. Perry Link, "Corruption and Indignation: Windows Into Popular Chinese Views of Right and Wrong," *Tocqueville on China* series, American Enterprise Institute for Public Policy Research, February 2008, http://www.aei.org/docLib/20080330_TocquevilleonChina_Link-3.pdf.

14. Cited in John Micklethwait, "Taming Leviathan: A Special Report on the Future of the State," *The Economist,* March 17, 2011, http://www.economist.com/node/18359954?story_id=18359954.

15. Warren I. Cohen, "China and the West in Historical Perspective," *Footnotes: The Newsletter of the FPRI's Wachman Center* 13, Foreign Policy Research Institute, no. 6 (April 2008), http://www.fpri.org/footnotes/1306.200804.cohen.chinawesthistorical.html.

16. International Trade Union Confederation, "Internationally Recognised Core Labour Standards in the People's Republic of China" (report for the World Trade Organization General Council Review of the Trade Policies of the People's Republic of China, Geneva, May 10 and 12, 2010), http://www.ituc-csi.org/IMG/pdf/Chinal_Final-2.pdf.

17. "An Alleyway in Hell: China's Abusive 'Black Jails,'" Human Rights Watch, November 12, 2009, http://www.hrw.org/en/reports/2009/11/12/alleyway-hell-0.

18. For an insightful description of China's financial system, see Carl Walter and Fraser Howie, *Red Capitalism: The Fragile Foundation of China's Extraordinary Rise* (Singapore: Wiley, 2011).

19. "Taiwan," *The World Factbook* (Washington, DC: Central Intelligence Agency, 2011), https://www.cia.gov/library/publications/the-world-factbook/geos/tw.html.

20. "Taiwan's Commonsense Consensus," *The Economist,* February 24, 2011, http://www.economist.com/node/18229208.

21. Pan, *Sons of the Yellow Emperor,* 372–3.

22. Ibid., 358–9.

23. "Tourism Peformance in 2010," Tourism Commission, Commerce and Economic Development Bureau, the Government of the Hong Kong Special Administrative Region, http://www.tourism.gov.hk/english/statistics/statistics_perform.html.

24. Author phone interview with Minky Worden, media director, Human Rights Watch, 2010.

25. Liu Xiaobo, interview with *Kaifang* [Open] magazine, Hong Kong, cited in Andrew Higgins, "How China Branded Nobel Winner Liu Xiaobo a Traitor," *Washington Post,* December 11, 2010, http://www.washingtonpost.com/wp-dyn/content/article /2010/12/10/AR2010121000111.html.

26. Liu Xiaobo et al., "Charter 08 for Reform and Democracy in China," December 10, 2008, http://www.charter08.eu/2.html. Translated from the Chinese by Perry Link.

27. Ibid.

28. Author interview, November 9, 2010.

29. Sorman, *The Empire of Lies,* 86.

30. "Chinese Reactions to Liu Xiaobo's Nobel Peace Prize—from Both Sides," Chinese Human Rights Defenders, December 10, 2010 (updated January 3, 2011), http://chrdnet .org/2010/10/14/nobel.

31. "No Awakening, but Crush It Anyway," *The Economist,* March 3, 2011, http://www .economist.com/node/18291529?story_id=18291529.

32. "Empty Chairs on the Cover of *Southern Metropolis Daily* Interpreted as Nobel Tribute," China Digital Times, December 13, 2010, http://chinadigitaltimes.net/2010/12 /netizens-interpret-empty-chairs-on-the-cover-of-southern-metropolis-daily.

33. Richard McGregor, *The Party: The Secret World of China's Communist Rulers* (London: Allen Lane, 2010), 229–62.

34. http://www.helplinfen.com/2011/04/persecution-photos.html, accessed June 24, 2011.

35. Author communication with Bob Fu, June 2011.

36. "International Religious Freedom Report 2010," US State Department, Bureau of Democracy, Human Rights, and Labor, November 17, 2010, http://www.state.gov/g/drl /rls/irf/2010/148863.htm.

37. Richard C. Morais, "China's Fight With Falun Gong," *Forbes,* February 9, 2006, http:// www.forbes.com/2006/02/09/falun-gong-china_cz_rm_0209falungong.html?boxes =custom.

38. Margherita Stancati, "Harvard Academic Inherits Dalai Lama's Political Role," *Wall Street Journal,* April 28, 2011, http://online.wsj.com/article/SB100014240527487040 99704576288221448496508.html.

39. "So Long, Farewell," Banyan blog, *The Economist,* March 14, 2011, http://www .economist.com/blogs/asiaview/2011/03/dalai_lama_resigns.

40. Cheng Li, "Shaping China's Foreign Policy: The Paradoxical Role of Foreign-Educated Returnees," *Asia Policy* 10 (July 2010): 69.

41. Cheng Li, remarks at "Chinese Foreign-Educated Returnees: Shaping China's Future?" symposium (Brookings Institution, Washington, DC), April 6, 2010, http:// www.brookings.edu/events/2010/0406_china_returnees.aspx.

42. Ibid.

43. Author interview, January 27, 2011.

44. Yu Keping, selected essays, published in English by the Brookings Institution, http:// www.brookings.edu/press/Books/2008/democracyisagoodthing.aspx.

45. Ibid.

46. Cited in James Miles, "Don't Worry, Be Happy," *The Economist,* March 17, 2011, http://www.economist.com/node/18388884.

47. Teng Biao, "A Hole to Bury You," *Wall Street Journal,* December 21, 2010, http:// online.wsj.com/article/SB10001424052970203731004576045152244293970.html.

48. Devesh Kapur, "Social Remittances: Migration and the Flow of Ideas," Chapter 5 in *Diaspora, Development and Democracy: The Domestic Impact of International Migration from India* (Princeton, NJ: Princeton University Press, 2010).

49. Clarisa Perez-Armendariz and David Crow, "Do Migrants Remit Democracy? International Migration, Political Beliefs, and Behavior in Mexico," *Comparative Political Studies* 43, no. 1 (January 2010): 119–48.

50. All 34 members of the Organisation for Economic Co-operation and Development are democracies: http://www.oecd.org/document/58/0,2340,en_2649_201185 _1889402_1_1_1_1,00.html.

51. Daron Acemoglu, Simon Johnson, James Robinson and Pierre Yared, "Income and Democracy," *American Economic Review* 98, no. 3 (2008): 808–42.

52. Erich Gundlach and Martin Paldam, "A Farewell to Critical Junctures: Sorting Out the Long-Run Causality of Income and Democracy," Kiel Working Paper No. 1410, Kiel Institute for the World Economy, March 2008, http://www.ifw-members.ifw-kiel .de/publications/a-farewell-to-critical-junctures-sorting-out-long-run-causality-of -income-and-democracy/KWP_1410_EG-MP-Democracy_KWP_19%20Mar%2008 .pdf.

53. See, for example, Carles Boix, "Development and Democratization," Princeton, 2009, http://www.princeton.edu/~cboix/development%20and%20democratization .pdf.

54. Sun Xiaoli, *State and Society in China's Modernization* (2001), cited in Bruce Gilley, *China's Democratic Future: How It Will Happen and Where It Will Lead* (New York: Columbia University Press, 2004), 63.

55. Alexis de Tocqueville, *Democracy in America*, trans. and ed. Harvey Mansfield and Delba Winthrop (Chicago: University of Chicago Press, 2000), 577.

56. Bret Stephens, "China and the Next American Century," *Wall Street Journal*, December 21, 2010, http://online.wsj.com/article/SB100014240527487038869045760313 32184760212.html.

57. Rana Mitter, "No Limits to Knowledge," *Times of India*, January 8, 2011, http:// articles.timesofindia.indiatimes.com/2011-01-08/edit-page/28357138_1_chinese -communist-party-peking-university-chinese-work.

58. Ying Chan, "Chinese Journalists Circumvent Government's Tight Restrictions," *Nieman Reports*, Nieman Foundation for Journalism at Harvard University, Spring 2011, http:// www.nieman.harvard.edu/reports/article/102604/Chinese-Journalists-Circumvent -Governments-Tight-Restrictions.aspx.

59. Oiwan Lam, "China: Yihuang Self-Immolation Incident and the Power of Micro-blogging," Globalvoicesonline.org, September 21, 2010, http://globalvoicesonline .org/2010/09/21/china-yihuang-self-immolation-incident-and-the-power-of-micro blogging.

60. Evgeny Morozov, *The Net Delusion: The Dark Side of Internet Freedom* (New York: PublicAffairs, 2011).

61. Ying Chan, "Chinese Journalists Circumvent Government's Tight Restrictions."

62. McGregor, *The Party*, 4.

63. Gilley, *China's Democratic Future*, 110–1.

64. Ibid., 118–47.

65. "2011 China Private Wealth Study," Bain & Company, cited in "To Get Out Is Glorious," Banyan blog, *The Economist*, April 30, 2011, http://www.economist.com/blogs /banyan/2011/04/chinas_itchy-footed_rich.

66. Quoted in *Kaifang* [Open] magazine, Hong Kong, May 2002; cited in Gilley, *China's Democratic Future*, 5.

CHAPTER 4: NETWORKS OF INNOVATION

1. "Putting the Smallest First," *The Economist*, September 23, 2010, http://www.economist .com/node/17090948?story_id=17090948.

2. Michael Lewis, *The New New Thing: A Silicon Valley Story* (New York: W. W. Norton, 2000), 114.

3. http://money.cnn.com/quote/quote.html?symb=WBMD.

4. "Overcoming Barriers: Human Mobility and Development," United Nations Human Development Report 2009 statistical tables, available at http://hdr.undp.org/en /reports/global/hdr2009.

5. Updates on the UID program's progress can be found at https://portal.uidai.gov.in/.

6. Bill Watterson, *There's Treasure Everywhere: A Calvin and Hobbes Collection* (London: Warner Books, 1996), 52. The Guest family copy has a broken spine thanks to frequent bedtime reading.

7. Atal Bihari Vajpayee, January 9, 2003 (Overseas Indians Day), New Delhi. Cited in Devesh Kapur, *Diaspora, Development and Democracy: The Domestic Impact of International Migration from India* (Princeton, NJ: Princeton University Press, 2010), 124.

8. Kapur, *Diaspora, Development and Democracy*, 62.

9. Stuart W. Leslie and Robert Kargo, "Exporting MIT: Science, Technology and Nation-Building in India and Iran," *Osiris* 21, no. 1 (2006): 110–30.

10. Kapur, *Diaspora, Development and Democracy*, 120.

11. Vivek Wadhwa, AnnaLee Saxenian, Ben Rissing and Gary Gereffi, "America's New Immigrant Entrepreneurs," Duke Science, Technology and Innovation Paper No. 23, 5, http://papers.ssrn.com/sol3/papers.cfm?abstract_id=990152.

12. "60,000 Indian Techies in US Return Home: Report," *Times of India*, May 14, 2007, http://articles.timesofindia.indiatimes.com/2007-05-14/indians-abroad/27875742_1 _anna-lee-saxenian-media-report-firms.

13. William R. Kerr, "Ethnic Scientific Communities and International Technology Diffusion," *The Review of Economics and Statistics* 90, no. 3 (August 2008): 518–37, http://www.people.hbs.edu/wkerr/KerrRestat08_EthProd.pdf, and author interview, April 16, 2010.

14. Edward L. Glaeser, "Making Sense of Bangalore," Legatum Institute, July 2010, 8, http://www.li.com/attachments/Making%20Sense%20of%20Bangalore%20-%20 Web.pdf.

15. Author interview, January 26, 2011.

16. C. K. Prahalad, *The Fortune at the Bottom of the Pyramid* (Upper Saddle River, NJ: Wharton School Publishing, 2005).

17. Author interviews with Jamshyd Godrej and G. Sunderraman, January 18, 2011; and with Uttam Ghoshal, February 3, 2011.

18. "Out of India," *The Economist*, March 5, 2011, http://www.economist.com/node /18285497. See also "First Break All the Rules: The Charms of Frugal Innovation," *The Economist*, April 15, 2010, http://www.economist.com/node/15879359.

19. "A $300 Idea That Is Priceless," Schumpeter blog, *The Economist*, April 30, 2011, http://www.economist.com/node/18618271?story_id=18618271, and author interview, September 3, 2010.

20. "Frugal Healing," *The Economist*, January 20, 2011, http://www.economist.com /node/17963427?story_id=17963427.

21. "Out of India," *The Economist*.

22. Figures supplied by GE, by email.

23. "First Break All the Rules: The Charms of Frugal Innovation," *The Economist*, April 15, 2010, http://www.economist.com/node/15879359.

24. World Health Statistics 2010, WHO, http://www.who.int/whosis/whostat/EN_WHS10 _Part2.pdf.

25. Author interview, January 11, 2011.

26. "Sun, Shopping and Surgery," *The Economist*, December 9, 2010, http://www .economist.com/node/17680806?story_id=17680806.

27. Author interview, September 7, 2010.

28. Author interview, March 23, 2009.

29. Email to author, quoted in "Life Is Expensive," *The Economist*, May 28, 2009, http:// www.economist.com/node/13686480.

CHAPTER 5: NETWORKS OF TRUST

1. Dilip Ratha et al., "Leveraging Migration for Africa: Remittances, Skills, and Investments," World Bank, March 30, 2011, http://siteresources.worldbank.org/EXT DECPROSPECTS/Resources/476882-1157133580628/AfricaStudyEntireBook.pdf.

2. Kevin O'Rourke, "The Economic Impact of the Famine in the Short and the Long Run," *American Economic Review* 84, no. 2 (2004): 309–13.

3. Robert E. B. Lucas, *International Migration and Economic Development: Lessons from Low-Income Countries* (Cheltenham, UK: Edward Elgar, 2005).

4. George J. Borjas, "Labor Outflows and Labor Inflows in Puerto Rico," *Journal of Human Capital* 2, no. 1 (2008). First published as National Bureau of Economic Research Working Paper no. 13669, November 2007, http://www.nber.org/papers/w13669.pdf.

5. Oded Stark, "Rethinking the Brain Drain," *World Development* 32, no. 1 (2004), http://www.esce.org/files/0401ESCE-RethinkingtheBrainDrain.pdf.

6. Michael Clemens and Lant Pritchett, "Income per Natural: Measuring Development As If People Mattered More Than Places," Center for Global Development Working Paper no. 143, February 5, 2008, 17.

7. Catia Batista, Aitor Lacuesta and Pedro Vicente, "Brain Drain or Brain Gain? Micro Evidence from an African Success Story," University of Oxford Department of Economics Discussion Paper Series no. 343 (August 2007), 25. Available online at http://ftp.iza.org/dp3035.pdf.

8. Michel Beine, Frederic Docquier and Hilel Rapoport, "On the Robustness of Brain Gain Estimates," Discussion Paper no. 18, Institut de recherches économiques et sociales, Université catholique de Louvain, June 2009, http://sites-final.uclouvain.be/econ/DP/IRES/2009018.pdf.

9. M. Beine, F. Docquier and H. Rapoport, "Brain Drain and LDCs' Growth: Winners and Losers," Milken Institute, October 2002, http://www.milkeninstitute.org/pdf/braindrain.pdf.

10. Ratha et al., "Leveraging Migration for Africa," 136.

11. Philippe Legrain, *Immigrants: Your Country Needs Them* (Princeton, NJ: Princeton University Press, 2006), 186.

12. Author interview, June 29, 2010.

13. For an excellent book on the history of Eritrea and Ethiopia, see Michela Wrong, *I Didn't Do It for You: How the World Betrayed a Small African Nation* (London: HarperCollins, 2005). For an account of the theft of aid money by Ethiopia's military regime, see David Rieff, "Dangerous Pity," *Prospect*, July 23, 2005, http://www.prospectmagazine.co.uk/2005/07/dangerouspity.

14. Cited in Ian Goldin, Geoffrey Cameron and Meera Balarajan, *Exceptional People: How Migration Shaped Our World and Will Define Our Future* (Princeton, NJ: Princeton University Press, 2011), 186.

15. Legrain, *Immigrants,* 182.

16. The numbers are from Goldin et al., *Exceptional People,* 189. The observations of the bar scene in Lesotho are my own. (I recommend the Maluti Lager.)

17. Ratha et al., "Leveraging Migration for Africa," 153.

18. Ibid., 54.

19. Ibid., 62.

20. Ibid., 62–4.

21. Dilip Ratha, "Leveraging Remittances for Development," policy brief, Migration Policy Institute, June 2007, http://www.migrationpolicy.org/pubs/MigDevPB_062507.pdf.

22. Ratha et al., "Leveraging Migration for Africa," 66.

23. Kathleen Newland, ed., *Diasporas: New Partners in Development Policy* (Washington, DC: Migration Policy Institute, 2010), 19.

24. Ibid., 76–81.

25. "The Method Behind Mugabe's Madness," *The Economist,* June 26, 2004, http://www.economist.com/node/2797085.

26. Steve Hanke, "RIP Zimbabwe Dollar," Cato Institute, Washington, DC, updated May 3, 2010, http://www.cato.org/zimbabwe.

27. Ratha et al., "Leveraging Migration for Africa," 76–8.

28. Ibid., 76.

29. Ibid., 81–2.

30. "M-PESA Service Goes Global Via Alliance With Western Union," Safaricom press release, March 31, 2011, http://www.safaricom.co.ke/index.php?id=1256.

31. A fuller account of this trip can be found in my book *The Shackled Continent: Power, Corruption and African Lives* (Washington, DC: Smithsonian, 2004).

32. Francis Fukuyama, *Trust: The Social Virtues and the Creation of Prosperity* (New York: Free Press, 1995).

33. Frances Williams, "Swiss Judge Sets Precedent in Global Corruption Fight," *Financial Times,* November 23, 2009, http://www.ft.com/cms/s/0/40b5a55e-d7d0-11de-b578 -00144feabdc0.html#axzz1IHHnwpKk.

34. For more on this, see Adams Bodomo, "The African Trading Community in Guangzhou: An Emerging Bridge for Africa-China Relations," *China Quarterly* no. 203, September 23, 2010, http://journals.cambridge.org/action/displayAbstract?fromPage =online&aid=7907533&fulltextType=RA&fileId=S0305741010000664.

35. Deborah Brautigam, *The Dragon's Gift: The Real Story of China in Africa* (Oxford: Oxford University Press, 2009), and author interview, June 17, 2010.

36. Wole Soyinka, *The Open Sore of a Continent: A Personal Narrative of the Nigerian Crisis* (Oxford: Oxford University Press, 1996), 124.

37. Newland et al., *Diasporas,* 115.

38. For a good modern history of Nigeria, see Karl Maier, *This House Has Fallen: Nigeria in Crisis* (London: Allen Lane, 2000), or Eghosa Osaghae, *Crippled Giant: Nigeria Since Independence* (Bloomington, IN: Indiana University Press, 1998). For a briefer take, see "Under New Management: A Survey of Nigeria," *The Economist,* January 13, 2000, http://www.economist.com/node/273161?story_id=E1_NSPTGT.

39. Author interview, February 10, 2011.

40. The phrase is from Clemens and Pritchett, "Income per Natural."

41. Clemens and Pritchett, "Income per Natural," 1–14.

42. Lant Pritchett, "Is Migration Good for Development? How Could You Even Ask?" Harvard Kennedy School presentation at Columbia University, February 13, 2009, http:// www.scribd.com/doc/13110177/Is-Migration-Good-for-Developmentcolumbia.

43. Ratha et al., "Leveraging Migration for Africa," 167.

44. Nicholas Norbrook, "Africa Doesn't Need Favours, Says Mo Ibrahim," *The Africa Report,* January 13, 2011, http://www.theafricareport.com/archives2/interviews /5135464-africa-doesnt-need-favours-says-mo-ibrahim.html.

45. "Zimbabwe," *The World Factbook* (Washington, DC: Central Intelligence Agency, 2011), https://www.cia.gov/library/publications/the-world-factbook/geos/zi.html. The CIA estimates that Zimbabwe's GDP was $400 per capita in 2010, while Botswana's was $13,500. Both figures are based on purchasing power parity. Statistics from Zimbabwe are unreliable, but the huge difference between the two countries is real enough.

46. "The Ibrahim Prize," Mo Ibrahim Foundation, accessed June 28, 2011, http://www .moibrahimfoundation.org/en/section/the-ibrahim-prize.

CHAPTER 6: NETWORKS OF HATE

1. Author interview, September 1, 2003.

2. "Mortality in the Democratic Republic of Congo," International Rescue Committee, January 2008, http://www.rescue.org/news/irc-study-shows-congos-neglected-crisis -leaves-54-million-dead-peace-deal-n-kivu-increased-aid—4331, and "Human Security Report 2009/10: The Causes of Peace and the Shrinking Costs of War," United Nations, December 2, 2010, http://www.hsrgroup.org/docs/Publications/HSR20092 010/20092010HumanSecurityReport-Part2-ShrinkingCostsOfWar.pdf. The International Rescue Committee estimates that 5.4 million people died as a result of the war between 1998 and 2007, mostly from disease or starvation. The UN offers a far lower estimate of 900,000 war-induced deaths between 2001 and 2007. Both figures are derived from estimating (1) how many people there are in Congo; (2) what the mortality rate was before the war; and (3) how much it rose as a result of the war—no better than an educated guess in either case. This is hardly surprising, given that Congo is a vast, chaotic country where few people keep records and roving bands of gunmen are liable to murder surveyors.

3. Author interview, September 1, 2003.

4. The best books on Congo's war are by Gérard Prunier, *Africa's World War* (Oxford: Oxford University Press, 2009), and Jason Stearns, *Dancing in the Glory of Monsters:*

The Collapse of the Congo and the Great War of Africa (New York: Public Affairs, 2011).

5. "The 'Jews' of Africa," *The Economist*, August 21, 2004, http://www.economist.com /node/3113203?story_id=3113203.
6. Ibid.
7. The definitive account of the Rwandan genocide is by Alison Des Forges, "Leave None to Tell the Story," Human Rights Watch, March 1, 1999, http://www.hrw.org/en/ reports/1999/03/01/leave-none-tell-story. It is 800 pages of scrupulously footnoted horror. Ms. Des Forges died in a plane crash in 2009. I was shocked; I had met her in Rwanda and spoken to her on the phone only a few weeks before she died. I paid tribute to her in a February 19 obituary in *The Economist:* http://www.economist.com/node/13137097.
8. Author interview, March 2004.
9. Philip Gourevitch, *We Wish to Inform You That Tomorrow We Will Be Killed With Our Families* (London: Picador, 1998), 211.
10. Ibid., 214.
11. Ibid., 218.
12. "HRW Alarmed About Hate Radio Broadcasts and the Incitement of Ethnic Violence in the DRC," Human Rights Watch, August 13, 1998, http://reliefweb.int/sites/reliefweb .int/files/reliefweb_pdf/node-38731.pdf.
13. Author interview, August 30, 2003.
14. Stearns, *Dancing in the Glory of Monsters,* 80.
15. "The 'Jews' of Africa," *The Economist*, August 21, 2004, http://www.economist.com /node/3113203?story_id=3113203.
16. See, for example, Jared Diamond, *Collapse: How Societies Choose to Fail or Succeed* (London: Viking Press, 2005).
17. "Conflict, Security, and Development," World Bank World Development Report 2011, http://wdr2011.worldbank.org/early-findings.
18. Author interview, March 2004.
19. Author interview, March 2004.
20. Author interview, August 24, 2003.
21. Author interview, August 2003.
22. Author interview, September 8, 2010.
23. Alastair Gee, "Mumbai Terror Attacks: And Then They Came for the Jews," *Sunday Times* (UK), November 1, 2009, http://www.timesonline.co.uk/tol/news/world/asia /article6896107.ece.
24. Chris Cuomo et al., "Alleged Fort Hood Shooter Nidal Malik Hasan was 'Calm,' Methodical During Massacre," ABC News, November 6, 2009, http://abcnews.go.com /story?id=9012995.
25. Joseph Rhee et al., "Accused Fort Hood Shooter Was a Regular at Shooting Range, Strip Club," ABC News, November 17, 2009, http://abcnews.go.com/Blotter/accused -fort-hood-shooter-nidal-hasan-visited-strip/story?id=9090116.
26. Katherine Zimmerman, "Militant Islam's Global Preacher: The Radicalizing Effect of Sheikh Anwar al-Awlaki," American Enterprise Institute for Public Policy Research Critical Threats Project, March 12, 2010, http://www.criticalthreats.org/yemen/militant -islams-global-preacher-radicalizing-effect-sheikh-anwar-al-awlaki.
27. "Lieberman Announces Senate Investigation into Ford Hood Shooting," Fox News, November 8, 2009, http://www.foxnews.com/politics/2009/11/08/lieberman -announces-investigation-fort-hood-shooting.
28. Chitra Ragavan, "The Imam's Very Curious Story," *US News and World Report,* June 13, 2004, http://www.usnews.com/usnews/news/articles/040621/21plot.htm.
29. Zimmerman, "Militant Islam's Global Preacher."
30. Tom Finn, "I Fear for My Son, Says Father of Anwar al-Awlaki, Tipped as New bin Laden," *The Observer* (UK), May 8, 2011, http://www.guardian.co.uk/world/2011/may/ 08/anwar-awlaki-yemen-al-qaida.
31. Zimmerman, "Militant Islam's Global Preacher."
32. "Muslim Americans: Middle Class and Mostly Mainstream," Pew Research Center, May 22, 2007, http://pewresearch.org/assets/pdf/muslim-americans.pdf.

33. Peter L. Bergen, *The Longest War: The Enduring Conflict Between America and al-Qaeda* (New York: Free Press, 2011), 205.
34. Ibid., 236.
35. Ibid., 237.
36. Ibid., 235.
37. Vali Nasr, *The Rise of Islamic Capitalism: Why the New Muslim Middle Class Is the Key to Defeating Extremism* (New York: Free Press, 2009), 26.
38. Author interview, January 4, 2010.
39. Author interview, January 4, 2010.
40. Ann Coulter, "This Is War," Universal Press Syndicate, September 13, 2001, http://classic-web.archive.org/web/20010914225811/http://www.nationalreview.com/coulter/coulter091301.shtml.
41. Michael Savage, *Liberalism Is a Mental Disorder* (Nashville, TN: Thomas Nelson, 2005), 32.
42. Kevin Sieff, "Florida Pastor Terry Jones's Koran Burning Has Far-reaching Effect," *Washington Post,* April 2, 2011, http://www.washingtonpost.com/local/education/florida-pastor-terry-joness-koran-burning-has-far-reaching-effect/2011/04/02/AFpiFoQC_story.html.
43. "Continuing Divide in Views of Islam and Violence," Pew Research Center for the People and the Press, March 9, 2011, http://pewresearch.org/pubs/1921/poll-islam-violence-more-likely-other-religions-peter-king-congressional-hearings.
44. "Muslim Americans: Middle Class and Mostly Mainstream," Pew Research Center.
45. "Muslim Americans: A National Portrait," Gallup Abu Dhabi Center, 2009, http://www.abudhabigallupcenter.com/144332/Muslim-Americans-National-Portrait.aspx.
46. "The Gallup Coexist Index 2009: A Global Study of Interfaith Religions," executive summary, Gallup Abu Dhabi Center, http://www.abudhabigallupcenter.com/144842/REPORT-Gallup-Coexist-Index-2009.aspx.
47. "Muslim Americans: Middle Class and Mostly Mainstream," Pew Research Center.
48. Gallup, "Muslim Americans," 10.
49. "The Year of the Drone," New America Foundation, http://counterterrorism.newamerica.net/drones, accessed June 30 2011.
50. Author interview, November 20, 2009.
51. "Muslim Americans: Middle Class and Mostly Mainstream," Pew Research Center, http://www.pewresearch.org/assets/pdf/muslim-americans.pdf.
52. Bergen, *The Longest War,* 297–9.
53. Author interview, November 1999.
54. "Osama bin Laden Largely Discredited Among Muslim Publics in Recent Years," Pew Global Attitudes Project, May 2, 2011, http://pewglobal.org/2011/05/02/osama-bin-laden-largely-discredited-among-muslim-publics-in-recent-years.
55. Peter Bergen, "Al-Qaeda: The Loser in Arab Revolutions," CNN.com, February 24, 2011, http://www.cnn.com/2011/OPINION/02/23/bergen.revolt.binladen/index.html?iref=allsearch.
56. Peter Bergen, "Al Qaeda Responds to Peter Bergen and CNN," New America Foundation, March 31, 2011, http://counterterrorism.newamerica.net/publications/articles/2011/al_qaeda_responds_to_cnn_47538.
57. Jerry Markon et al., "VA Suspects in Pakistan Say Mission Was Jihad Not Terrorism," *Washington Post,* January 5, 2010, http://www.washingtonpost.com/wp-dyn/content/article/2010/01/04/AR2010010400800.html.
58. Moises Naim, *Illicit: How Smugglers, Traffickers and Copycats Are Hijacking the Global Economy* (New York: Anchor Books, 2006), 1–37.
59. Aimar Alkholt, "Nigerian Criminal Networks: A Comparative Analysis" (master's thesis, University of Bergen, December 2010), https://bora.uib.no/bitstream/1956/4655/1/78479924.pdf.
60. Alkholt, "Nigerian Criminal Networks."
61. Naim, *Illicit,* 220–4.

62. Ibid., 72–3.
63. Ibid., 220.
64. Kathryn Cullen-DuPont, *Human Trafficking* (New York: Facts On File, 2009), 78.
65. Jørgen Carling, "Trafficking in Women from Nigeria to Europe," *Migration Information Source,* Migration Policy Institute, July 2005, http://www.migrationinformation .org/feature/display.cfm?ID=318.
66. Somini Sengupta, "Oldest Profession Is Still One of the Oldest Lures for Young Nigerian Women," *New York Times,* November 5, 2004, http://query.nytimes.com/gst /fullpage.html?res=9504E0DB143CF936A35752C1A9629C8B63.
67. "Failed States and Failed Policies: How to Stop the Drug Wars," *The Economist,* March 5, 2009, http://www.economist.com/node/13237193?story_id=13237193.

CHAPTER 7: "A PONZI SCHEME THAT WORKS"

1. This important subject is examined in detail in "The Meaning of America: Where Men are Men and Pumpkins Are Nervous," *The Economist,* November 10, 2005, http:// www.economist.com/node/5139909?story_id=5139909.
2. This number fluctuates a lot, and so should be treated with caution, but on May 12, 2011, it was 32.8 percent, according to the Realclearpolitics.com average of various polls: http://www.realclearpolitics.com/epolls/other/direction_of_country-902.html.
3. "How the Great Recession Has Changed Life in America," Pew Research Center, Social and Demographic Trends, June 30, 2010, http://pewsocialtrends.org/2010/06/30 /interactive-how-the-great-recession-has-changed-life-in-america.
4. "American Dream Declared Dead as Final Believer Gives Up," *The Onion,* March 29, 2011, http://www.theonion.com/video/american-dream-declared-dead-as-final -believer-giv,19846.
5. Neli Esipova and Julie Ray, "700 Million Worldwide Desire to Migrate Permanently," Gallup, November 2, 2009, http://www.gallup.com/poll/124028/700-million-world wide-desire-migrate-permanently.aspx.
6. Author interview, September 21, 2005.
7. Author interview, April 28, 2005.
8. Robert Rector, "Understanding Poverty: What the Census Bureau Doesn't Count," Heritage Foundation, September 11, 2009, http://www.heritage.org/Research /Commentary/2009/09/Understanding-Poverty-in-America-What-the-Census-Bureau -doesnt-count.
9. Ibid.
10. Ibid.
11. "GDP per Head, US$, Constant Prices, Constant PPPs, Reference Year 2000," Organisation for Economic Co-operation and Development Statextracts, http://stats.oecd .org/index.aspx?queryid=559.
12. Author interview, September 4, 2009.
13. "International Migration 2009," United Nations Department of Economic and Social Affairs, Population Division, http://www.un.org/esa/population/publications /2009Migration_Chart/ittmig_wallchart09.pdf.
14. Data compiled by the Migration Policy Institute and provided to the author by Michael Fix, September 2009.
15. Jonathan Wynne-Jones and Patrick Hennessy, "Tony Blair: Mention God and You're a 'Nutter,'" *Daily Telegraph,* November 25, 2007, http://www.telegraph.co.uk/news /politics/1570417/Tony-Blair-Mention-God-and-youre-a-nutter.html.
16. Author interview, September 9, 2009.
17. Author interview, September 8, 2009.
18. Ayaan Hirsi Ali, *Infidel* (New York: Free Press, 2007), 9.
19. Author interview, September 15, 2009.
20. The AHA Foundation can be found online at: http://www.theahafoundation.org.
21. CIA World Factbook, https://www.cia.gov/library/publications/the-world-factbook /geos/us.html, accessed June 30, 2011.

22. "Annual Projections of the Total Resident Population as of July 1: Middle, Lowest, and Highest and Zero International Migration Series, 1999 to 2100," US Census Bureau, revised February 14, 2000, http://www.census.gov/population/projections /nation/summary/np-t1.pdf.

23. Amar Bhidé, *The Venturesome Economy: How Innovation Sustains Prosperity in a More Connected World* (Princeton, NJ: Princeton University Press, 2008).

24. Author interview, 2009.

25. Ariana Eunjung Cha, "Looming Population Crisis Forces China to Revisit One-Child Policy," *Washington Post,* December 12, 2009, http://www.washingtonpost.com/wp -dyn/content/article/2009/12/11/AR2009121104378.html.

26. Gordon G. Chang, "China Alone?" *National Review,* November 23, 2009, http://nrd .nationalreview.com/?q=MjAwOTExMjM=.

27. "Population Aging and Development 2009," United Nations Department of Economic and Social Affairs, http://un.org/esa/population/publications/ageing/ageing2009chart.pdf.

28. Michael Fitzpatrick, "No, Robot: Japan's Elderly Fail to Welcome Their Robot Overlords," BBC News, February 4, 2011, http://www.bbc.co.uk/news/business-12347219.

29. Cited in Richard Florida, *Who's Your City? How the Creative Economy Is Making Where to Live the Most Important Decision of Your Life* (New York: Basic Books, 2008), 66.

30. "Table 1: Human Development Index and Its Components," United Nations Human Development Report 2010, http://hdr.undp.org/en/media/HDR_2010_EN_Table1 _reprint.pdf.

31. "2010 Legatum Prosperity Index Table Rankings," Legatum Institute, http://www .prosperity.com/rankings.aspx.

32. Bruce Western, testimony to Joint Economic Committee, US Congress, October 4, 2007, http://www.wjh.harvard.edu/soc/faculty/western/pdfs/western_jec_testimony .pdf.

33. Online Briefing: Latest International Comparisons of Crime in OECD Countries, Civitas, 2010, http://www.civitas.org.uk/crime/crimestats6.php.

34. See, for example, Laura Vanderkam, "Where Did the Korean Greengrocers Go?" *City Journal,* Winter 2011, http://www.city-journal.org/2011/21_1_nyc-koreans.html.

35. Richard Florida, *The Flight of the Creative Class: The New Global Competition for Talent* (New York: HarperCollins, 2007), 275, and author interview, September 10, 2009.

36. Adam Sitte, "US, Canada Show More Interfaith Cohesion Than Europe," Gallup, May 7, 2009, http://www.gallup.com/poll/118273/canada-show-interfaith-cohesion -europe.aspx.

37. Author interview, 1996.

38. "In Praise of Boise," *The Economist,* May 13, 2010, http://www.economist.com /node/16112080.

39. Author interview, May 5, 2010.

40. CIA World Factbook, https://www.cia.gov/library/publications/the-world-factbook /geos/us.html, accessed June 30, 2011.

41. Joel Kotkin, *The Next Hundred Million: America in 2050* (New York: Penguin, 2010), 114.

42. CIA World Factbook, https://www.cia.gov/library/publications/the-world-factbook /geos/us.html, accessed June 30, 2011.

43. Author interview, May 5, 2010.

44. Author interview, May 10, 2010.

45. Tom Tancredo, *In Mortal Danger: The Battle for America's Border and Security* (Nashville, TN: Cumberland House, 2006).

46. Patrick J. Buchanan, *State of Emergency: The Third World Invasion and Conquest of America* (New York: Thomas Dunne, 2006).

47. Barack Obama, speech in New Orleans, October 15, 2009. Transcript at: http:// www.realclearpolitics.com/printpage/?url=http://www.realclearpolitics.com/articles/ 2009/10/15/transcript_obama_new_orleans_town_hall_meeting_98761.html.

48. Samuel Huntington, "The Hispanic Challenge," *Foreign Policy*, March 1, 2004, http://www.foreignpolicy.com/articles/2004/03/01/the_hispanic_challenge.

49. Author interview, June 7, 2006.

50. Author interview, March 20, 2006.

51. "Blood, Sweat, and Fear: Workers' Rights in US Meat and Poultry Plants," Human Rights Watch, January 24, 2005, http://www.hrw.org/en/reports/2005/01/24/blood -sweat-and-fear.

52. "Census of Fatal Occupational Injuries," Bureau of Labor Statistics, http://data.bls .gov/pdq/querytool.jsp?survey=fi. According to these statistics, in 2008, there were 58 deaths among 46,000 taxi drivers, and 10 deaths among 500,000 animal slaughter-house workers. Since deaths are rare even in dangerous industries, this ratio varies a lot from year to year.

53. "Between Two Worlds: How Young Latinos Came of Age in America," Pew Hispanic Center, December 11, 2009, http://pewhispanic.org/reports/report.php?ReportID =117.

54. Jeffrey S. Passel, "Hispanics Account for More Than Half of Nation's Growth in Past Decade," Pew Hispanic Center, March 24, 2011, http://pewhispanic.org/reports /report.php?ReportID=140.

55. See John Kasarda and James Johnson, "The Economic Impact of the Hispanic Population on the State of North Carolina," Frank Hawkins Kenan Institute of Private Enterprise, University of North Carolina at Chapel Hill, January 2006, figure 1, http://www.ime.gob.mx/investigaciones/2006/estudios/migracion/economic_impact _hispanic_population_north_carolina.pdf, and Passel, "Hispanics Account for More Than Half of Nation's Growth in Past Decade."

56. Author interview, June 6, 2006.

57. George Borjas, "Increasing the Supply of Labor Through Immigration: Measuring the Impact on Native-Born Workers," *Backgrounder*, Center for Immigration Studies, May 2004, http://www.hks.harvard.edu/fs/gborjas/Papers/cis504.pdf.

58. David Card, "Is the New Immigration Really So Bad?" *Economic Journal* 115, November 2005, http://emlab.berkeley.edu/~card/papers/new-immig.pdf.

59. Gianmarco I. P. Ottaviano and Giovanni Peri, "Rethinking the Effects of Immigration on Wages," National Bureau of Economic Research Working Paper no. 12497, August 2006, http://www.creativeclass.com/rfcgdb/articles/Peri%20and%20Ottavanio,%20 Rethinking%20Immigrations%20Effect.pdf.

60. Author interview, June 5, 2006.

61. "Statistical Portrait of Hispanics in the United States 2009," Pew Hispanic Center, February 2011, Table 36, http://pewhispanic.org/files/factsheets/hispanics2009/Table %2036.pdf.

62. Ibid., Table 20, http://pewhispanic.org/files/factsheets/hispanics2009/Table%2020.pdf.

63. Ibid., Table 22, http://pewhispanic.org/files/factsheets/hispanics2009/Table%2022.pdf.

64. In 2010, 0.34 percent of the US adult population started a business each month. The rate for Latinos was 0.56 percent. See Robert Fairlie, "The Kauffman Index of Entrepreneurial Activity 1996–2010," Kauffman Foundation, Kansas City, March 2011, http://www.kauffman.org/research-and-policy/Kauffman-Index-of-Entrepreneurial -Activity-1996-2010.aspx.

65. Author interview, June 5, 2006.

66. Mark Krikorian, *The New Case Against Immigration: Both Legal and Illegal* (New York: Sentinel, 2008), 14.

67. Scott Bittle and Jonathan Rochkind, "A Place to Call Home: What Immigrants Say Now About Life in America," Public Agenda, September 2009, http://www.public agenda.org/files/pdf/Immigration.pdf.

68. "Turks Feel Unwanted in Germany," *Der Spiegel* online, international edition, March 13, 2008, http://www.spiegel.de/international/germany/0,1518,541216,00.html.

69. Michael Lind, "The Next Big Thing: America," *Foreign Policy*, April 15, 2009, http://www.foreignpolicy.com/articles/2009/04/15/the_next_big_thing_america.

CHAPTER 8: THE HUB OF THE WORLD

1. Author interview, October 7, 2010.
2. Author interview, January 10, 2011.
3. Monish Suvarna, personal communication, May 2011.
4. Goldin et al., *Exceptional People,* 168–9.
5. UNESCO Science Report 2010, executive summary, United Nations Educational, Scientific, and Cultural Organization, 1–31, http://unesdoc.unesco.org/images/0018 /001898/189883E.pdf.
6. Ibid.
7. "Patents Yes; Ideas Maybe," *The Economist,* October 10, 2010, http://www.economist .com/node/17257940.
8. "Patents Yes; Ideas Maybe," *The Economist,* October 14, 2010, http://www.economist .com/node/17257940.
9. "Knowledge, Networks and Nations: Global Scientific Collaboration in the 21st Century," Royal Society, March 2011, 59–60, http://royalsociety.org/uploadedFiles /Royal_Society_Content/Influencing_Policy/Reports/2011-03-28-Knowledge -networks-nations.pdf.
10. Ibid., 6.
11. Ibid., 55.
12. Ibid., 62.
13. Ibid., 49.
14. William R. Kerr and William F. Lincoln, "The Supply Side of Innovation: H1-B Visa Reforms and US Ethnic Invention," *Journal of Labor Economics* 28, no. 3 (July 2010): 473–508, http://www.people.hbs.edu/wkerr/Kerr_LincolnJOLE10_H1B.pdf.
15. Author interview, March 30, 2010.
16. "To Err Is Human: Building a Safer Health System," US National Academies Institute of Medicine, November 1, 1999, http://www.iom.edu/~/media/Files/Report%20 Files/1999/To-Err-is-Human/To%20Err%20is%20Human%201999%20%20report %20brief.pdf.
17. Author interview, April 16, 2010.
18. Author interview, June 17, 2010.
19. "Knowledge, Networks and Nations," 27.
20. "Kauffman Index of Entrepreneurial Activity, 1996–2010," Ewing Marion Kauffman Foundation, March 7, 2011, 10, http://www.kauffman.org/uploadedFiles/KIEA_2011 _report.pdf.
21. "Growth and Competitiveness in the United States: The Role of Its Multinational Companies," McKinsey & Company, June 2010, http://www.mckinsey.com/mgi /publications/role_of_us_multinational_companies/index.asp.
22. "The Fiscal Year 2009 Pentagon Spending Request—Global Military Spending," Center for Arms Control and Non-Proliferation, February 22, 2008, http://armscontrol center.org/policy/securityspending/articles/fy09_dod_request_global.
23. Joseph S. Nye, "The Future of American Power," *Foreign Affairs,* November/December 2010, 2, http://www.foreignaffairs.com/articles/66796/joseph-s-nye-jr/the-future -of-american-power.
24. Joseph S. Nye, "Chapter 4: Soft Power," in *The Future of Power* (New York: Public Affairs, 2011).
25. "How to Improve China's Soft Power?" *People's Daily* Online, March 11, 2010, http://english.peopledaily.com.cn/90001/90776/90785/6916487.html.
26. L. Gordon Crovitz, "The VOA Is Losing Its Voice," *Wall Street Journal,* April 18, 2011, http://online.wsj.com/article/SB10001424052748704495004576264880231253582.html.
27. Xinhua news, online edition (English), http://www.xinhuanet.com/english2010, accessed April 18, 2011.
28. "China Hits Back with Report on US Human Rights," Xinhua news agency, April 11, 2011, http://news.xinhuanet.com/english2010/video/2011-04/11/c_13823315 .htm.

29. "Ai Is Out," *The Economist,* June 23, 2011, http://www.economist.com/blogs/banyan/2011/06/china-and-its-dissidents.

30. Geoff Dyer, "Beijing's Push for Soft Power Runs Up Against Hard Absolutes," *Financial Times,* January 4, 2010, http://www.ft.com/cms/s/0/c67477f4-f8cf-11de-beb8-00144feab49a.html#axzz1JUlLLown.

31. "Bigger Abroad," *The Economist,* February 27, 2011, http://www.economist.com/node/18178291.

32. Andy Goldberg, "In Hollywood, Even Superheroes Are Getting Outsourced," Deutsche Presse Agentur, March 22, 2011, http://www.earthtimes.org/articles/news/372792,superheroes-outsourced-feature.html.

33. Robert Putnam, "E Pluribus Unum: Diversity and Community in the 21st Century" (Johan Skytte Prize Lecture, Uppsala, Sweden, September 30, 2006). Published in *Scandinavian Political Studies* 30, no. 2, 141, http://www.utoronto.ca/ethnicstudies/Putnam.pdf.

34. Roger Runningen, "Actor Kal Penn Joins Obama White House as Asian-American Link," *Bloomberg News,* April 8, 2009, http://www.bloomberg.com/apps/news?pid=newsarchive&sid=aFXnt_hqV._8.

35. Author interview, May 24, 2010.

36. Liu Zhongde, quoted in "CPPCC: Exterminate the SuperGirls," *China Times,* English translation posted April 26, 2006, http://www.danwei.org/trends_and_buzz/cppcc_exterminate_the_super_girls.php.

37. Nye, *The Future of Power,* Chapter 4.

38. "The Lozi Lost," *The Economist,* September 2, 1999, http://www.economist.com/node/236417?story_id=E1_NPGQTS.

39. Author interview, May 24, 2010.

40. "Academic Ranking of World Universities 2010," Jiao Tong University Shanghai, http://www.arwu.org/ARWU2010.jsp, accessed July 5, 2011. The only non-American universities in the top 20 were Cambridge, Oxford and Tokyo.

41. Nye, *The Future of Power,* Chapter 4.

42. Author interview, October 1, 2010.

43. Carol Atkinson, "Does Soft Power Matter? A Comparative Analysis of Student Exchange Programs, 1980–2006," *Foreign Policy Analysis* 6, no. 1 (January 2010): 3, http://iis-db.stanford.edu/pubs/22948/Atkinson_Does_Soft_Power_Matter.pdf.

44. Ibid.

45. Fouad Ajami, "Egypt's 'Heroes With No Names,'" *Wall Street Journal,* February 12, 2011, http://online.wsj.com/article/SB10001424052748704132204576136442019920256.html?mod=WSJ_Opinion_LEADTop.

46. "Global Destinations for International Students at the Post-Secondary Level, 2001 and 2009," Atlas of International Student Mobility, Institute of International Education, http://www.atlas.iienetwork.org/?p=48027, accessed July 5, 2011.

47. Ben Wildavsky, *The Great Brain Race: How Global Universities Are Reshaping the World* (Princeton, NJ: Princeton University Press, 2010), 15–16.

48. Ibid., 16.

49. Edward B. Roberts and Charles Eesley, "Entrepreneurial Impact: The Role of MIT," Ewing Marion Kauffman Institute, February 2009, http://www.kauffman.org/uploadedFiles/MIT_impact_full_report.pdf.

50. Author interview, October 7, 2010.

51. Roberts and Eesley, "Entrepreneurial Impact: The Role of MIT," 5.

52. "Teacher Attendance," as described on the Abdul Latif Jameel Poverty Action Lab website, http://www.povertyactionlab.org/policy-lessons/education/teacher-attendance, accessed July 5, 2011. See also Esther Duflo and Abhijit Banerjee, *Poor Economics: A Radical Rethinking of the Way to Fight Global Poverty* (New York: PublicAffairs, 2011).

53. Author interview, November 4, 2010.

54. According to a BBC World Service/GlobeScan/PIPA poll of residents of 28 countries, 2010 was the first year since 2005 that views of the United States' influence in the world were, on average, more positive than negative: http://www.globescan.com/news_archives/bbc2010_countries/BBC_2010_countries.pdf. America's num-

bers improved slightly in 2011: http://www.bbc.co.uk/pressoffice/pressreleases/stories /2011/03_march/07/poll.pdf.

55. Simon Anholt, "The $2 Trillion Man: How Obama Saved Brand America," *Foreign Policy*, December 17, 2009, http://www.foreignpolicy.com/articles/2009/12/17/the _two_trillion_dollar_man. Additional information via author interview, 2010.

56. "2005–2009 American Community Survey 5-Year Estimates," US Census Bureau. Louisiana: http://factfinder.census.gov/servlet/ACSSAFFFacts?_event=Search&geo_id=&_ geoContext=&_street=&_county=&_cityTown=&_state=04000US22&_zip=& _lang=en&_sse=on&pctxt=fph&pgsl=010; South Carolina: http://factfinder.census.gov /servlet/ACSSAFFFacts?_event=Search&_lang=en&_sse=on&geo_id=04000US45& _state=04000US45, accessed July 5, 2011.

57. Fred Kaplan, "Egomania, Inc.," *Slate*, March 8, 2004, http://www.slate.com/id /2096813/.

58. Mark Krikorian, *The New Case Against Immigration: Both Legal and Illegal* (New York: Sentinel, 2008), 21–45.

CONCLUSION: A MOBILE WORLD

1. Author interview, November 17, 2005.

2. "Come Hither," *The Economist*, December 1, 2005, http://www.economist.com /node/5249522?story_id=5249522.

3. "Throwing Good Money After Bad: Immigration Enforcement," Immigration Policy Center, May 26, 2010, http://www.immigrationpolicy.org/just-facts/throwing-good -money-after-bad-immigration-enforcement#_edn3.

4. "Unauthorized Immigrant Population: National and State Trends 2010," Pew Hispanic Center, February 11, 2011, http://pewhispanic.org/files/reports/133.pdf.

5. "Immigration Enforcement Actions 2007," US Department of Homeland Security Annual Report, December 2008, http://www.dhs.gov/xlibrary/assets/statistics /publications/enforcement_ar_07.pdf.

6. Wayne Cornelius et al., "Controlling Unauthorized Immigration from Mexico: The Failure of 'Prevention Through Deterrence' and the Need for Comprehensive Reform," Immigration Policy Center, University of California, San Diego, June 10, 2008, http://www.immigrationforum.org/images/uploads/CCISbriefing061008.pdf.

7. Author interview, November 18, 2005.

8. Raul Hinojosa-Ojeda, "Raising the Floor for American Workers," Center for American Progress, January 7, 2010, http://www.americanprogress.org/issues/2010/01 /raising_the_floor.html.

9. "Immigration Reform and US Economic Performance," Council on Foreign Relations, March 14, 2011, http://www.cfr.org/immigration/immigration-reform-us-economic -performance/p24358#expert_roundup_author_7619.

10. Gianmarco I. P. Ottaviano, Giovanni Peri and Greg C. Wright, "Immigration, Offshoring and American Jobs," National Bureau of Economic Research Working Paper No. 16439, October 2010, http://www.nber.org/papers/w16439.pdf.

11. Council on Foreign Relations, "Immigration Reform and US Economic Performance."

12. Ibid.

13. Author interview, May 2010.

14. Edward Alden, "America's National Suicide," *Newsweek*, April 10, 2011, http:// www.newsweek.com/2011/04/10/america-s-national-suicide.html.

15. "Travel Poll," RT Strategies and Discover America Partnership, October–November 2006, http://www.poweroftravel.org/dap/pdf/DAP_Nov_SurveyResults.pdf.

16. "Bin Laden's Legacy," *The Economist*, January 16, 2010, http://www.economist.com /node/15270716.

17. "The Open Society and Its Discontents," *The Economist*, June 5, 2010, http://www .economist.com/node/16274061.

18. Cited in Alden, "America's National Suicide."

19. Scott Keeter, "Where the Public Stands on Immigration Reform," Pew Hispanic Center, November 23, 2009, http://pewresearch.org/pubs/1421/where-the-public-stands -on-immigration-reform.

20. Ibid.
21. Marshall Fitz et al., "The Costs of Mass Deportation," Center for American Progress, March 19, 2010, http://www.americanprogress.org/issues/2010/03/deportation_cost.html.
22. Hinojosa-Ojeda, "Raising the Floor for American Workers."
23. Author interview, November 2005.
24. "Come Hither," *The Economist.*
25. "South Africa: Events of 2008," Human Rights Watch World Report 2009, http://www.hrw.org/en/node/79205.
26. US unemployment was 9.6 percent for 2010. It fell to 9.1 percent by mid-2011. http://www.bls.gov/cps/, accessed July 5, 2011.
27. Author interview, April 27, 2010.
28. Timothy B. Gravelle et al., "What Makes 700 Million Adults Want to Migrate?" Gallup, February 18, 2010, http://www.gallup.com/poll/126065/Makes-700-Million-Adults-Migrate.aspx.
29. Author interview, April 16, 2010.
30. For an outstanding book on this subject, see Edward Alden, *The Closing of the American Border* (New York: HarperCollins, 2008).
31. T. Lindsay Baker, *Ghost Towns of Texas* (Norman: University of Oklahoma Press, 1986); *More Ghost Towns of Texas,* (Norman: University of Oklahoma, 2005).
32. Baker, *Ghost Towns of Texas,* vii.
33. "Table A-1: Annual Geographical Mobility Rates, by Type of Movement, 1947–2009," US Census Bureau, http://www.census.gov/population/socdemo/migration/tab-a-1.pdf.
34. "Fannie Mae and Freddie Mac: End of Illusions," *The Economist,* July 17, 2008, http://www.economist.com/node/11751139.
35. John Gittelsohn, "US 'Underwater' Homeowners Increase to 28 Percent, Zillow Says" Bloomberg News, May 9, 2011, http://www.bloomberg.com/news/2011-05-09/u-s-underwater-homeowners-increase-to-28-percent-zillow-says.html.
36. Fernando Ferreira, Joseph Gyourko and Joseph Tracy, "Housing Busts and Household Mobility," *Journal of Urban Economics* 68, no. 1 (July 2010): 34–45, http://ideas.repec.org/a/eee/juecon/v68y2010i1p34-45.html#abstract.
37. Author interview, March 16, 2009.
38. Andrew Oswald, "The Missing Piece of the Unemployment Puzzle" (lecture, Warwick, UK, November, 1997), http://www2.warwick.ac.uk/fac/soc/economics/staff/academic/oswald/inaugura.pdf.
39. Scott Adams, "Employer-Provided Health Insurance and Job Change," *Contemporary Economic Policy* 22, no. 3 (July 18, 2008), http://onlinelibrary.wiley.com/doi/10.1093/cep/byh026/abstract.
40. Author interview, December 11, 2008.
41. Author interview, March 5, 2009.
42. Shoba Narayan, "Return to India: One Family's Journey to America and Back," special report, *Knowledge@Wharton,* November 1, 2007, http://knowledge.wharton.upenn.edu/india/papers/Return_to_India.pdf.
43. Apolonija Oblak Flander, "Immigration to EU Member States Down by 6 Percent and Emigration Up by 13 Percent in 2008," *Statistics in Focus,* Eurostat, January 2011, http://epp.eurostat.ec.europa.eu/cache/ITY_OFFPUB/KS-SF-11-001/EN/KS-SF-11-001-EN.PDF.
44. Giampaolo Lanzieri, "First Demographic Estimates for 2009," *Data in Focus,* Eurostat, April 2009, http://epp.eurostat.ec.europa.eu/cache/ITY_OFFPUB/KS-QA-09-047/EN/KS-QA-09-047-EN.PDF.
45. Goldin et al., *Exceptional People,* 265.
46. In practice, I don't think discriminatory policies are ever a good idea, but that is too complex an argument to enter here. See Robert Guest, *The Shackled Continent* (London: Macmillan, 2003), Chapter 5.
47. Author interview, October 3, 2008.

INDEX